SOFTWARE
TESTING
TECHNIQUES

SOFTWARE TESTING TECHNIQUES

Boris Beizer
Data Systems Analysts, Inc.
Pennsauken, New Jersey

Van Nostrand Reinhold Electrical/Computer Science and Engineering
Series

VNR VAN NOSTRAND REINHOLD COMPANY
NEW YORK CINCINNATI TORONTO LONDON MELBOURNE

Library of Congress Catalog Card Number: 82-8446
ISBN: 0-442-24592-0

Manufactured in the United States of America

Published by Van Nostrand Reinhold Company, Inc.
135 West 50th Street, New York, N.Y. 10020

Van Nostrand Reinhold Publishing
1410 Birchmount Road
Scarborough, Ontario M1P 2E7, Canada

Van Nostrand Reinhold Australia Pty. Ltd.
17 Queen Street
Mitcham, Victoria 3132, Australia

Van Nostrand Reinhold Company Limited
Molly Millars Lane
Wokingham, Berkshire, England

15   14   13   12   11   10   9   8   7   6   5   4   3   2   1

Library of Congress Cataloging in Publication Data

Beizer, Boris, 1934–
  Software testing techniques.

  (Van Nostrand Reinhold electrical/computer science
and engineering series)
  Includes bibliographical references and index.
  1. Computer programs—Testing.   I. Title.   II. Series.
QA76.6.B433   1982   001.64'25'0287   82-8446
ISBN 0-442-24592-0   AACR2

Dedicated to several unfortunate, very bad software projects for which I was privileged to act as a consultant (albeit briefly). They provided lessons on the difficulties this book is intended to circumvent and led to the realization that this book is needed. Their failure could have been averted—requiescat in pace.

Van Nostrand Reinhold
Electrical/Computer Science and Engineering Series
Sanjit Mitra, Series Editor

HANDBOOK OF ELECTRONIC DESIGN AND ANALYSIS PROCEDURES US-ING PROGRAMMABLE CALCULATORS, by Bruce K. Murdock

COMPILER DESIGN AND CONSTRUCTION, by Arthur B. Pyster

SINUSOIDAL ANALYSIS AND MODELING OF WEAKLY NONLINEAR CIR-CUITS, by Donald D. Weiner and John F. Spina

APPLIED MULTIDIMENSIONAL SYSTEMS THEORY, by N.K. Bose

MICROWAVE SEMICONDUCTOR ENGINEERING, by Joseph F. White

INTRODUCTION TO QUARTZ CRYSTAL UNIT DESIGN, by Virgil E. Bottom

DIGITAL IMAGE PROCESSING, by William B. Green

SOFTWARE TESTING TECHNIQUES, by Boris Beizer

LIGHT TRANSMISSION OPTICS, Second edition, by Dietrich Marcuse

The Tester's Soliloquy

To test, or not to test; that is the question:
Whether 'tis nobler for the tester's soul to suffer
The barbs and snickers of outraged designers,
Or to take arms against a sea of failures,
And by testing, end them? To try: to test; to test
Yet more; and by such tests to say we end
All software and the thousand myriad faults
That it is heir to—'tis a consummation
Devoutly to be wished. To try: to test;
To test; perchance to work; ay, there's the rub;
For if it works, what tasks may come
When we have passed the final code
Must give us pause. There's the fact
That makes calamitous too good a test;
For who would copious errors bear,
The printouts long, the endless loops,
The pangs of cracked software, the work's delay,
The indolence of labor, and the spurns
The tester, unmerited, from the coder takes,
When we ourselves, by passing all routines,
Might our quietus make? Who would insults bear,
Or grunt and sweat under a bleary light,
But that the dread of testing ended,
In whose wake no more debugging lurks,
Makes us rather bear those ills we suffer,
Than seek employment of an honest kind.
Thus expedience doth make cowards of us all;
And thus the routine's resolution
Is studied o'er with the pale cast of doubt,
And enterprises of great pith and moment
With grinding fits, they jump back to a halt
And lose the name of action.

PREFACE

This book concerns testing techniques that are applied to individual routines. The companion volume, *Software System Testing and Quality Assurance,* is concerned with integration testing, development of system test plans, software quality management, test teams, and software reliability. Most software is produced by the cooperative effort of many designers and programmers working over a period of years. The resulting product cannot be fully understood by any one person. Consequently, quality standards can only be achieved by emplacing effective management and control methods. However, no matter how elegant the methods used to test a system, how complete the documentation, how structured the architecture, the development plans, the project reviews, the walkthroughs, the data-base management, the configuration control—no matter how advanced the entire panoply of techniques— all will come to nothing, and the project will fail, if the unit-level software, the individual routines, have not been properly tested. Quality assurance that ignores unit-level testing issues is a construct built on a foundation of sand.

Although I set out to write a book on software quality assurance, it became clear to me as I progressed that I was assuming that programmers know how to do unit testing. Good programmers *do* know how to do unit testing—it is one of the things that makes them good programmers—but their knowledge and their techniques are hard won; and if they communicate those lessons to others, it is as master to apprentice. The literature of programming is dominated by design issues. Some otherwise excellent textbooks have nothing to say about testing other than "try everything" or "be sure to test thoroughly." And those texts that do address testing explicitly do not give testing an emphasis that even remotely reflects the 50% or more of labor that is expended in testing. The same can be said for programming courses. Typically, although testing will consume more than half of a programmer's professional life, less than 5% of the programmer's education will be devoted to testing.

Yet there has evolved a large body of techniques and an abundant technical literature on testing. The purpose of this book is to extract from that

ix

literature those techniques that are most useful to the individual programmer, to merge and modify them by the lessons of practice—the lessons of the art of testing as it is actually done—and to present a tool kit that the programmer can use to design and execute comprehensive unit tests. I have stressed unit-level testing, but the reader will realize that most of the techniques can be applied at all system levels and should be.

Although this is a text, it does not include problems to solve. Programmers have enough real problems, and I don't think that it is appropriate to add contrived ones to those they already have. Testing should be taught in a testing laboratory course. In the ideal course, as I see it, the student does not write one line of original code. Small modules of 50 to 100 statements are provided as exercises. These modules are bad pieces of code–ugly, convoluted horrors with hidden own-data, self-modification, inadvertent recursions, and bugs—lots and lots of bugs. Each exercise is given a fixed computer-time budget. The student's progress is measured by the number of known bugs discovered in that time. The student who carefully structures the test cases, who does proper desk checking, and who thinks about test objectives, is more likely to find the bugs in the budgeted time than the student who relies on intuition as a sole tool. The language used and the nature of the exercises should be tailored to the environment—in terms of factors that include computer availability, terminals, and built-in test tools. The language is not important, although assembly language and older languages, such as FOR-TRAN and COBOL, have the distinct advantage of permitting entire categories of bugs, which are impossible in modern languages such as Pascal.

Boris Beizer
Abington, Pennsylvania

ACKNOWLEDGMENTS

My thanks to Data Systems Analysts for the support they gave to this work and, as ever, my appreciation and affection to Adrienne Bilotta who typed the manuscript and who knows how to translate my arbitrary orthography into a recognizable standard.

CONTENTS

PREFACE vii

1—INTRODUCTION 1

1. The Purpose of Testing 1
   1.1. What We Do 1
   1.2. Productivity and Quality in Software 2
   1.3. Goals for Testing 3
   1.4. Test Design 4
2. Some Dichotomies 4
   2.1. Structure Versus Function 4
   2.2. The Designer Versus the Tester 5
   2.3. Modularity Versus Efficiency 7
   2.4. The Builder Versus The Buyer 7
3. A Model for Testing 8
   3.1. The Project 8
   3.2. Overview 10
   3.3. The Environment 10
   3.4. The Program 11
   3.5. Bugs 11
   3.6. Tests 12
   3.7. The Role of Models 12
4. Is Complete Testing Possible? 12

2—THE TAXONOMY OF BUGS 15

1. Synopsis 15
2. The Consequences of Bugs 15
3. A Taxonomy for Bugs 16
   3.1. General 16
   3.2. Function–Related Bugs 17
   3.3. System Bugs 18
   3.4. Process Errors 23
   3.5. Data Errors 25

3.6. Code Errors   32
3.7. Testing and Style   33
4. Some Bug Statistics   33

3—FLOWCHARTS AND PATH TESTING   37

1. Synopsis   37
2. Flowcharts as Models   37
    2.1. Flowcharts   37
    2.2. Path Selection   41
    2.3. Loops   50
    2.4. Effectiveness of Path Testing   54
3. Path Sensitizing   55
    3.1. General   55
    3.2. Path Predicates   55
    3.3. Independence and Correlation of Variables and Predicates   56
    3.4. Examples   58
    3.5. Desk Checking   64
4. Test Case Generation and Instrumentation   67
    4.1. Automatic Test Case Generation   67
    4.2. Instrumentation   68
    4.3. Implementation   71
    4.4. Limitations   72
5. Summary   72

4—PATH TESTING AND TRANSACTION FLOWS   75

1. Synopsis   75
2. Generalizations   75
3. Transaction Flows   75
    3.1. Definitions   75
    3.2. Example   76
    3.3. Usage   78
    3.4. Implementation   78
    3.5. Complications   81
4. Transaction-Flow Testing   82
    4.1. Get the Transaction Flows   82
    4.2. Test Design   83
    4.3. Path Selection   83
    4.4. Hidden Languages   85
    4.5. Instrumentation   86
5. Summary   87

5—GRAPHS, PATHS AND COMPLEXITY   89

1. Synopsis   89
2. Graphs   89

2.1. Notation   89
2.2. Names and Weights   91
2.3. Path Bases   92
2.4. Circuits   93
3. McCabe's Metric   96
   3.1. What is a Metric?   96
   3.2. Structural Complexity   97
   3.3. Applications   100
4. Summary   105

6—PATHS, PATH PRODUCTS, AND REGULAR EXPRESSIONS   107

1. Synopsis   107
2. Path Products and Path Expressions   107
   2.1. Basic Concepts   107
   2.2. Path Products   108
   2.3. Path Sums   110
   2.4. Distributive Law   111
   2.5. Absorption Rule   111
   2.6. Loops   112
   2.7. Null Sets and Nonpaths   113
3. A Reduction Procedure   113
   3.1. Overview   113
   3.2. Cross Term   114
   3.3. Parallel Term   116
   3.4. Loop Term   117
   3.5. Comments, Identities, and Node-Removal Order   119
4. Applications   120
   4.1. General   120
   4.2. How Many Paths in a Flowchart?   121
   4.3. Approximate Minimum Number of Paths   125
   4.4. The Probability of Getting There   129
   4.5. The Mean Processing Time of a Routine   133
   4.6. Push/Pop, Get/Return, Set/Reset   136
   4.7. Limitations and Solutions   141
5. Regular Expressions, Initialization, and Sequence Problems   142
   5.1. The Problem   142
   5.2. The Method   143
   5.3. An Example   144
   5.4. Generalizations, Limitations, and Comments   146
6. Summary   146

7—DATA VALIDATION AND SYNTAX TESTING   148

1. Synopsis   148
2. Garbage   148

2.1. A Protest 148
2.2. Casual and Malicious Users 149
2.3. Operators 149
2.4. The Internal World 150
2.5. What To Do 150
3. A Grammar for Formats 151
3.1. Objectives 151
3.2. BNF Notation 151
4. Test Case Generation 154
4.1. Generators, Recognizers, and Approach 154
4.2. Where Does the BNF Specification Come From? 155
4.3. Test Case Design 157
4.4. The Source of the Syntax 164
4.5. Where Did the Good Guys Go? 165
4.6. Running Syntax Tests 166
4.7. Ad-Lib Tests 167
5. Higher-Order Format Thinking 168
6. Summary 169

8—DATA-BASE-DRIVEN TEST DESIGN 170

1. Synopsis 170
2. The Data Base 170
2.1. Size and Scope 170
2.2. The Data Dictionary 171
2.3. Objectives of Data-Base-Driven Test Design 172
3. The Process 173
3.1. Overview and Prerequisites 173
3.2. Read the Documentation 173
3.3. The Master File 175
3.4. Data-Base Solitaire 177
3.5. The Interviews 178
3.6. The Confrontation 181
3.7. The Resolution 181
3.8. Scope and Effort 182
4. Specifics 182
4.1. Simple Fields and Parameters 182
4.2. Semantic Shifts 183
4.3. Type Changes 185
4.4. Representation Changes 186
4.5. Splatters, Mergers, and Overlaps 187
4.6. Access Changes 187
4.7. Dynamic Resources 187
4.8. Inconsistent Hooks and Changes 188
5. Other Uses and Other Scopes 190
6. Summary 190

9—DECISION TABLES AND BOOLEAN ALGEBRA   191

1. Synopsis   191
2. Decision Tables   191
   2.1. Definitions and Notations   191
   2.2. Decision Table Processors and Implementation   193
   2.3. Decision Tables as a Basis for Test Case Design   194
   2.4. Expansion of Immaterial Cases   195
   2.5. Test Case Design   197
   2.6. Decision Tables and Structure   198
3. Path Expressions Again   200
   3.1. General   200
   3.2. Notation   201
   3.3. Boolean Algebra   201
   3.4. Boolean Equations   206
4. Summary   208

10—BOOLEAN ALGEBRA THE EASY WAY   209

1. Synopsis   209
2. The Problem   209
3. K-V Charts   209
   3.1. Simple Forms   209
   3.2. Three Variables   213
   3.3. Four Variables and More   216
4. Specifications   219
   4.1. General   219
   4.2. Finding and Translating the Logic   219
   4.3. Ambiguities and Contradictions   222
   4.4. Don't-Care and Impossible Terms   223
5. Summary   226

11—STATES, STATE GRAPHS, AND TRANSITION TESTING   227

1. Synopsis   227
2. State Graphs   227
   2.1. States   227
   2.2. Inputs and Transitions   228
   2.3. Outputs   229
   2.4. State-Table Representation   231
   2.5. Software Implementation   231
3. Good State Graphs and Bad   233
   3.1. General   233
   3.2. State Bugs   235
   3.3. Transition Bugs   241
   3.4. Output Errors   247

3.5. Impact of Bugs   247
4. State Testing   247
   4.1. General Principles   247
   4.2. Limitations   248
   4.3. What to Model   249
5. Summary   250

12—GRAPH MATRICES AND APPLICATIONS   251

1. Synopsis   251
2. The Problem   251
3. The Matrix of a Graph   252
   3.1. Basic Principles   252
   3.2. A Simple Weight   253
   3.3. Further Notation   254
4. The Powers of a Matrix   255
   4.1. Principles   255
   4.2. Matrix Powers and Products   258
   4.3. The Set of All Paths   258
   4.4. Loops   260
5. Node-Reduction Method   261
   5.1. General   261
   5.2. Some Matrix Properties   261
   5.3. The Algorithm   262
   5.4. Applications   264
   5.5. Some Hints   267

REFERENCES   269

INDEX   283

SOFTWARE
TESTING
TECHNIQUES

1

INTRODUCTION

1. THE PURPOSE OF TESTING

1.1. What We Do

Testing consumes at least half of the labor required to produce a working program (BOEH75C, BROW73, GOOD79, WOLV75). Few programmers like testing and fewer like test design—especially if testing and test design are likely to take longer than program design and coding. This attitude is understandable. Software is ephemeral: you can't point to something physical. I think, deep down, most of us don't really believe in software—at least not the way we believe in hardware. If software is insubstantial, then how much more insubstantial is software testing? There isn't even debugged code to point to when we're through with test case design. The effort put into test design and testing seems wasted, especially if the tests don't reveal any bugs.

There's another, deeper problem with testing and test design that's related to the reason we have to do it in the first place (MILL78B). It's done to catch bugs. There's a myth that if we were really good at our jobs, there would be no bugs to catch. If only we could really concentrate, there would be no bugs. If only everyone used structured coding techniques, or top-down design, or decision tables, or if all programs had to be written in DOITALL or SQUISH, or if all programs were specified in terms of inverse-recursive-produlations, then there would be no bugs. So goes the myth. There are bugs, the myth insists, because we are bad at what we do; and if we are bad at what we do, we should feel guilty about it. Therefore, testing and test design is an admission of failure, which instills a goodly dose of guilt. And the tedium of testing is just punishment for our errors. Punishment for what? For being human? Guilt for what? For failing to achieve inhuman perfection? For failing to distinguish between what another programmer thinks and what he says? For not being telepathic? For not solving human communication problems that have been kicked around by philosophers and theologians for forty centuries?

The statistics indicate that programming, done well, will still have of the order of one bug per hundred statements (AKIY71, ALBE76, BOEH75B, ENDR75, SHOO75, THAY77). Certainly, if you have of the order of 10% errors, then you either need reeducation in programming or you deserve reprimand *and* guilt.* There are some persons who claim that they can write bug-free programs. There's a saying among sailors on the Chesapeake River, whose sandy, shifting bottom outdates charts before they're printed, "If you haven't run aground on the Chesapeake, you haven't sailed the Chesapeake much." So it is with programming and bugs: I have them, you have them, we all have them—and the point is to do what we can to prevent them and discover them but not to feel guilty about them. Programmers! Cast out your guilt! Spend half of your time in joyous testing and debugging! Thrill to the excitement of the chase! Stalk bugs with care, and with method, and with reason. Build traps for them. Be more artful than those devious bugs and taste the joys of guiltless programming!

1.2. Productivity and Quality in Software

Consider the manufacture of a mass-produced gadget. However great the cost of the design effort, when it is amortized over a large production run, it is a small part of the total cost. Once in production, every stage of manufacture is subjected to quality control and testing from the source inspection of components to the final testing prior to shipping. If errors or malfunctions are discovered at any stage, the gadget or part of it will either be discarded or will be cycled back for rework and correction. The productivity of the assembly line is measured by the sum of the costs of the materials, the rework, the discarded components, and the cost of quality assurance and testing. There is a trade between quality assurance costs and manufacturing costs. If insufficient effort is spent in quality assurance, the reject rate will be high and the net cost will be high. Conversely, if inspection is so good that all faults are caught as they occur, inspection costs will dominate, and again net cost will suffer. The designers of a manufacturing process attempt to establish a level of testing and quality assurance that minimizes net cost for a given quality objective. The cost of testing and quality assurance for manufactured products can be as low as 2% in consumer products or as high as 80% in products such as spaceships, atomic reactors, and aircraft, where failures are life threatening.

The relation between productivity and quality in software is distinctly different than in manufactured goods. The "manufacturing" cost of a copy

---

*The worst I ever saw was a five-hundred-instruction assembly language routine with an average of 2.2 bugs per instruction after syntax checking by the assembler. That person, obviously, did not belong in programming.

of software is trivial. It is the cost of the tape or disc and a few minutes of computer time. Furthermore, software "manufacturing" quality assurance is fully automated through the use of check-sums and other error-detecting methods. Software costs are almost completely expended in development. Software maintenance is totally unlike hardware maintenance. It is really an extended development in which enhancements are designed and installed, and deficiencies corrected. It is clear that the single largest component of software cost is the cost of bugs: the cost of detecting them, the cost of correcting them, the cost of designing tests that discover them, and the cost of executing those tests. Consequently, the primary aim of software quality assurance should be bug prevention.

1.3. Goals for Testing

Testing and test design, as components of quality assurance, should also focus on bug prevention. To the extent that testing and test design do not prevent bugs, they should discover symptoms caused by bugs, and finally, tests should provide clear diagnoses so that bugs can be easily corrected. Bug prevention is the primary goal of testing. A prevented bug is more desirable than a detected and corrected bug, because there is no code to correct if the bug is prevented, no retesting to confirm that the correction was valid, no one is embarrassed, no memory is consumed, and prevented bugs cannot adversely affect a schedule. More than the act of testing, the act of *designing* tests is one of the most effective bug preventers known. The thinking and analysis that must be done to create a useful test can discover and eliminate bugs before they are coded—indeed, test-design thinking can discover and eliminate bugs at every stage in the creation of software, from conception to specification, to design, coding, and the rest. The ideal test activity would be so successful at this that it would not be necessary to run the tests, because all bugs would have been found and fixed during test design.*

Unfortunately, this ideal cannot be achieved. Despite our effort, because we are human, there will be bugs. To the extent that testing fails to reach its primary goal of bug prevention, it must reach its secondary goal of clearly identifying that there is a bug. Bugs are not always obvious. A bug is manifested in deviations from expected behavior. A test design must document expectations, the test procedure in detail, and the results of the actual test—all of which are subject to error. But knowing that a program is incorrect does not imply knowing the bug. Different bugs can have the same

---

*I think that's what good programmers do—they test continuously and at every opportunity. "Test early and often" is their motto. It's not that they have fewer bugs, but that the habit of continual testing has kept their bugs private, and consequently cheaper.

manifestations, and one bug can have many symptoms. The symptoms and the causes can be disentangled only by using many small detailed tests.

1.4. Test Design

While programmers and programming managers know that code must be designed and tested, many appear to be unaware that tests themselves must be designed and tested—designed by a process no less rigorous and no less controlled than that which is used for code. Too often, test cases are attempted without prior analysis or careful consideration of the program's requirements or structure. Such test design, if you can call it that, is nothing more than a haphazard series of ad lib cases that are not documented either before or after the tests are executed. Because they were not formally designed, they cannot be precisely repeated, and no one is sure if there was a flaw or not. After the bug has been ostensibly corrected, no one is sure if the retest was identical to the test that found the flaw. Ad hoc tests are useful during debugging, where their primary purpose is to help locate the bug. However, ad hoc tests done in support of debugging, no matter how exhausting, are not substitutes for *designed* tests.

The test-design phase of programming should be explicitly identified. Instead of "design, code, desk check, test, and debug," the programming process should be described as: "design, test design, code, test code, program desk check, test desk check, test debugging, test execution, program debugging." Giving test design an explicit place in the scheme of things provides more visibility to that amorphous 50% of the labor that now goes under the name "test and debug." It makes it less likely that test design will be given short shrift when the budget's meager and the schedule's tight and there's a vague hope that maybe this time, just this once, the whole system will go together without bugs.

2. SOME DICHOTOMIES

2.1. Structure Versus Function

Tests can be designed from a functional or a structural point of view. In **functional testing** the program or system is treated as a black box. It is subjected to inputs, and its outputs are verified for conformance to specified objectives. The software's ultimate user should be concerned only with function, and the program's implementation details should not matter. Functional testing inherently takes the user's point of view.

Conversely, **structural testing** does look at the implementation details. Such things as programming style, control method, source language, database design, and coding details dominate structural testing. However, the boundary between function and structure is fuzzy. Good systems are built in layers—from the outside to the inside. The ultimate user sees only the outermost layer, the layer of pure function. Each layer inward is less related to the system's functions and more constrained by its structure. Therefore, what is structure to one layer is function to the next. For example, the outside user of an online system is not aware that the system has a memory-resource-allocation routine. For the user, such things are structural details. The memory-management routine's designer, however, is working from a specification for that routine. The specification is a definition of "function" at that layer. The resource-management routine uses a link-block subroutine. The resource-management routine's designer writes a "functional" specification for a link-block subroutine, thereby defining a further layer of structural detail and function. At deeper levels, the programmer views the operating system as a structural detail, while the operating system's designer treats the computer's hardware logic as the structural detail.

Most of this book is devoted to the exposition of models of programs and the tests that can be designed by using those models. A given model, and the associated tests may be first introduced in a structural context but later used again in a functional context, or vice versa. The initial choice of how to present a model was based on the context that seemed most natural for that model and in which it was most likely that the model would be used for test design. Just as you can't clearly distinguish function from structure, you can't fix the utility of a model to structural tests or functional tests. If it helps you design effective tests, then use the model in whatever context it seems to work.

There is no controversy concerning the use of structural versus functional tests at any level. Both methods are effective and both have limitations. Functional tests can, in principle, detect all bugs but would take infinite time to do so. Structural tests are inherently finite but cannot detect all errors, even if completely executed. The art of testing, in part, consists of making judicious choices between structural and functional tests.

2.2. The Designer Versus the Tester

If testing were totally based on functional specifications and independent of all implementation details, then it would be possible to completely separate the designer and the tester. Conversely, to design a test plan based completely on a system's structural details would require as great a knowledge of the design as that which the designer had, and it could only be done by the designer. The more you know about the design the more likely you are to eliminate useless test cases, which despite functional differences, are actually handled by the same routines over the same paths. However, the more you know about the design, the more likely you are to have the same misconceptions that the designer has. Ignorance of structure is the tester's best friend and worst enemy. The naive tester has no biases and no preconceptions as to what is or is not possible and can therefore design tests that the program's designer would never think of and many tests that never should be thought of. Knowledge, which is the designer's forte, brings efficiency to testing but also blindness to missing functions and strange cases. Tests designed and executed by the software's designers are by nature biased towards structural considerations and therefore suffer the limitations of structural testing. Tests designed and executed by an independent test team are bias free and can never be finished. Part of the artistry of testing is to balance knowledge and its attendant biases against ignorance and its attendant inefficiencies.

Throughout this book, I discuss the "tester," "test-team member," or "test designer" in contrast to the "programmer" and "program designer," as if they were distinct persons. As one goes from unit-level testing, to unit integration, to system testing, and finally to formal system functional testing, it is increasingly more effective if the "tester" and "programmer" actually are different persons. Most of the techniques presented in this book can be used at all levels of testing—from unit to system. When the technique is used at the system level, the designer and tester are probably different individuals. However, when the same technique is used in unit-level testing, the tester and programmer merge into one person, who sometimes acts as a programmer and sometimes as a tester.

You must be a constructive schizophrenic. Be clear about the difference between your role as a programmer and as a tester. The tester in you must be suspicious, uncompromising, hostile, and compulsively obsessed with destroying, utterly destroying, the programmer's software. The tester in you is your Mister Hyde—your Incredible Hulk. He must exercise what Gruenberger calls "low cunning." (HETZ 73) The programmer in you is trying to do a job in the simplest and cleanest way possible, on time, and within budget. Sometimes you achieve this by having great insights into the programming problem which reduce complexity and labor and which are almost correct. And with that Tester/Hulk lurking in the background of your mind, it pays to have a healthy paranoia concerning bugs. Remember, therefore, that when I refer to the "test designer" and "programmer" as separate individuals, the extent to which they are separated depends on the testing level and the context in which the technique is applied. This saves me the effort of writing about the same technique twice and you the tedium of reading it twice.

2.3. Modularity Versus Efficiency

Both tests and systems can be modular. A module is a discrete, well-defined, relatively small, component of a system. The smaller the module the easier it is to understand. However, each module implies interfaces with other modules, and *all* interfaces are sources of confusion. The smaller the module, therefore, the greater the likelihood of interface bugs. Large modules reduce external interfaces but have complicated internal logic that may be difficult or impossible to understand. Part of the artistry of software design consists of establishing module size and boundaries at points which balance internal complexity against interface complexity to achieve an overall minimization of complexity.

Testing can and should be organized into modules. Small, independent test cases have the virtue of simple repeatability. If an error is found as a result of testing, only the small test, not a large module that consists of a sequence of hundreds of interdependent tests, need be rerun to confirm that a bug has been fixed. Similarly, if the test has a bug, only that test need be changed and not a whole test plan. Microscopic test cases, however, require individual setup and each such setup (e.g. data base, inputs) can have bugs. As with system design, artistry comes into test design in establishing the scope of each test and groups of tests, so that test design, test debugging, and test execution labor are minimized without compromising effectiveness.

2.4. The Builder Versus The Buyer

Most software is written and used by the same organization. Unfortunately, this situation is inherently dishonest because it clouds accountability. More and more organizations are recognizing the virtue of independent software development and operation, because it leads to better software, better security, and better testing. Independent software development does not mean that all software should be bought from software houses or consultants, but that the software development entity and the entity that pays for the software are sufficiently separated as to make accountability clear. I've heard of instances in which the software development group and the operational group within the same company negotiate and sign formal contracts with one another—with lawyers present. If there is no separation between builder and buyer, there can be no accountability. If there is no accountability, the primary motivation for software quality disappears and with it any serious attempt to do proper testing. It might seem that I have a bias toward independent software houses, because throughout this book I've referred to builder and buyer as if they are separated. Just as programmers and testers can merge and become one, so can builder and buyer. There are several other persons in the software development cast of characters who, like the above, can also be separated or merged:

1. The **builder** who designs for and is accountable to
2. The **buyer**—who pays for the system in the hope of making a profit by providing services to
3. The **user**—the ultimate beneficiary or victim of the system. The user's interests are guarded by
4. The **tester**—who is dedicated to the builder's destruction and
5. The **operator**—who has to live with the builder's mistakes, the buyer's murky specifications, the tester's oversights, and the user's complaints.

3. A MODEL FOR TESTING

3.1. The Project

Testing is applied to anything from subroutines to systems that consist of millions of program statements. The archetype system, however, is one that allows the exploration of all aspects of testing without the managerial and organizational complications that have nothing to do with testing, but which affect any very large project. Testing a standalone routine that consists of a few hundred instructions is very different from testing a routine of the same size that must be integrated into a working program of a few hundred thousand instructions. Testing the interfaces between different parts of your own mind is very different from testing the interface between you and other programmers separated from you by geography, language, time, and disposition. Testing a one-shot routine that will be run only a few times is very different from testing one that must run for decades and may be modified by some unknown future programmer. While all the problems of the solitary routine occur for the routine that is embedded in a system, the converse is not true: many kinds of bugs simply cannot exist in solitary routines. The real world of programming is dominated by cooperative efforts and programming staffs of tens to hundreds. There is an implied context for the test methods discussed in this book—a real-world context, which can be characterized by the following model project:

Application—The specifics of the application are unimportant. It is a real-time system that must provide timely responses to user requests for services. It is an online system, which is connected to remote terminals by communications links.

Staff—The programming staff consists of 20 to 30 programmers—large enough to warrant some formality, but not too large to manage effectively—large enough to use specialists for various aspects of the system's design.

Schedule—The project will take 24 months from the start of design to formal acceptance by the customer. Acceptance will be followed by a six-month cutover period. There will be almost adequate computer resources for development and testing.

Specification—The specification is good. It is functionally detailed without constraining the design. There are, however, undocumented "understandings" concerning the requirements.

Acceptance Test—The system will be accepted only after a formal acceptance test. The application is not new and, therefore, part of the formal test already exists. The customer will initially intend to design the acceptance test, but later, it will become the software design team's responsibility.

Personnel—The staff is professional and experienced in programming and in the application. Half of the staff has programmed for that computer before, and most know the source language. One third, mostly at the junior level, have no experience with the application. The typical programmer has been employed by the programming department for two years and knows (likes and dislikes) 25% of the group. The general attitude is open and frank. Management's attitude is positive and knowledgeable about the realities of such projects.

Standards—There are programming standards and they are usually followed. There is an implicit understanding of the role of interfaces and the need for interface standards. Documentation is good. There is an internal, semi-formal, quality-assurance function. The data base is centrally developed and administered.

Objectives—The system is the first of many similar systems that will be implemented in the future. No two will be identical, but they will have 75% of the code in common. Once installed, the typical system is expected to operate profitably for ten or more years.

History—One programmer will quit before his module is tested. Another programmer will be fired before testing begins. The work will be excellent, but the documentation poor. One module will have to be totally redone after unit testing. It will be a superb piece of work that defies integration. The customer will insist on five major changes and twenty minor ones. There will be at least one nasty problem that nobody, not customer, not programmer, not management, nor the hardware vendor suspected. A facility and/or hardware-delivery problem will delay testing for several weeks and force second- and third-shift work. Several important milestones will slip but the delivery date will be met.

In other words, our model environment is typical of a reasonably well-run, successful project with a share of glory and catastrophe. Not a utopian project, but not a slice of hell either.

3.2. Overview

Figure 1-1 is a model of the testing process. The process starts with a program embedded in an environment, such as a computer, an operating system, or a calling program. There is an implicit understanding of human nature and its suceptibility to error. This understanding leads us to create three models: a model of the environment, a model of the program, and a model of the bugs expected. From these models we create a set of tests which are then executed. The result of each test is either expected or unexpected. If unexpected, it may lead us to revise the test, our model or concept of how the program behaves, our concept of what bugs are possible, or the program itself. Only rarely would we attempt to modify the environment.

3.3. The Environment

A program's environment is the hardware and software required to make it run. In online systems, the environment may include communications lines and facilities, other systems, terminals, and operators. The environment also

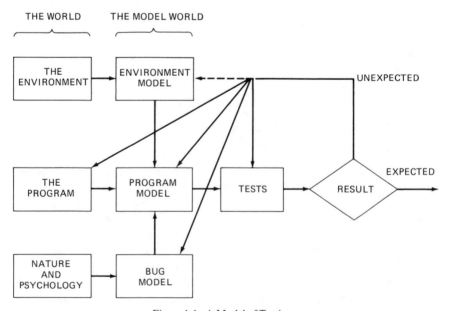

Figure 1-1. A Model of Testing.

includes all programs that interact with, and that are used to create, the program under test, such as an operating system, a loader, a linkage editor, a compiler, utility routines.

Programmers should learn early in their careers that it is not effective to quickly blame the environment (that is, hardware and firmware) for bugs. Hardware bugs are rare. So are bugs in manufacturer-supplied software. This isn't because logic designers and operating system programmers are better than application programmers, but because such hardware and software is stable, tends to be in operation for a long time, and consequently, most bugs will have been found and fixed by the time the typical programmer uses that hardware or software. New computers and new operating systems, of course, present a totally different situation. Because hardware and firmware are stable, we don't have to consider all of the environment's complexity. Instead, we work with a simplification of it, in which only the features most directly related to the program at hand are considered. Our model of the environment includes our *beliefs* regarding such things as the workings of the computer's instruction set, operating system macros and commands, and what a higher-order language statement will do. If testing reveals an unexpected result, it may be necessary to change our beliefs, (our model of the environment) to find out what went wrong. Occasionally, the environment may be wrong: the bug could be in the hardware or firmware after all.

3.4. The Program

Most programs are too complicated to be understood in detail. We must simplify our concept of the program in order to test it. Therefore, while a real program is being exercised on the test bed, we are in our brains dealing with a simplified version of it: a version in which most of the details are ignored. If the program calls a subroutine, we tend not to think about the subroutine's details unless its operation is suspect. Similarly, we may ignore processing details to focus on the program's control structure or ignore the control structure to focus on the processing. As with the environment, if the simple model of the program does not explain the unexpected behavior, we may have to modify that model to include more facts and more detail. And if that fails, we may have to modify the program.

3.5. Bugs

Bugs tend to be more insidious than ever we expect them to be. Yet it is convenient to categorize them: initialization, call-sequence, wrong variable, and so on. Our notion of what is or is not a bug is also variable. A poorly written specification may lead us to mistake proper behavior for bugs and vice versa. An unexpected test result may lead us to change our notion of what constitutes a bug—which is to say, our model of bugs.

3.6. Tests

Tests are formal procedures. Inputs must be prepared, outputs predicted, tests documented, commands executed, and results observed; all these steps are subject to error. There is nothing magical about testing and test design that immunizes testers against bugs. An unexpected test result is as often due to a test bug as it is to a real bug. Bugs can creep into the documentation, the inputs, and the commands and becloud our observation of results. An unexpected test result, therefore, may lead us to revise the tests. Because the tests are themselves in an environment, we also have a mental model of the tests, and instead of revising the tests, we may have to revise that mental model.

3.7. The Role of Models

Testing is a continuing process in which we create mental models of the environment, the program, human nature, and the tests themselves. Each model is used until either correct behavior is demonstrated or until the model is no longer sufficient for the purpose. Unexpected test results always force a revision of some mental model, which in turn may lead to a revision of that which is being modeled. The revised model may be more detailed, which is to say more complicated, or more abstract, which is to say simpler. The art of testing consists of creating, selecting, exploring, and revising models. Our ability to do this depends on the number of different models we have at hand and their ability to express a program's behavior.

4. IS COMPLETE TESTING POSSIBLE?

If the objective of testing were to *prove* that a program is free of bugs, then not only would testing be practically impossible, but it would also be theoretically impossible. Three different approaches can be used to demonstrate that a program is correct: tests based purely on structure, tests based purely on function, and formal proofs of correctness. Each approach leads to the conclusion that complete testing, in the sense of a *proof* is not theoretically possible, and certainly not practically possible (MANN78).

Functional Testing—Every program operates on a finite number of inputs. Whatever pragmatic meaning those inputs might have, they can always be interpreted as a binary bit stream. A complete functional test would consist of subjecting the program to all possible input streams. For each input, the routine either accepts the stream and produces a correct output, or accepts the stream and produces an incorrect output, or it rejects the stream and tells us that it did so. Because the rejection message is itself an output, the problem is reduced to verifying that the correct output is produced for every input. However, a ten-character input string has 2^{80} possible input streams and corresponding outputs. So complete functional testing in this sense is clearly impractical.*

Unfortunately, even theoretically, we cannot execute a purely functional test this way because we don't really know the length of the string to which the system is responding. Let's say that the routine should respond to a ten-character string. It should be reset after the tenth character, and the next ten characters should constitute a new test. However, the routine has a huge buffer and is actually responding to 10,000-character strings. The bug is such that the program will appear to provide a proper output for every ten-character sequence the first thousand times and fail on the 1001st attempt. Without a limit to the routine's memory capacity, which is a structural concept, it is impossible even in principle to prove that the routine is correct.

There are two additional problems: the input sequence generator and the output comparator. Is it to be assumed that the hardware and software used to generate the inputs, used to compare the real outputs to the expected outputs, and used to document the expected outputs themselves, are bug free? Pure functional testing is at best conditional on a nonverifiable assumption that all test tools and test preparation tools are correct and that only the routine being tested is at fault; in the real world of testing, that assumption is silly.

Structural Testing—One should design a sufficient number of tests to assure that every path through the routine is exercised at least once. Right off that's impossible, because some loops might never terminate. Brush that problem aside by observing that the universe and all that's in it is finite. Even so, the number of paths through a small routine can be awesome, because each loop multiplies the path count by the number of times through the loop. A small routine can have millions or billions of paths. Total path testing is not generally practical. Total path testing can be done for some routines. Say we do it. This has the virtue of eliminating the problems of unknown size that we ran into for purely functional testing, but it does not eliminate the problem of preparing a bug-free input, a bug-free response list, and a bug-free test observation. We still need those

---

*At one test per microsecond, approximately four times the current estimated age of the universe.

things, because purely structural testing does not assure us that the routine is doing the right thing in the first place.

Correctness Proofs—Formal proofs of correctness rely on a combination of functional and structural concepts. Requirements are stated in a formal language (e.g. mathematics), and each program statement is examined and used in a step of an inductive proof that the routine will produce the correct output for all possible input sequences. The practical issue here is that such proofs are very expensive and have been applied only to numerical routines or to formal proofs for crucial software such as a system's security kernel or portions of compilers. But there are theoretical objections to formal proofs of correctness that go beyond the practical issues. How do we know that the specification is achievable? It's consistency and completeness must be proven, and in general, that is a provably unsolvable problem. Assuming that the specification has been proven correct, then the mechanism used to prove the program, the steps in the proof, the logic used, and so on, must be proven (GOOD75). Mathematicians and logicians have no more immunity to bugs than programmers or testers have. This also leads to never-ending sequences of unverifiable assumptions.

Manna and Waldinger (MANN78) have clearly summarized the theoretical barriers to complete testing:

"We can never be sure that the specifications are correct."
"No verification system can verify every correct program."
"We can never be certain that a verification system is correct."

Not only are all known approaches to absolute demonstrations of correctness impractical, but they are impossible as well. Therefore, our objective must shift from an absolute proof to a suitably convincing demonstration—from a deduction to a seduction. That word "suitable," if it is to have the same meaning to everyone, implies a quantitative measure, which in turn implies a statistical measure of software reliability. Our goal, then, should be to provide sufficient testing to assure that the probability of failure due to hibernating bugs is sufficiently low to be acceptable. "Sufficient" implies judgment. What is sufficient to a videogame is not sufficient to a nuclear reactor. We can expect that each application will eventually evolve its own software reliability standards. Concurrently, test techniques will evolve to the point where it will be possible, on the basis of test results, to provide a quantitative prediction of the routine's reliability. But this is still in the future. For now, it seems that all testing, in most applications, must be substantially increased (perhaps by an order of magnitude) before such measures can be applied and interpreted with confidence.

2

THE TAXONOMY OF BUGS

1. SYNOPSIS

What are the possible consequences of bugs? Bugs are categorized. Statistics and frequency of occurrence of various bugs are given.

2. THE CONSEQUENCES OF BUGS

Every bug has consequences that range from mild to catastrophic, or worse. These consequences should be measured in human rather than in machine terms, because it is ultimately for humans that we write programs. If you answer the question, "What are the consequences of this bug?" in machine terms by saying, for example, "Bit so-and-so will be set instead of reset," you are avoiding responsibility for the bug. Although it may be difficult to do in the scope of a subroutine, programmers should attempt to measure the consequences of bugs in their routine in human terms. Here are some consequences on a scale of one to ten:

1. *Mild*—The symptoms of the bug offend us aesthetically; a misspelled output or a badly aligned printout.
2. *Moderate*—Outputs are misleading or redundant. The bug has a small but measurable impact on the system's performance.
3. *Annoying*—The system's behavior, because of the bug, is dehumanizing. Names are truncated or arbitrarily modified. Bills for $0.00 are sent. Operators must use unnatural command sequences and must trick the system into a proper response for unusual, bug-related cases.
4. *Disturbing*—It refuses to handle legitimate transactions. The money machine refuses to cash your paycheck. My credit card is not accepted at the bookstore.
5. *Serious*—It loses track of transactions: not just the transaction itself (your paycheck), but the fact that the transaction occurred. Accountability is lost.

15

6. *Very Serious*—Instead of losing your paycheck, the system credits it to another account or converts a deposit into a withdrawal. The bug causes the system to do the wrong transaction.

7. *Extreme*—The above problems are not limited to a few users or to a few transaction types. They occur frequently and arbitrarily, instead of sporadically for strange cases.

8. *Intolerable*—Long-term, irrecoverable corruption of the data base occurs. Furthermore, this corruption is not easily discovered. Serious consideration is given to shutting the system down.

9. *Catastrophic*—The decision to shut down is taken out of our hands. The system fails.

10. *Infectious*—What can be worse than a failed system? One that corrupts other systems even though it does not fail itself; that erodes the social or physical environment; that melts nuclear reactors or starts wars; whose influence, because of malfunction, is far greater than expected, or wanted; a system that kills.

Any of these consequences could follow from that wrong bit. Programming is a serious business, and testing is more serious still. It pays to have nightmares about undiscovered bugs once in a while (SHED80). When was the last time one of your bugs violated someone's human rights?

3. A TAXONOMY FOR BUGS

3.1. General

There is no universally correct way to categorize bugs. This taxonomy is not rigid. Bugs are difficult to categorize, because they usually have several symptoms. A given bug can be put into one or another category depending on the history of the bug and the programmer's state of mind. For example, a one-character error in a source statement changes the statement, but unfortunately, it passes syntax checking. As a result, data are corrupted in an area far removed from the actual bug. That in turn leads to an improperly executed function. Is this a keypunch error, a coding error, a data error, or a functional error? If the bug is in our own program, we are tempted to blame it on keypunching; if in another programmer's code, on carelessness. And if our job is to critique the system, we might say that the fault lies in its inadequate internal data-validation mechanism. The broad categories are: function bugs, system bugs, data bugs, and code errors. The function bugs can be subdivided into specification errors, incorrect functions, testing errors, and validation-criteria errors. System bugs include external interfaces, internal interfaces, hardware-achitecture problems, operating system problems, software architecture problems, control and sequence bugs, and resource-management bugs. Process errors can involve basic manipulations, initialization, control and sequence, and static logic.

3.2. Function-Related Bugs

3.2.1. Specification Problems

Specifications can be incomplete, ambiguous, or self-contradictory. They can be misunderstood or incapable of being understood. The specification may assume, but not mention, additional specifications and prerequisites which are known to the specifier but not the designer. And specifications that do not have these flaws may change while the design is in progress. Functions are modified, added, and deleted. The designer has to hit a moving target and occasionally misses.

3.2.2. Function Errors

Specification problems usually create corresponding functional problems. A function can be wrong, missing, or superfluous. A missing function is the easiest to detect and correct. A wrong function could have deep design implications. Extra functions were at one time considered desirable. It is now recognized that "free" functions are rarely free. Any increase in generality that does not contribute to software reliability, modularity, maintainability, and system robustness should be suspected. Gratuitous enhancements can, if they increase the system's complexity, accumulate into a fertile compost heap that breeds future bugs, and they can burrow holes that can be converted into system security breaches. Conversely, one cannot rigidly forbid additional features that might be a consequence of good design. Removing the features might complicate the software, require additional resources, and foster additional bugs.

3.2.3. Testing

Testers have no immunity to bugs; neither do specification writers. Tests, particularly system-level functional tests, require complicated scenarios and data bases. They require code or the equivalent to execute, and consequently, they can have bugs. The virtue of independent functional testing is that it provides an unbiased point of view. But that lack of bias creates an opportunity for different, and possibly incorrect, interpretations of the specification. While test bugs are not system bugs, it's hard to tell them apart, and considerable labor can be expended in making the distinction.

3.2.4. Test Criteria

The specification is correct, it is correctly interpreted and implemented, and in principle, a proper test has been designed. However, the criterion by which the system's behavior is judged is incorrect or impossible. How would you, for example, "prove that the entire system is free of bugs?" If a criterion is quantitative, such as a throughput or processing delay, the act of measuring the performance can perturb the performance measured. The more complicated the criteria, the more likely they are to have bugs.

3.2.5. Remedies

Most function-related bugs are rooted in human-to-human communication problems. One of the proposed solutions being researched is the use of high-level, formal, specification languages (BOEH79, FISC79, YEHR80). Such languages may or may not help. If the specification language were really good, and it were possible, even theoretically, to create an unambiguous, complete specification with an unambiguous, complete test, and completely consistent test criteria, then a specification written in that language would be theoretically capable of automatic conversion into code (ignoring efficiency and practicality issues). But this is just programming in HOL squared. The specification problem has been shifted to a higher level but not eliminated. The real impact of formal specification languages will probably be that they will influence the design of ordinary programming languages so that more of the specification can be formalized. This will reduce, but not eliminate, specification-related errors.

Assurance of functional correctness is provided by an independent interpretation of the specification and independent, system-level, functional testing. The remedy for test bugs is testing and debugging the tests. The differences between test debugging and program debugging are not fundamental. Generally, test debugging is easier, because tests, when properly designed, are simpler than programs and do not have to make concessions to efficiency. Programmers have the right to ask how quality in independent testing and test design is monitored. Should we implement test testers and test-tester tests? This sequence does not converge. Methods for test quality assurance are discussed in *Software System Testing and Quality Assurance* (BEIZ83).

3.3. System Bugs

3.3.1. External Interfaces

The external interfaces are the means the system uses to communicate with the world. These include devices, actuators, sensors, input consoles, printers, and communication lines. Often, there is a person on the other side of the interface. That person may be ingenious or ingenuous, but often malevolent. The principal design criterion for an interface with the outside world is robustness. All external interfaces, human or machine, employ a formally or informally specified protocol. Protocols are complicated and hard to understand. The protocol itself may be wrong, especially if it's new, or it may be implemented incorrectly. Other external interface errors include: invalid timing or sequence assumptions related to external signals; misunderstanding external input and output formats; insufficient tolerance to bad input data. The test design methods of Chapters 7and ll are suited to testing external interfaces.

3.3.2. Internal Interfaces

Internal interfaces are in principle not different from external interfaces, but there are differences in practice because the internal environment is more controlled. While the external environment is fixed, and the system must adapt to it, the internal environment, which consists of interfaces with other programs, can be negotiated. Internal interfaces have the same problems external interfaces have and a few more that are more closely related to implementation details: protocol-design errors, input- and output-format errors, inadequate protection against corrupted data, wrong subroutine call sequence, call-parameter errors, misunderstood entry or exit parameter values.

To the extent that internal interfaces, protocols, and formats are formalized, the test methods of Chapters 7, 8, and ll will be helpful. The real remedy, however, is in the design and in project standards. Internal interfaces should be standardized and not just allowed to grow. They should be formal, and there should be as few as possible. There is an inherent trade between the number of different internal interfaces and the complexity of the interfaces. One universal interface would have so many parameters that it would be inefficient and subject to abuse, misuse, and misunderstanding. Unique interfaces for every pair of communicating routines would be efficient, but N programmers could lead to N^2 interfaces, most of which wouldn't be documented and all of which would have to be tested (but wouldn't be). The primary objective of system integration testing is to test all internal interfaces (BEIZ83).

3.3.3. Hardware Architecture

It's easy to forget that hardware exists. It's possible to have a programming career and never see a computer. When you are working through successive layers of application executive, operating system, compiler, and other intervening software, it's understandable that the hardware architecture appears abstract and remote. It is neither practical nor economical for every programmer in a large project to be knowledgeable in all aspects of the hardware architecture. Software bugs related to hardware architecture arise mainly from misunderstanding how the hardware works. Here are examples: paging mechanism ignored or misunderstood, address-generation error, I/O-device operation or instruction error, I/O-device address error, misunderstood device-status code, improper hardware simultaneity assumption, hardware race condition ignored, data format wrong for device, wrong format expected, device protocol error, device instruction-sequence limitation ignored, expecting the device to respond too quickly, waiting too long for a response, ignoring channel throughput limits, assuming that the device is initialized, assuming that the device is not initialized, incorrect interrupt handling, ignoring hardware fault or error conditions, ignoring operator malice.

The remedy for hardware architecture and interface problems is twofold: 1) good programming and testing, and 2) centralization of hardware interface software in programs that are written by hardware interface specialists. Hardware interface testing is complicated by the fact that modern hardware has very few buttons, switches, and lights. Old computers had lots of them, and it was possible to abuse those buttons and switches to create wonderful anomalous interface conditions that could not be simulated any other way. Today's highly integrated black boxes rarely have such controls*, and consequently, considerable ingenuity may be needed to simulate and test hardware interface status conditions. Modern hardware is better and cheaper without the buttons and lights, but also harder to test. This paradox can be resolved by hardware that has special test modes and test instructions that do what the buttons and switches used to do. The hardware manufacturers as a group, have yet to provide adequate features of this kind.

3.3.4. Operating System

Program bugs related to the operating system are a combination of hardware architecture and interface bugs, mostly due to misunderstanding what it is the operating system does. And of course, the operating system could have bugs of its own. Operating systems can lull the programmer into believing that all hardware interface issues are handled by it. Furthermore, as the operating system matures, bugs in it are found and corrected, but some of these corrections may leave quirks. Sometimes the bug is not fixed at all, but

---

*You don't have to believe this, but there is one minicomputer with fake buttons and lights silk-screened on the front panel—as if the manufacturer had to conform to the cartoonist's notion of what computers should look like. So much for nostalgia.

a notice of the problem is buried somewhere in the documentation—if only you knew where to look for it.

The remedy for operating system interface bugs is the same as for hardware bugs: use operating system interface specialists, and use explicit interface modules or macros for all operating system calls. This may not eliminate the bugs, but at least it will localize them and make testing easier.

3.3.5. Software Architecture

Software architecture bugs are the kind that are called "interactive." Routines can pass unit and integration testing without revealing such bugs. Many of these bugs are load dependent and occur only when the system is stressed. They tend to be the most difficult kind of bug to find and exhume. Here is a sample of the causes of such bugs: assumption that there will be no interrupts, failure to block or unblock interrupts, assumption that code is reentrant or not reentrant, bypassing data interlocks, failure to close or open an interlock, assumption that a called routine is resident or not resident, assumption that a calling program is resident or not resident, assumption that registers or memory were initialized or not initialized, assumption that register or memory location content did not change, local setting of global parameters, and global setting of local parameters.

The first line of defense against these bugs is the design. The first bastion of that defense is that there be a design for the overall software architecture. Failure to create an explicit software architecture is an unfortunate but common disease. The most elegant test techniques will be helpless in a complicated system whose architecture "just growed" without plan or structure. All test techniques are applicable to the discovery of software architecture bugs, but experience has shown that careful integration of modules and subjecting the final system to a brutal stress test are particularly effective (BEIZ83).

3.3.6. Control and Sequence Errors

These are system-level control and sequence errors. They include: ignoring timing, assuming that events occur in a specified sequence, initiating a process before its prerequisites are met (e.g., attempting to work on data before it has arrived from disc), waiting for an impossible combination of prerequisites, failing to recognize when prerequisites have been met, specifying wrong priority, program state, or processing level, missing process step, using wrong process step, redundant process step, superfluous process step.

The remedy for these bugs is in the design. Highly structured sequence control is helpful. Specialized, internal, sequence-control mechanisms, such as an internal job control language, are useful. Sequence steps and prerequisites stored in tables and processed interpretively by a sequence-control processor or dispatcher make process sequences easier to test and to modify if bugs are discovered. **Path testing** as applied to **transaction-flow diagrams**, as discussed in Chapter 4, is particularly effective in detecting control and sequence bugs at the system level.

3.3.7. Resource Management Problems

Memory is subdivided into dynamically allocated resources such as buffer blocks, queue blocks, task-control blocks, and overlay buffers. Similarly, external mass storage units such as discs, are subdivided into memory-resource pools. Here are some resource usage and management bugs: required resource not obtained (rare), wrong resource used (common, if there are several resources with the same structure or different kinds of resources in the same pool), resource already in use, race condition in getting a resource, resource not returned to the right pool, fractionated resources not properly recombined (some resource managers take big resources and subdivide them into smaller resources, and Humpty Dumpty isn't always put together again), failure to return a resource (common), resource deadlock (a type A resource is needed to get a type B, a type B is needed to get a type C, and a type C is needed to get a type A), resource use forbidden to the caller, used resource not returned, resource linked to the wrong kind of queue, forgetting to return a resource.

A design remedy that prevents bugs is always preferable to a test method that discovers them. The design remedy in resource management is to keep the resource structure simple: the fewest different kinds of resources, the fewest pools, and no private resource management. Complicated resource structures are often designed in an attempt to save memory and not because they are essential. The system has to handle, say, large-, small-, and medium-length transactions, and it is reasoned that memory will be saved if three different-sized resources are implemented. This reasoning is often faulty because:

1. Memory is cheap and getting cheaper.
2. Complicated resource structures and multiple pools need software; that software needs memory, and the increase in program space could be bigger than the expected data space saved.
3. The complicated scheme takes additional processing time, which means that all resources are held in use a little longer. The size of the pools will have to be increased to compensate for this additional holding time.

4. The basis for sizing the resource is often wrong. A typical choice is to make the buffer block's length equal to the length required by an average transaction. This is usually a poor choice. A correct analysis (see BEIZ78, pages 301-302) shows that in most cases, the optimum resource size is proportional to the square root of the transaction's length. Square root laws are relatively insensitive to parameter changes. Consequently, the wastage entailed in using many short blocks for a long transaction or in using a large block to store a short transaction is not as bad as intuition might suggest.

The second design remedy is to centralize the management of all pools, either through centralized resource managers, common resource-management subroutines, resource-management macros, or a combination of these.

I mentioned resource loss three times—it was not a writing bug. Resource loss is the most frequent resource-related bug. Common sense tells you why programmers lose resources. You need the resource to process—so it's unlikely that you'll forget to get it. Once the job is done, however, the successful conclusion of the task will not be affected if the resource is not returned. A well-designed routine attempts to get resources as early as possible and at a common point and also attempts to return them at a common point. However, strange paths may require additional resources, and you could forget that you have two resource units instead of one. Furthermore, an exception-condition handler that responds to system threatening illogical conditions may bypass the normal exit and jump directly to an executive level—there goes the resource. The design remedies are to centralize resource fetch-and-return within each routine and to provide macros that return all resources rather than just one. Resource-loss problems are exhumed by path testing (Chapters 3 and 4), the methods of Chapter 6, and stress testing (BEIZ83).

3.4. Process Errors

3.4.1. Arithmetic and Manipulative Bugs

These bugs include arithmetic errors and their extension into algebra, function evaluation, and general processing. Many problems in this area are related to incorrect conversion from one data representation to another. This is particularly true in assembly language programming. Other problems include: ignoring overflow, ignoring the difference between positive and negative zero, improper use of greater, greater-than-or-equal, less-than, less-than-or-equal, assumption of equality to zero in floating point, and improper comparison between different formats as in ASCII to binary or integer to floating point.

The best design remedy is in the source language. A **strongly typed language**, that is, language that does not permit the inadvertent combination of different data types or that warns the programmer when such operations are attempted, can minimize this kind of error. If such language facilities are not available, the use of macros and arithmetic subroutines, particularly in assembly language programming, are effective.

3.4.2. Initialization Bugs

Initialization-related bugs are among the most common. Both the failure to initialize properly and superfluous initialization occur. The latter tends to be less harmful but can affect performance. Typical errors are: forgetting to initialize working space, registers, or data areas before first use or assuming that they are initialized elsewhere; error in the first value of a loop-control parameter; accepting an initial value without a validation check; and initializing to the wrong format, data representation, or type.

The remedies here are in the kinds of tools the programmer has. The source language is also helpful. Forcing explicit declaration of all variables, as in Pascal, helps to reduce some initialization problems. Preprocessors, either built into the language or run separately, can detect some but not all initialization problems. The test methods of Chapter 6 are helpful in designing tests and in debugging initialization problems.

3.4.3. Control and Sequence Bugs

These are similar to control and sequence errors at the system level, but they are usually easier to test and debug, because they tend to have more localized effects: paths left out, unreachable code, improper nesting of loops, loop-back or loop-termination criteria incorrect, missing process steps, error in process step, duplicated processing, unnecessary processing, improper assumption about processing by-products, and unwanted by-products.

Control and sequence errors at all levels are caught by testing, particularly structural testing, combined with a bottom-line functional test based on a specification. The problem at the unit level is that there often is no formal specification of what is wanted. While informal or absent design specifications are appropriate for throwaway code, even small routines in a large system must have formal design specifications.

3.4.4 Static Logic

Static-logic errors are errors in logic, particularly those related to misunderstanding how case statements and elementary logic operators behave singly and in combinations: nonexistent cases, improper layout of cases, "impossible" case is not impossible, a "don't-care" case matters, improper negation of boolean expression (for example, using "greater than" as the negation of "less than"), improper simplification and combination of cases, overlap of exclusive cases, confusing "exclusive-or" with "inclusive-or."

These errors are not really different in kind from arithmetic errors. They are more likely to occur than arithmetic errors because programmers, like most people, have less formal training in logic at an early age than they do in arithmetic. The best defense against this kind of bug is a systematic analysis of cases. The methods of Chapters 9 and 10 are helpful.

3.5. Data Errors

3.5.1. General

Data errors include all errors that arise from the specification of data elements, their formats, the number of such elements, and their initial values. Data errors are at least as common as code errors, but they are often treated as if they did not exist at all. The underestimation of the frequency of data-related bugs is due to bad bug accounting. In some projects, bugs in data declaration statements are simply not counted, and for that matter, data declaration statements are not counted as part of the code. The separation of code and data is, of course, artificial because their roles can be interchanged at will. At the extreme, one can write a 20-instruction program that will suffice to simulate any computer (a Turing machine) and have all "programs" recorded as data and manipulated as such. Furthermore, this can be done in any language on any computer—but who would want to do it?

Software is evolving toward programs in which more and more of the control and processing functions is stored in tables. Because of this, there is an increasing awareness that coding errors are only half the battle and that data-base problems should be given equal attention. Examine a piece of contemporary source code—you may find that half of the statements are data declarations. Although these statements do not result in executable code, because they are specified by humans, they are as subject to error as operative statements. If a program is designed under the assumption that a certain data item will be set to zero and it isn't, while the operative statements of the program are not at fault, there is still an initialization error, which, because it is in a data declaration, could be much harder to find than if it had been an error in executable code.

This increase in the proportion of the source statements devoted to data declaration is a direct consequence of two factors: 1) the dramatic reduction in the cost of main memory and disc storage, and 2) the high cost of creating and testing software. Generalized processors that are controlled by tables are not efficient of processing time and memory. Computer costs, especially memory costs, have decreased to the point where the additional inefficiencies of generalized table-driven code are not usually significant. The increasing cost of software as a percentage of total system cost has shifted the emphasis in the software industry away from single-purpose, unique software, to an increased reliance on prepackaged, generalized programs. This trend is evident in the computer manufacturers' software and in the existence of a healthy proprietary software industry. Generalized packages must satisfy a wide range of options, host configurations, operating systems, and computers. The designer of a generalized package achieves generality, in part, through heavy parameterization of the program. Things like array sizes, memory partition, and file structure, may be parametric. It is not unusual for a large application package to have several hundred parameters. Setting the parameter values particularizes the program to the specific installation. The parameters are interrelated, and errors in those relations can cause illogical conditions and therefore, bugs.

Another source of increase in data-base complexity is the use of control tables in lieu of code. The simplest example is the use of tables that turn processing options on and off, either permanently or dynamically. A more complicated form of control table is used when a system must execute a set of closely related processes that have the same control structure but are different in details. An early, classical example, is found in telephony, where the details of setting up and controlling a telephone call are table driven. This allows a generalized call-control processor to handle calls from and to different kinds of lines. The system is loaded with a set of tables that corresponds to the protocols required for that telephone exchange. Another example is the use of generalized device-control software that is particularized by data stored in device tables. This allows the operating system to be used with new, undefined devices, if those devices' parameters can fit into a set of very broad values. The culmination of this trend is the use of complete, internal, transaction-control languages that are designed for the application. Instead of being coded as computer instructions or language statements, the steps required to process a transaction are stored as a sequence of constants in a transaction-processing table. The state of the transaction, that is, the current processing step, is stored in a transaction-control block. The generalized transaction-control processor uses the combination of transaction state and the control tables to direct the transaction to the next step. The transaction-control table is actually a program which is processed interpretively by the transaction-control processor. That program may contain the equivalent of addressing, conditional-branch instructions, looping statements, case statements, and so on. In other words, an internal programming language has been created. It is an effective design technique because it allows fixed software to handle many different transaction types, individually and simultaneously. Furthermore, modifying the control tables to incorporate new transaction types is usually easier than making the same modifications in code.

In summary, current programming trends are leading to the increasing use of undeclared, internal, specialized programming languages. These are really languages—make no mistake about that—even if they are simple by normal language standards. However, the syntax of these languages might not have been debugged.There is no assembler or compiler for them. The programs in these languages are inserted as octal or hexadecimal codes—as if we were programming back in the early days of UNIVAC-I. Large, low-cost, memory will continue to strengthen this trend, and consequently, there will be an increased incidence of code masquerading as data. Bugs in this kind of hidden code are as, if not more, difficult to find as bugs in normal code. The first step in the avoidance of data-related errors, whether that data is used as pure data, as parameters, or as pseudo-code, is the realization that *all* source statements, particularly data declarations, must be counted, and that all source statements, whether or not they result in object code, are bug prone.

The categories used for data bugs are different from those used for code bugs. Each way of looking at data provides a different perspective on the possible bugs. These categories for data bugs overlap and are no stricter than the categories used for code bugs.

3.5.2. Dynamic Versus Static

Dynamic data is transitory. Whatever its purpose, it has a relatively short lifetime, typically the processing time of a single transaction. A storage element may be used to hold dynamic data of different types, with different formats, attributes, and residues. Failure to properly initialize a shared structure will lead to data-dependent bugs because of possible residues from a previous use of that block by another transaction. Note that the culprit transaction is long gone when the bug's symptoms are discovered. Because the effect of corruption of dynamic data can be arbitrarily far removed from the cause, such bugs are among the most difficult to catch. The design remedy is complete documentation of all shared memory structures, defensive code that does thorough data-validation checks, and centralized resource managers.

The basic problem is leftover garbage in a shared resource. This can be handled in one of three ways: 1) cleanup after use by the user, 2) common cleanup by the resource manager, and 3) no cleanup. The latter is the method usually used. This means that all resource users must be aware of and must program under the assumption that the resource contains garbage when gotten from the resource manager. Common cleanup is used in very secure systems where it is imperative that no subsequent user of a resource could inadvertently read data that had been left by a previous user in a higher security or privacy category.

Static data is fixed in form and content. Whatever its purpose, it appears in the source code or data base, directly or indirectly, as, for example, a number, a string of characters, or a bit pattern. Static data need not appear explicitly in the source code. Some languages allow **compile-time processing**. This is particularly useful in general purpose routines that are particularized by interrelated parameters. Compile-time processing is an effective measure against parameter-value conflicts. Instead of relying on the programmer to calculate the correct values of interrelated parameters, a program , which is executed at compile time (or assembly time) calculates the parameter's values. Alternatively, if compile-time processing is not a language feature, then a specialized preprocessor can be built which checks the parameter values and calculates those values that are derived from others. As an example, a large commercial telecommunications system has several hundred parameters that dictate the number of lines, the layout of all storage media, the hardware configuration, the characteristics of the various lines, the allowable user options for those lines, and so on. These are processed by a site-adapter program that not only sets the parameter values but builds data declarations, sizes arrays, creates constants, and inserts processing routines from a library. A bug in the site adapter, or in the data given to the site adapter, can result in bugs in the static data used by the object programs for that site.

Any preprocessing code, any code executed at compile or assembly time or before, can lead to faulty static data and therefore bugs—even though such code and the execution thereof does not represent object code at run time. We tend to take compilers, assemblers, and utilities for granted and do not suspect them to be bug sources. This is not a bad assumption for standard utilities or translators. However, if a highly parameterized, generalized system uses site-adapter software or preprocessors or compile-/assembly-time processing, and if such processors and code are being developed concurrently with the working software of the application—watch out!

All software used in the production of object code is suspect until validated. All new software must be subjected to rigorous testing, even if it is not part of the application's mainstream. Static data can be just as wrong as any other kind and can have just as many bugs. Do not treat a routine that creates static data as "simple" because it "just stuffs a bunch of numbers into a table." Subject such code to the same degree of rigorous testing that you use for running code.

The design remedy is in the source language. If the language permits compile-time processing that can be used to particularize parameter values and data structures, and if the syntax of the compile-time statements is identical to the syntax of the rest of the language, then the code will be subjected to the same validation and syntax checking as ordinary code. Such language facilities effectively eliminate the need for most specialized preprocessors, table generators, and site adapters.

3.5.3. Information, Parameter, and Control

Static or dynamic data can serve in one of three roles, or in a combination of roles: as a parameter, for control, or for information. What constitutes control or information is a matter of perspective and can shift from one processing level to another. A scheduler receives a request to initiate a process. The identity of the process is, to the scheduler, information to be processed, but at another level, it is control. My name is used to generate a hash code that will be used to access a disc record. My name is information, but to the disc hardware, its translation into an address is control (e.g., move to track so-and-so).

Information is usually dynamic and tends to be local to a single transaction or task. As such, errors in information (when data are treated as information, that is) do not constitute bugs. The bug, if any, is in the lack of protective data-validation code or in the failure to protect the routine's logic from out-of-range data or data in the wrong format. The only way we can be sure that there is data-validation code in a routine is to put it there. Assuming that the other routine will validate data invites latent bugs and maintenance problems.The program evolves and changes, and it is forgotten that the modified routine did the data validation for several other routines. If a routine is vulnerable to bad data, the only sane thing to do is to block such data within the routine or to redesign it so that it is no longer vulnerable.

Lack of data validation often leads to finger pointing. The calling routine's author is blamed, the called routine's author blames back, they both blame the system's operators. This leads to a lot of ego confrontation and guilt. "If only the other programmers did their job correctly," you say, "we would have no need for all this redundant data validation and defensive code. I have to put in all this extra junk because I'm surrounded by slobs!" This attitude is understandable, but not productive. Furthermore, if you really feel that way, it's likely that you'll also feel some guilt about it too. There is no need to blame your fellow programmer or to feel guilt. Nature has conspired against us, but also given us a convenient scapegoat. One of the unfortunate side effects of large-scale integrated circuitry stems from the use of microscopic logic elements that work at very low energy levels. Modern circuitry is vulnerable to electronic noise, electromagnetic radiation, cosmic rays, neutron hits, stray alpha particles, and other noxious disturbances. No kidding—alpha particle hits that can change the value of a bit are a serious problem, and the semiconductor manufacturers are spending a lot of money and effort to reduce the random modification of data by alpha particles. Therefore, even if your fellow programmers did thorough, correct data validation, dynamic data, static data, parameters, and code can be corrupted. Program without rancor and guilt! Put in the data-validation checks and blame the need on sunspots and alpha particles!

3.5.4. Contents, Structure, and Attributes

Data specifications consist of three components:

Contents—The actual bit pattern, character string, or number put into a memory location or data structure. Content is a pure bit pattern and has no meaning unless it is interpreted by a hardware or software processor. All data bugs result in the corruption or misinterpretation of content.

Structure—The size and shape and numbers that describe the data element, i.e., the memory locations used to store the content: 16 characters aligned on a word boundary, 122 blocks of 83 characters each, bits 4 through 14 of word 17, and so on. Structures can have substructures and can be arranged into superstructures. A given hunk of memory may have several different structures defined over it—e.g., a two-dimensional array treated elsewhere as N one-dimensional arrays.

Attributes—The specification of meaning, i.e., the semantics associated with the contents of a data element. For example: an integer, an alphanumeric string, a subroutine.

The severity and subtlety of bugs increases as we go from content to attributes, because things get less formal in that direction. Content has been dealt with adequately earlier in this section. Structural errors can take the form of declaration errors, but these are not the worst kind of structural bugs. A particularly serious potential for bugs occurs when data are used with different structures. Here is a piece of clever design. The programmer has subdivided the problem into eight cases and uses a three-bit field to designate the case. Another programmer has four different cases to consider and uses a two-bit field for the purpose. A third programmer is interested in the combination of the other two sets of cases and treats the whole as a five-bit field that leads to 32 combined cases. We cannot judge, out of context, if this is a good design or an abomination. However, we can note that there is a different structure in the minds of the three programmers and therefore a possibility for bugs. The practice of interpreting a given memory location under several different structures is not inherently bad. Often, the only alternative would be a large increase in the amount of memory needed and many additional explicit data transfers.

Attributes of data are the meanings we associate with data. While some bugs are related to misinterpretation of integers for floating point and other basic representation problems, the more subtle attribute-related bugs are embedded in the application. Consider a 16-bit field. It could represent, among other things, a number, a loop-iteration count, a control code, a pointer, or a link field. Each interpretation is a different attribute. There is no way for the computer to know that it is proper or improper to add a control code to a link field to yield a loop count. We have used the same data with different meanings. In modern parlance, we have changed the **data type**. It is generally incorrect to logically or arithmetically combine objects whose types are different. Conversely, it is almost impossible to create an efficient system without doing so. Shifts in interpretation usually occur at interfaces, particularly the human interface that is behind every software interface. See GANN76 for a summary of **type errors**.

The preventive measures for data-type errors are in the source language, documentation, and coding style. Explicit documentation regarding the contents, structure, and attributes of all data elements is essential. The database documentation should be centralized. All alternate interpretation of a given data element should be listed along with the identity of all routines that have access to that element. A proper **data dictionary** (which is what the database documentation is called) can be as large as the narrative description of the code. The data dictionary and the data base it represents must also be designed. This design is done by a high-level design process which is as important as the design of the system software hierarchy. It is an integral part of the system's architecture. My point of view here is admittedly dogmatic. Individual routines should not have their own data declarations. All data structures should be globally defined and centrally administered. Exceptions, such as a private work area, should be ruled on and justified individually. Under no circumstances should such private data structures ever be used by any other routine. If there is more than one user, then the structure should be documented in the data dictionary.

It's impossible to properly test a system of any size (say more than 10,000 instructions) without central data-base management and a controlled data dictionary. I was once faced with such a Herculean challenge, and my first step was to try to create the missing data dictionary preparatory to any attempt to define tests. The act of dragging the murky bottoms of a hundred minds for hidden data declarations and semiprivate space in an attempt to create a data dictionary revealed so many data-type and structure bugs that it was evident that the system would defy integration. I never did get to design any tests for that project—it collapsed, and a new design was started surreptitiously from scratch.

The second remedy is in the source language. **Strongly typed languages** prohibit the mixed manipulation of data that are declared as different types. A conversion in usage from pointer type to counter type, say, requires an explicit statement that will do the conversion. Such statements may or may not result in object code. Conversion from floating point to integer, would, of course, require object code, but conversion from pointer to counter, might not. Strong typing in a language forces the explicit declaration of attributes and provides compiler facilities to check for mixed-type operations. The ability of the user to specify types, as in Pascal, is mandatory. These data-typing facilities force the specification of data attributes into the source code, which makes them more amenable to automatic verification by the compiler and to test design than when the attributes are described in a separate data dictionary. In assembly language programming, or in source languages that do not have user-defined types, the remedy is the use of **field-access macros**. No programmer is allowed to directly access a field in the data base. Access can only be obtained through the use of a field-access macro. The macro code does all the extraction, stripping, justification, and type conversion necessary. If the data-base structure has to be changed for any reason, the affected field-access macros are changed, but the source code that uses the macros does not (usually) have to be changed. The attributes of the data are documented with the field-access macro documentation. In one system, the data dictionary is automatically produced from the specifications of the field-access macro library.

3.6. Code Errors

Code errors of all kinds can create any of the aforementioned bugs. Syntax errors are generally not important in the scheme of things, if the source language translator has adequate syntax checking. Failure to catch a syntax error is a bug in the translator. A good translator will also catch undeclared data, undeclared routines, dangling code, and many initialization problems. Any kind of error that is normally caught by the translator (assembler, compiler, or interpreter) does not materially affect the design and execution of tests, because testing cannot start until such errors are eliminated. Whether it takes a programmer one, ten, or a hundred passes before a syntactically valid, testable routine is achieved should concern software management but not test design. However, if a program has many source-syntax errors, we should expect many logic and coding errors as well—after all, a slob is a slob is a slob.

Given good source-syntax checking, the most common pure coding errors are typographical, followed by errors due to failure to understand the operation of an instruction or statement or the byproducts of an instruction or statement. Coding errors are the wild cards of programming. Unlike logic or process errors, which have their own perverse rationality, wild cards are arbitrary.

3.7. Testing and Style

This is a book on test design, yet this chapter has dealt heavily with programming style and design. You might wonder why the productivity of one programming group is as much as ten times higher than that of another group working on the same application, the same computer, in the same language, and under similar constraints. It should be obvious—bad designs lead to bugs and bad designs are very difficult to test; therefore, the bugs remain. Good designs inhibit bugs before they occur and are easy to test thoroughly. These two factors are multiplicative, which explains the large productivity differences. The best test techniques are useless when applied to abominable code and systems that were not designed. It is sometimes easier to totally redesign a bad routine than to attempt to create tests for it. The labor required to produce new code plus the test design and execution labor for the new code can be significantly less than the labor required for the design of thorough tests for an undisciplined, unstructured, monstrosity. Good testing works best on good code and good design. And no test technique can ever convert garbage into gold.

4. SOME BUG STATISTICS

The frequency of bugs taken from several different sources (DNIE78, RUBE75, SCHN79A, ENDR75) shows approximately 1.6 bugs per hundred statements. However, because most of the sample did not include nonexecutable statements, the real value is probably lower. The norm appears to be 1 bug per hundred statements. A further breakdown into categories, especially the categories discussed in this chapter is difficult to achieve, because different schemes were used to categorize the bugs. The breakdown shown in Table 2-1 is rough and is based on interpreting the reported results according to my

TABLE 2-1. Sample Bug Statistics.

SIZE OF SAMPLE—126,000 STATEMENTS (MOSTLY EXECUTABLE)
TOTAL REPORTED BUGS—2070
BUGS PER STATEMENT—1.63%

FUNCTIONAL		
Specification	404	
Function	147	
Test	7	
Total	558	27%
SYSTEM		
Internal Interface	29	
Hardware (I/O devices)	63	
Operating System	2	
Software Architecture	193	
Control or Sequence	43	
Resources	8	
Total	338	16%
PROCESS		
Arithmetic	141	
Initialization	15	
Control or Sequence	271	
Static Logic	13	
Other	120	
Total	560	27%
DATA		
Type	36	
Structure	34	
Initial Value	51	
Other	120	
Total	201	10%
CODE	78	4%
DOCUMENTATION	103	5%
STANDARDS	166	8%
OTHER	62	3%

categories. The biggest swing could occur between process-level errors and system-level errors. Most of the data did not distinguish between them. I suspect that many of the control/sequence errors, which I ascribed to individual processes, were actually system-level errors. The low value for data errors is also likely to be apocryphal, because part of the source data (ENDR75) was based on a combination of new code and modified code, in which the impact of data errors would be somewhat less than for new code.

You should examine the sources for these statistics yourself so that you can rearrange the categories to better match your own situation. Other references with useful statistics are: AKIY71, BELF79, BOEH75, BOIE72, DNIE78, ELSH76B, ENDR75, GANN76, GILB77, GOEL78B, HAUG64, HOFF77, ITOH73, LITE76, REIF79, RUBE75, SCHI78, SCHN75, SCHN79A, SCHW71, SHOO75, THAY77 (especially), and WAGO73.

3

FLOWCHARTS AND PATH TESTING

1. SYNOPSIS

Path testing based on the use of the program's control flow as a structural model is the cornerstone of testing. Methods for generating tests from the program's control flow, criteria for selecting paths, and how to determine path-forcing input values are discussed.

2. FLOWCHARTS AS MODELS

2.1. Flowcharts

A **flowchart** is a graphical representation of a program's control structure. It uses the elements shown in Figure 3-1.

A **process** has one entry and one exit. It performs an operation on data. A process can consist of a single statement or instruction, a sequence of statements or instructions, a single-entry/single-exit subroutine, a macro or function call, or a combination of these. The program does not (rather, is not intended to) jump into or out of processes. From the point of view of test cases designed from flowcharts, the details of the operation carried out by the process are unimportant if those details do not affect the control flow. A sequence of processing statements that is uninterrupted by **junctions** or **decisions** is usually put into one process block. If the processing affects the flow of control, that effect will be manifested at a subsequent decision or case statement.

A decision is a program point at which the control flow diverges. Machine language conditional branch-and-skip instructions are examples of decisions. The FORTRAN IF and the Pascal IF-THEN-ELSE constructs are decisions, although they also contain processing components. While most decisions are two-way or **binary**, some, such as the FORTRAN IF are three-way branches in control flow. The design of test cases is generally easier with two-way

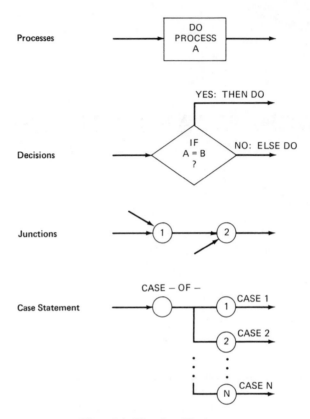

Figure 3-1. Flowchart Elements.

branches than with three-way branches, and there are also more powerful test design tools that can be used. A **case statement** is a multi-way branch or decision. Examples of case statements are: a jump table in assembly language, the FORTRAN computed GOTO and assigned GOTO, and the Pascal CASE statement. From the point of view of test design, there are no fundamental differences between decisions and case statements.

A **junction** is a point in the program where the control flow merges. The target of a jump or skip instruction in assembly language, a label which is the target of a GOTO and the END-IF and CONTINUE statements in FOR-TRAN, and the Pascal statement labels, END and UNTIL are examples of junctions.

Unconditional branches such as FORTRAN's GOTO or assembly language unconditional jump instructions are not fundamental to programming. They are used primarily to transform the two-dimensional representation of control flow shown in a flowchart to the one-dimensional representation of code. While it can be proven (BOHM66) that unconditional branches are not essential to programming, their use is ubiquitous and often practically unavoidable.

A flowchart* is a pictorial representation of a program and not the program itself, just as a topographic map, no matter how detailed, is not the terrain it represents. This is an important distinction: failure to make it can lead to bugs. You cannot always associate the elements of a program in a unique, one-for-one manner with flowchart elements, because many program structures, such as IF-THEN-ELSE constructs, consist of a combination of decisions, junctions, and processes. Furthermore, the translation from a flowchart element to a statement and vice versa is not always unique. Myers (MYER77) cites an anomaly based on different representations of the FOR-TRAN statement "IF (A = 0) .AND. (B = 1) THEN. . . ." It has the alternate representation shown in Figure 3-2.

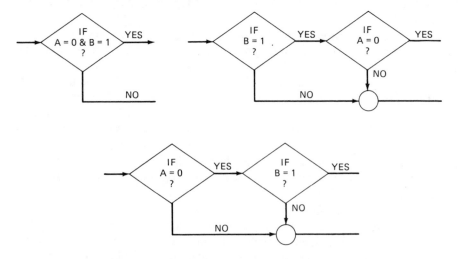

Figure 3-2. Alternate Flowcharts for the Same Logic.

---

*Whatever is said here about flowcharts applies with little change when programs are designed using a program-design language (PDL) or pseudo-code as a starting point. I am not advocating the exclusive use of flowcharts as a program representation and the avoidance of program-design languages. In fact, I favor PDL's; but flowcharts have an archaic charm, keep artists employed, and are conceptually close to graphs (see chapter 5). What counts is the control flow and the graph that represents it. Translation problems from a PDL specification of a program to the code that implements that specification can also exist and are analogous to those that occur for the conversion of flowcharts to code. If you favor PDL specifications over flowcharts, substitute "PDL specification" for "flowchart" in the sequel; also substitute "handwritten" for "hand-drawn."

A FORTRAN DO contains three parts: a decision, an end-point junction, and a process that iterates the DO variable. The FORTRAN IF-THEN-ELSE has a decision, a junction, and three processes (including the processing associated with the decision itself). Therefore, neither of these statements can be translated into a single flowchart element. Some computers have looping, iterating, and EXECUTE instructions or other instruction options and modes that prevent the direct correspondence between instructions and flowchart elements. Such differences are so familiar to us that we often code without conscious awareness of their existence. It is, however, important that the distinction between a program and its flowchart representation be kept in mind during test design. An improper translation during coding can lead to bugs, and an improper translation during test design can lead to missing test cases and consequently, to undiscovered bugs. When faced with a possibly ambiguous translation from code to flowchart or from flowchart to code, as in the above example, it is better to pick the more complicated representation rather than the simpler one. At worst, you will have designed a few extra test cases.

Flowcharts can be: 1) hand-drawn by the programmer, 2) automatically produced by a flowcharting program based on a mechanical analysis of the source code, or 3) semiautomatically produced by a flowcharting program based in part on structural analysis of the source code and in part on directions given by the programmer. The semiautomatic flowchart is most common with assembly language source code. All three kinds of flowcharts would be identical in a perfect world, but often, they are not. The programmer's original flowchart is a statement of intentions and not a program. Those intentions become corrupted through the action of malevolent forces such as keypunch operators, compilers, and programmers. A typographical error in a case statement can cause a different path to be implemented or can make a path inaccessible. In assembly language, the possibility of manipulating addresses, registers, page boundaries, or even instructions (inadvertently, it is to be hoped) makes the potential differences between the specification flowchart and the actual control flow wilder yet. If you have automatically produced flowcharts, then it is effective to check the correspondence between the specification flowchart and the one produced from code. Better yet, have someone else, preferably someone who has never seen the specification flowchart, translate the code back into a flowchart, or compare the automatically produced flowchart with the specification flowchart. Many bugs can be caught this way. It may seem like a lot of extra work, but consider which you would rather do:

1. A calm, manual retranslation of the code back into a flowchart with an unbiased comparison?

or:

2. A frenzied plea to a colleague in the heat of the test floor late at night, to: "Look this over for me, will you? I just can't find the bug."

2.2. Path Selection

2.2.1. Paths, Nodes, and Links

A **path** through a program is a sequence of instructions or statements that starts at a junction or decision and ends at another, or possibly the same, junction or decision. A path may go through several junctions, processes, or decisions, one or more times. The word "**node**" is used to mean either junction, decision, or both. Paths consist of **segments**. The smallest segment is a single process that lies between two nodes, e.g., junction-process-junction, junction-process-decision, decision-process-junction, decision-process-decision. A direct connection between two nodes, as in an unconditional GOTO, is also called a "process" by convention, even though no actual processing takes place. The collective term for flowchart lines that join nodes is "**link**." A flowchart then, consists of nodes and links. A path segment is a succession of consecutive links that belongs to some path. The word "path" is also used in the more restrictive sense of a path that starts at the routine's entrance and ends at its exit.

2.2.2. Multi-Entry, Multi-Exit Routines

Throughout this book I make an implicit assumption that all routines and programs have a single entry and a single exit. While there are circumstances in which it is proper to jump out of a routine and bypass the normal control structure and exit method, I cannot conceive of any rational reason why one would want to jump into the middle of a routine or program.* You might want to jump out of a routine when an illogical condition has been detected for which it is clear that any further processing along that path could cause significant damage to the system's operation or data base. Under such circumstances, the normal return path must be bypassed. In such cases, though, there is only one place to go—to the system's recovery-processing module. Jumping into a routine, however, is almost always done in an attempt to save some code or coding labor (to be paid for by a three-fold

---

*Not to be confused with instances in which a collection of independent routines are accessed by a common name. For example, the set of routines is called "SET" and it is loaded as a set in order to have efficient overlays; but within "SET" there are independent, single-entry subroutines. It might superficially seem that "SET" is a multi-entry, multi-exit routine.

increase in test design and debugging labor). If the routine performs several variations on the same processing, and it is effective to bypass part of the processing, the correct way to design the routine is to provide an entry parameter which within the routine, say by a case statement, directs the control flow to the proper point. Similarly, if a routine can have several different kinds of outcomes, then an exit parameter should be used. Instead of using direct linkages between multiple exits and entrances, we handle the control flow by examining the values of the exit parameter which can serve as an entry parameter for the next routine or a return parameter for the calling routine. Note that the parameter does not have to be passed explicitly between the routines—it can be a value in a register or in a common memory location.

The trouble with multi-entry and multi-exit routines is that it can be extremely difficult to determine what the interprocess control flow is, and consequently, it is easy to miss important test cases. Furthermore, the use of multi-exit and multi-entrance routines increases the number of entries and exits, and therefore, the number of interfaces. This leads to more test cases than would otherwise be needed.

Unfortunately, we may not be lucky and we may have to test a program that has multi-entry and/or multi-exit routines. The solution, assuming that we cannot get the routines changed, is to create fictitious single-entry segments with fictitious case statements and fictitious processes that set fictitious exit parameters and go to a fictitious common junction. This fictitious code (providing you do not get trapped into confusing it with real code) will help you organize the test case design and keep the control flow relatively clean from an analytical point of view (see Figure 3-3).

This is a lot of extra work because you must examine the cross-reference listings to find all references to the labels that correspond to the multiple entries. But it can be rewarding. Present the fictitious input case statement and the list of entrances to the designer of the multi-entry routine, and you may be rewarded with a statement like, "That's not right! So-and-so isn't supposed to come in via that entry point." Similarly, every exit destination corresponding to your pseudo-exit parameter should be discussed with the designer of the multi-exit routine, and again you may find that some targets are not correct, although this is less likely to happen because multiple entries are more likely to be misused than multiple exits. After all, the designers of routines should know where they want to go, but it's difficult to control an entry that can be initiated by many other programmers.

In assembly language it's possible to calculate the address of the entry point either in absolute terms or relative to the routine's origin. Such multiple entries are truly abominable, because absolute address calculations make the

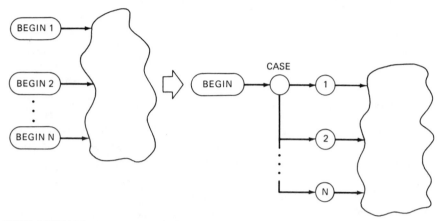

A MULTI-ENTRY ROUTINE IS CONVERTED TO AN EQUIVALENT SINGLE-ENTRY ROUTINE WITH
AN ENTRY PARAMETER AND A CONTROLLING CASE STATEMENT.

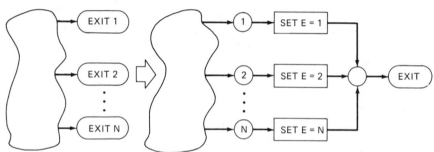

A MULTI-EXIT ROUTINE IS CONVERTED TO AN EQUIVALENT SINGLE-EXIT ROUTINE WITH AN
EXIT PARAMETER.

Figure 3-3. Conversion of Multi-Exit or Multi-Entry Routines.

routine's operation dependent upon location, and relative address calculations change the control flow when the routine is modified. Furthermore,
there is no way to tell, without effectively simulating the machine's operation,
just what is going on. Absolute addressing for control purposes should be
forbidden in almost all instances, although there are mitigating circumstances
in which it is not only desirable, but mandatory. In some computers, it is not
possible to write an interrupt-handling routine or a device-control routine
without resorting to absolute addresses. Where this is essential, all such code
should be centralized, tightly controlled, and approved in writing, one such
address at a time.

Therefore, the proper way to test multi-entry or multi-exit routines is:

1. Get rid of them.
2. Completely control those you can't get rid of.
3. Augment the flowchart with fictitious, equivalent, input case statements and exit parameters to help you organize the tests for those that remain.

2.2.3. Fundamental Path Selection Criteria

There are many paths between the entry and exit of a typical routine. Every decision doubles the number of potential paths, and every loop multiplies the number of potential paths by the number of different iteration values possible for the loop. If a routine contains one loop, each pass through that loop, once, twice, three times, and so on, constitutes a different path through the routine, even though the same code is traversed each time. Even small routines can have an incredible number of potential paths (see Chapter 6 for path-counting methods). A lavish test approach might consist of testing all known paths, but that would not be a complete test, because a bug could create unwanted paths or make mandatory paths impossible. And just because all paths are right doesn't mean that the routine is doing the required processing along those paths. Such possibilities aside for the moment, how might we do "complete testing"?

1. Exercise every path from entry to exit.
2. Exercise every statement or instruction at least once.
3. Exercise every branch and case statement, in each direction, at least once.

If prescription 1 is followed, then prescriptions 2 and 3 are automatically followed. However, prescription 1 is impractical for most routines. It can be done only for routines that have no loops, in which case it is equivalent to a combination of prescriptions 2 and 3. Prescriptions 2 and 3 might appear to be equivalent, but they are not. Here is a correct version of a routine:

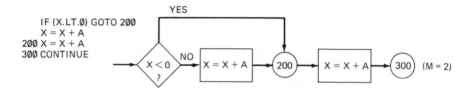

For X negative, the output is X + A, while for X greater than or equal to zero, the output is X + 2A. Following prescription 2 and executing every instruction, but not every branch, would not reveal the bug in the following incorrect version:

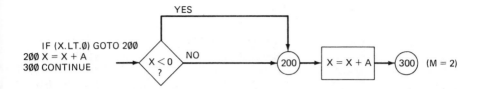

A negative value produces the correct answer. Every instruction can be executed, but if the test cases do not force each branch to be taken in all directions, the bug can remain hidden. The next example uses a test based on executing each branch in all directions but does not force the execution of all instructions:

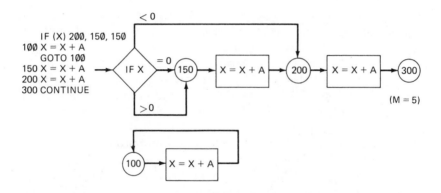

The hidden loop around label 100 is not revealed by tests based on prescription 3 alone, because no test forces the execution of statement 100 and the following GOTO statement. Furthermore, label 100 is not flagged by the compiler as an unreferenced label, and the subsequent GOTO does not refer to an undefined label.

In general, a **static analysis** (that is, an analysis based on examining the source code or structure) cannot determine if a piece of code is or is not reachable. There could be subroutine calls with parameters that are subroutine labels, or in the above example, there could be a GOTO that targeted label 100 but could never achieve a value that would send the program to that label. Generally, only a **dynamic analysis** (that is, an analysis based on the code's behavior while running) can determine if code is reachable or not and therefore distinguish between the ideal structure we think we have and the actual structure that contains bugs.

While real bugs are rarely as blatant as the above examples, the examples demonstrate that prescriptions 2 and 3 alone are insufficient. Any testing strategy based on path tracing must at least both exercise every instruction *and* take all branches in all directions. A set of tests that does this is not complete in an absolute sense, but it is complete in the sense that anything less must leave something untested.

The term **"complete cover,"** or **"cover"** alone, when context is clear, is used to mean that a set of tests has the potential for executing every instruction and taking all branches in all directions. Complete coverage is a minimum mandatory testing requirement. One can argue that it is a lot of work, to which I reply that debugging is a lot more work. Why not use a judicious sampling of paths? What's wrong with leaving some code, particularly code that has a low probability of execution, untested? Common sense and experience shows why such proposals are ineffectual:

1. Typographical bugs are ramdon. Not testing a piece of code leaves a residue of bugs in the program in proportion to the size of the untested code and the probability of typographical bugs.
2. The high-probability paths are always thoroughly tested if only to demonstrate that the system works properly. If you had to leave some code untested at the unit level, it would be more rational to leave the normal, high-probability paths untested, because someone else is sure to exercise them during system integration or system functional testing.
3. Logic errors and fuzzy thinking are inversely proportional to the probability of the path's execution.
4. The subjective probability of executing a path as seen by the routine's designer and its objective execution probability are far apart. Only analysis can reveal the probability of a path, and most programmers' intuition with regard to path probabilities is poor (see BEIZ78).
5. The subjective evaluation of the importance of a code segment as judged by its programmer is biased by aesthetic sense, ego, and familiarity. Elegant code might be heavily tested to demonstrate its elegance or to defend the concept, while straightforward code might be given cursory testing because: "How could anything go wrong with that?"

Any testing based on less than complete coverage requires decisions regarding what code should be left untested. Such decisions are inevitably biased, rarely rational, and always grievous. Realistically, the practice of putting untested code into systems is common, and so are system failures. The excuse I've most often heard for putting in untested code is that there wasn't enough time left or enough money left to do the testing. What magic is there in untested code that eliminates its bugs? If there wasn't enough time and money to test the routine, then there wasn't enough time and money to create it in the first place—for what you think is code, before it has been properly tested, is not code, but the mere promise of code—not a program, but a perverse parody of a program. If you put such junk into a system, its bugs will show, and because there hasn't been a rigorous unit test, you'll have a difficult time finding out just what caused the bugs. As Hannah Cowley said, "Vanity, like murder, will out." For it's vanity to think that untested code has no bugs, and murder to put such code in.

It is better to leave out untested code altogether than to put it in. Code that does not exist cannot corrupt good code. A function that has not been implemented is known not to work. An untested function may or may not work itself (probably not), but it can make other functions fail that would otherwise work. If I could, I would legislate a minimum standard that required the execution under test of every single line of code and every decision's direction. In case I haven't made myself clear, leaving untested code in a system is stupid, shortsighted, and irresponsible.

2.2.4. Which Paths

You must pick enough paths to provide full coverage. The question of what are the fewest number of such paths is interesting to the designer of test tools that help automate path testing, but it is not crucial to the pragmatic design of tests. It's better to take many simple paths than a few complicated paths. Furthermore, there's no harm in taking paths that will exercise the same code more than once. As an example of how to go about selecting paths, consider the unstructured monstrosity of Figure 3-4:

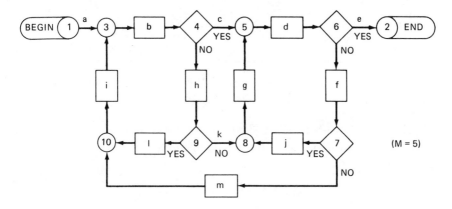

Figure 3-4. An Example Flow Chart.

Start at the beginning and take the most obvious path to the exit—it typically corresponds to the normal path. The most obvious path in Figure 3-4 is 134562, if we name it by nodes, or *abcde,* if we name it by links. Then take the next most obvious path, *abhkgde.* All other paths in this example lead to loops. Take a simple loop first, building, if possible, on a previous path, such as *abhlibcde.* Then take another loop, *abcdfjgde.* And finally, *abcdfmibcde.* Here are some practical suggestions:

1. Reduce the flowchart or combine its parts so that it fits on a single sheet of paper.* Work with a simplified version that lumps all straight-line code sequences into single, equivalent processes.
2. Make several copies—as many as you'll need for coverage and several more.**
3. Use a yellow highlighting marker to trace paths. Copy the paths onto a master sheet.
4. Continue tracing paths until all lines on the master sheet are covered, indicating that you appear to have achieved coverage.

I say "appear," because some of the paths you've selected might not be achievable. This is discussed in Section 3.

As you trace the paths, create a table that shows the paths, the coverage status of each process, and each decision. The above paths lead to the following table:

PATHS	DECISIONS				PROCESS–LINK												
	4	6	7	9	a	b	c	d	e	f	g	h	i	j	k	l	m
abcde	YES	YES			√	√	√	√	√								
abhkgde	NO	YES		NO	√	√		√	√		√	√			√		
abhlibcde	NO, YES	YES		YES	√	√	√	√	√			√	√			√	
abcdfjgde	YES	NO, YES	YES		√	√	√	√	√	√	√			√			
abcdfmibcde	YES	NO, YES	NO		√	√	√	√	√	√			√				√

After you have traced a covering path-set on the master sheet and filled in the table for every path, check for the following:

1. Does every decision have a YES and a NO in its column?
2. Has every case of all case statements been marked?

---

*This procedure doesn't work if you have to deal with a tangle of off-page connectors; do it from the code or PDL, if that's what you're using.
**See Chapters 5 and 6 for how many copies you might need.

3. Is every three-way branch (less, equal, greater) covered?
4. Is every link (process) covered at least once?

Select successive paths as small variations of previous paths. Try to change only one thing at a time—only one decision's outcome if possible. It's better to have several paths, each differing by only one thing, than one path that covers more but along which several things change. The *abcd* segment in the above example is common to many paths. If this common segment has been debugged, and a bug appears in a new path that uses this segment, it's more likely that the bug is in the new part of the path (say *fjgde*) rather than in the part that's already been debugged. Using small changes from one test to the next may seem like more work, but:

1. Small changes from path to path mean small, easily documented, and gradual changes in the test set-up. Setting up long, complicated paths that share nothing with other test cases is also a lot of extra work.
2. Testing is an experimental process. All experimental processes are based on the notion of changing only one thing at a time. The more you change from test to test, the more likely you are to get confused.
3. The costs of extra paths are a few more microseconds of computer time, the elapsed time to run another case, and the cost of additional documentation. Many more and different kinds of tests are required beyond path testing. A few extra paths represent only a small increment in the total test labor.

You could select paths with the idea of achieving coverage without knowing anything about what the routine is supposed to do. Path selection based on pure structure without regard to function has the advantage of being free of bias. Conversely, such paths are likely to be confusing, counter-intuitive, and hard to understand. I favor paths that have some sensible functional meaning.* With this in mind, the path-selection rules can be revised as follows:

1. Pick the simplest, functionally sensible path from entrance to exit.
2. Pick additional paths as small variations from previous paths. Pick paths that do not have loops rather than paths that do. Favor short paths over long paths, simple paths over complicated paths, and paths that make sense over paths that don't.

---

*The term "function" is here understood to mean function in the context of the routine's specification and not necessarily in the sense of overall function as viewed at the user or system level.

3. Pick additional paths that have no obvious functional meaning only if it's necessary to provide coverage. But ask yourself first why such paths exist at all. Why wasn't coverage achieved with functionally sensible paths?
4. Be comfortable with the paths you pick. Play your hunches and give your intuition free reign as long as you achieve coverage.
5. Don't follow rules slavishly—except for coverage.

2.3. Loops

2.3.1. The Kinds of Loops

I had a physics professor who use to say that there were only two kinds of mensuration systems: the metric and the barbaric. I say that there are only three kinds of loops: nested, concatenated, and horrible. Figure 3-5 shows examples of each kind.

2.3.2. Cases For A Single Loop

A single loop can be covered with two cases: looping and not looping. However, experience shows that many loop-related bugs are not discovered by simple coverage. Bugs lurk in corners and congregate at boundaries—in the case of loops, at or around the minimum and maximum number of times the loop can be iterated. The minimum number of iterations is often zero, but it need not be.

Case 1—Single Loop, Zero Minimum, N Maximum, No Excluded Values

1. Try bypassing the loop (zero iterations). If you can't, you either have a bug, or zero is not the minimum and you have the wrong case.
2. Could the loop-control variable be negative? Could it appear to specify a negative number of iterations? What happens to such a value?
3. One pass through the loop.
4. Two passes through the loop. The reason for this is discussed below.
5. A typical number of iterations, unless covered by a previous test.
6. One less than the maximum number of iterations.
7. The maximum number of iterations.
8. Attempt one more than the maximum number of iterations. What prevents the loop-control variable from having this value? What will happen with this value if it is forced?

The reason for two passes through the loop is based on a theorem by Huang (HUAN79) that states that some initialization problems can only be

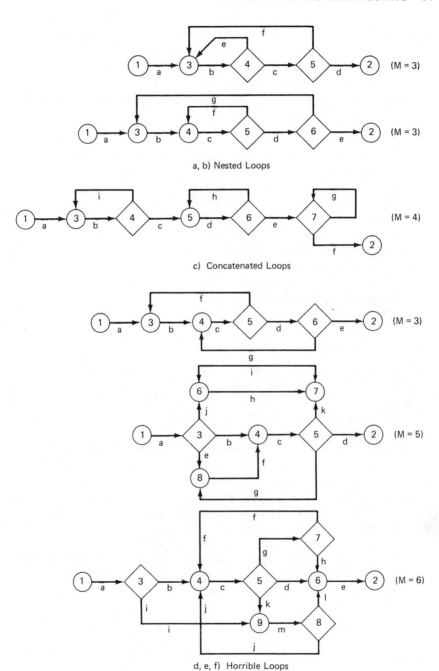

a, b) Nested Loops

c) Concatenated Loops

d, e, f) Horrible Loops

Figure 3-5. Examples of Loop Types.

detected by two or more passes through the loop. The problem occurs when data are initialized within the loop and referenced after leaving the loop. If, because of bugs, a variable is defined within the loop but is not referenced or used in the loop, only two traversals of the loop would show the double initialization. Similar problems are discussed in further detail in Chapter 6.

Case 2—Single Loop, Nonzero Minimum, No Excluded Values

1. Attempt one less than the expected minimum. What happens if the loop control variable's value is less than the minimum? What prevents the value from being less than the minimum?
2. The minimum number of iterations.
3. One more than the minimum number of iterations.
4. Once, unless covered by a previous test.
5. Twice, unless covered by a previous test.
6. A typical value.
7. One less than the maximum value.
8. The maximum number of iterations.
9. Attempt one more than the maximum number of iterations.

Case 3—Single Loops With Excluded Values

Treat single loops with excluded values as two sets of tests consisting of loops without excluded values, such as Cases 1 and 2 above. Say that the total range of the loop-control variable was 1 to 20, but that values 7,8,9 and 10 were excluded. The two sets of tests are 1-6 and 11-20. The test cases to attempt would be 0,1,2,4,6,7, for the first range and 10, 11,15,19,20,21, for the second range. The underlined cases are not supposed to work, but they should be attempted. Similarly, you might want to try a typical value within the excluded range, such as 8. If you had two sets of excluded values, you would have three sets of tests, one for each allowed range. If the excluded values are very systematic and easily typified, this approach would entail too many tests. Say that all odd values were excluded. I would test the extreme points of the range as if there were no excluded values, for the extreme points, for the excluded values, and also for typical excluded values. For example, if the range is 0 to 20 and odd values are excluded, try −1,0,1,2,3,10,11,18,19,20,21,22.

2.3.3. Nested Loops

If you had five tests (assuming that one less than the minimum and one more than the maximum were not achievable) for one loop, a pair of nested loops would require 25 tests, and three nested loops would require 125. This is heavy even by my standards. You can't test all combinations of nested loops' iteration values. Here's a tactic to use to discard some of these values:

1. Start at the innermost loop. Set all the outer loops to their minimum values.
2. Test the minimum, minimum + 1, typical, maximum − 1, and maximum for the innermost loop, while holding the outer loops at their minimum-iteration-parameter values. Expand the tests as required for out-of-range and excluded values.
3. If you've done the outermost loop, GOTO step 5, ELSE move out one loop and set it up as in Step 2—with all other loops set to typical values.
4. Continue outward in this manner until all loops have been covered.
5. Do the five cases for all loops in the nest simultaneously.

This works out to twelve tests for a pair of nested loops, sixteen for three nested loops, and nineteen for four nested loops. Practicality may prevent testing in which all loops achieve their maximum values simultaneously. You may have to compromise. Estimate the processing time for the loop and multiply by the product of loop-iteration variables to get an estimate of the total time spent in the loop (for details in the general case and precise methods, see BEIZ78). If the expected execution time is several years or centuries, ask yourself if this is reasonable. Why isn't there a check on the combination of values? Unbounded processing time could indicate a bug.

These cases can be expanded by taking into account potential problems associated with initialization of variables and with excluded combinations and ranges. In general, Huang's twice-through theorem should also be applied to the combination of loops to assure catching data-initialization problems. Hold the outer loops at the minimum values and run the inner loop through its cases. Then hold the outer loop at one and run the inner loop through its cases. Finally, hold the outer loop at two and run through the inner-loop cases. Next, reverse the role of the inner and outer loop and do it over again, excluding cases that have been tried earlier. A similar strategy can be used with combinations of allowed values in one loop and excluded values in another.

2.3.4. Concatenated Loops

Concatenated loops fall between single and nested loops with respect to test cases. Two loops are **concatenated** if it's possible to reach one after exiting the other while still on a path from entrance to exit. If the loops cannot be on the same path, then they are not concatenated and can be treated as individual loops. Even if the loops are on the same path and you can be sure that they are independent of each other, you can still treat them as individual loops. If however, the iteration values in one loop are directly or indirectly related to the iteration values of another loop, and they can occur on the same path, then treat them as you would nested loops. The problem of excessive processing time for combinations of loop-iteration values should not occur, because the loop-iteration values are additive rather than multiplicative as they are for nested loops.

2.3.4. Horrible Loops

While the methods of Chapter 6 may give you some insight into the design of test cases for horrible loops, the resulting cases are not definitive and are usually too many to execute. The thinking required to check the endpoints and looping values for intertwined loops appears to be unique for each program. The use of code that jumps into and out of loops, intersecting loops, hidden loops, and cross-connected loops, makes iteration-value selection for test cases an awesome and ugly task, which is another reason such structures should be avoided.

2.4. Effectiveness of Path Testing

2.4.1. Effectiveness and Limitations

Approximately 65% of all bugs can be caught in unit testing, which is dominated by path testing. Precise statistics based on controlled experiments on the effectiveness of path testing are not available. What statistics there are show that path testing catches approximately half of all bugs caught during unit testing or approximately 35% of all bugs (BOEH75B, MILL77C, ENDR75, GANN79, HOWD76, KERN76, HOWD78D, THAY77). When path testing is combined with other methods, such as limit checks on loops, the percentage of bugs caught rises to 50% to 60% in unit testing. But the statistics also indicate that path testing as a sole technique is limited. Here are some of the reasons:

1. Planning to cover does not mean you will cover. Path testing may not cover if you have bugs.
2. Path testing may not reveal totally wrong or missing functions.
3. Interface errors, particularly at the interface with other routines, may not be caught by unit-level path testing.
4. Data-base errors may not be caught.

5. The routine can pass all of its tests at the unit level, but the possibility that it interferes with or perturbs other routines cannot be determined by unit-level path tests.
6. Not all initialization errors are caught by path testing.

2.4.2. A Lot Of Work?

Indeed, examining the flowchart, converting it into a simplified model, selecting a set of covering paths, finding input data values to force those paths, setting up the loop cases and combinations—all that is a lot of work. Perhaps as much work as it took to design the routine and certainly more work than it took to code it. The statistics indicate that you will spend half of your time doing test and debugging—presumably that time includes the time required to design and document test cases. I would rather spend a few quiet hours in my office doing test case design than twice those hours on the test floor debugging, going half-deaf from the clatter of a high-speed printer that's producing massive dumps, the reading of which will make me half-blind. Furthermore, *the act of careful, complete, systematic, test design will catch as many bugs as the act of testing.* It's worth repeating here and several times more in this book: *the test design process, at all levels, is at least as effective at catching bugs as is running the test designed by that process.* Personally, I believe that it's far more effective, but I don't have statistics to back that claim. And when you consider the fact that bugs caught during test design cost less to fix than bugs caught during testing, it makes test-design bug catching even more attractive.

3. PATH SENSITIZING

3.1. General

Selecting a path does not mean that it is achievable. If all decisions are based on variables whose values are independent of the processing and of one another, then all combinations of decision outcomes are possible (2^n outcomes for n binary decisions) and all paths are trivially achievable. However, in general, this is not so. Finding a set of input values that will cause the desired path to be taken is called **sensitizing** the path.

3.2. Path Predicates

The direction taken at a decision depends on the value of decision variables. For binary decisions, the processing associated with the decision ultimately results in the evaluation of a logical function whose outcome is either TRUE or FALSE, or equivalently, YES or NO, ONE or ZERO, et cetera. While the function evaluated for the decision may be numeric or alphanumeric, when the decision is actually made, it is based on a logical function's truth value. The logical function evaluated for a decision is called a **predicate** (GOOD75, HUAN75). Here are some examples: "A is greater than zero," "the character in the fifth position has a numerical value of 31," "A is either negative or equal to 10," "A + B = 3 × 2 − 44," "Flag 21 is set." Every path corresponds to a succession of TRUE/FALSE values for the predicates that are met along that path. As an example:

" 'A is greater than zero' is TRUE."

AND

" 'A + B = 3 × 2 − 44' is FALSE."

AND

" 'A is either negative or equal to 10' is TRUE."

represents a sequence of path predicates whose logical values would cause the routine in which those predicates occurred to take a particular path. **Path sensitizing** is the act of finding a set of input *data values* (including values that may reside in the data base) that force the path predicates to the *truth values* (TRUE/FALSE) that correspond to the desired path.

3.3. Independence and Correlation of Variables and Predicates

The path predicates take on truth values (TRUE/FALSE) based on the values of input variables, either directly or indirectly, singly or in combination. If a variable's value does not change as a result of processing, that variable is said to be **independent** of the processing. Conversely, if the variable's value can change as a result of the processing, the variable is said to be **process dependent**. Similarly, a *predicate* whose truth functional value can change as a result of the processing is said to be **process dependent**, and one whose truth functional value does not change as a result of the processing is **process independent**. Note that dependence of a path predicate does not follow from dependence of the input variables on which that path predicate might be based. For example, the input variables are X and Y and the path predicate is "X + Y = 10." The processing increments X and decrements Y each time through a loop. While the numerical values of X and Y are process dependent, the predicate which is based on their values is process independent. As another example, the predicate is "X is odd," and the process increments X by an even number. Again, X's value is process dependent but the predicate based on X's value is process independent. However, if all the variables on which a predicate is based are process independent, it follows that the predicate must be process independent. Also keep in mind that we are looking only at those variables whose values can affect the flow of control in the routine and not at all variables whose values may change as a result of the processing. Furthermore, an "input" variable in this context does not necessarily appear in the routine's calling sequence.

Variables, whether process dependent or independent, may be correlated to one another. Two variables are **correlated** if every combination of their values cannot be independently specified. For example, two variables of 8 bits each should lead to 2^{16} possible combinations. If there is a restriction on their sum, say the sum must be less than or equal to 2^8, then only 2^9 combinations are possible. Variables whose values can be specified independently without restriction are **uncorrelated**. By analogy, a pair of predicates whose outcomes depend on one or more variables in common (whether or not those variables are correlated) are said to be **correlated predicates**. As an example, let A and B be two input variables which are independent of the processing and which are not correlated with one another. Let decision 10 be based on the predicate "A = B" and decision 12 on the statement "A + B = 8." It is clear that having selected values for A and B in order to satisfy decision 10, we may have forced the logical value for decision 12 and may not be able to make that predicate go the way we wish. Every path through a routine is achievable only if all predicates in that routine are uncorrelated. If a routine has a loop, then at least one decision's predicate must depend on the processing or there is an input value which will cause the routine to loop indefinitely.

There is no general procedure that will allow you to sensitize paths. Here is a workable heuristic approach:

1. Identify all input variables that can directly or indirectly affect the outcome of decisions. Classify the variables according to whether they are process dependent or independent. Identify all correlated input variables. For all dependent variables, write down the exact nature of the process dependency as an equation, function, or whatever is convenient and clear. For all correlated variables, similarly write down the logical, arithmetic, or functional relation that expresses the correlation.
2. Identify all predicates (i.e., decision statements) and classify them as to whether they are dependent or independent. Any predicate based only on

independent input variables must be independent. Identify correlated predicates and document the nature of the correlation either as a function, logical relation, table, or whatever is clear and concise. If the same predicate appears at more than one decision, the two decisions are obviously correlated.

3. Start path selection with uncorrelated, independent predicates. Cover as much as you can this way. If you achieve coverage and you had identified supposedly dependent predicates, something is wrong. Here are some of the possibilities:

   a. The predicates are correlated and/or dependent in such a way as to nullify the dependency. The routine's logic can probably be simplified. See the methods of Chapters 9 and 10.

   b. You have classified your predicates incorrectly. Check your work.

   c. Your path tracing is faulty. Look for a missing path or incomplete coverage.

   d. There is a bug.

4. If coverage has not been achieved using independent uncorrelated predicates, extend the coverage by using correlated predicates; preferably those whose resolution is independent of the processing.

5. If coverage has not been achieved, extend the cases to those that involve dependent predicates (typically required to cover loops), preferably those that are not correlated.

6. Lastly, use correlated, dependent predicates.

7. For each path selected above, list the input variables corresponding to the predicates required to force the path. If the variable is independent, list its value. If the variable is dependent, list relation that will make the predicate go the right way. If the variable is correlated, state the nature of the correlation to other variables. Examine forbidden combinations (if any) in detail. Determine the mechanism by which forbidden combinations of values are prohibited. If nothing prevents such combinations, what will happen if they are supplied as inputs?

8. Each path will yield a set of conditions, call them equations or inequalities, which must be simultaneously satisfied to force the path. More on this later.

3.4. Examples

3.4.1. Simple, Independent, Uncorrelated Predicates

The uppercase letters in the decision boxes of Figure 3-6 represent the predicates. For example, "A" might mean "X = 0?" The capital letters on

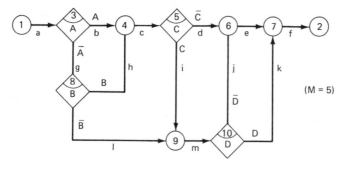

Figure 3-6. Predicate Notation.

the links following the decisions indicate whether the predicate is true (unbarred) or false (barred) for that link. There are four decisions in this example and, consequently, four predicates. Because they are uncorrelated and independent by assumption, each can take on a TRUE or FALSE value independently, leading to $2^4 = 16$ possible values. However, the number of possible paths is far less (8) and the number of covering paths is smaller still. A set of covering paths and their associated predicate truth values can be trivially obtained from the flowchart:

Path	Predicate Values
abcdef	A $\overline{C}$
aghcimkf	$\overline{A}$ B C D
aglmjef	$\overline{A}$ $\overline{B}$ $\overline{D}$

A glance at the path column shows that all links are represented at least once. The predicate value column shows all predicates appearing both barred and unbarred. Therefore, every link has been covered and every decision has been taken both ways. I violated my own rules here because the second path had two things changing at once. Using a few more but simpler paths with fewer changes to cover the same flowchart, I get:

Path	Predicate Values
abcdef	A $\overline{C}$
abcimjef	A C $\overline{D}$
abcimkf	A C D
aghcdef	$\overline{A}$ B $\overline{C}$
aglmkf	$\overline{A}$ B $\overline{D}$

Because you know what each predicate means (e.g., A means "X = 0?"), you can now determine the set of input values corresponding to each path.

3.4.2. Correlated, Independent Predicates

The two decisions in Figure 3-7 are correlated because they used the identical predicate (A). If you picked paths *abdeg* and *acdfg*, which seem to provide coverage, you would find that neither of these paths are achievable. If the A branch (c) is taken at the first decision, then the A branch (e) must also be taken at the second decision. There are two decisions and therefore a potential for four paths, but only two of them, *abdfg* and *acdeg*, are possible. The flowchart can be replaced with the flowchart of Figure 3-8.

The correlation of predicates will not often be so blatant as when both decisions have exactly the same tests on the same variables. Suppose you did not know or did not realize that two or more predicates were correlated. You would find that setting one decision's variables would force another and that you did not have complete freedom to choose the rest of the path. In general, correlated predicates mean that some paths are not achievable, although this does not mean that coverage is unachievable. If you select paths from the design flowchart or the PDL specification without considering the details of path sensitization (which is a good idea) and subsequently you find that a path is not achievable, even though it was selected on the basis of seemingly meaningful cases, it is an occasion for joy rather than frustration. One of the following must be true:

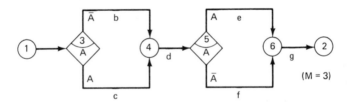

Figure 3-7. Correlated Decisions.

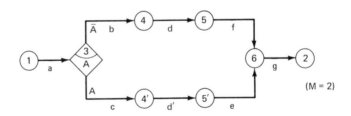

Figure 3-8. Correlated Decision of Figure 3-7 Removed.

1. You found a bug.
2. The design can be simplified by removing some decisions, possibly at the cost of a new subroutine or repeated code.
3. You have gained a better understanding of how the decisions are interrelated.

The real question to ask, however, is how did the decisions come to be correlated? Correlated decisions are to some extent redundant. If you have n decisions in a routine and less than 2^n paths, there is a degree of redundancy in the design, even though you might not be able to take advantage of the redundancy. If n decisions give you only 2^{n-1} paths, then one decision is targeted for removal. If n decisions give 2^{n-2} paths, then two decisions should be targeted. Generally, $\log_2$ (number of paths) tells you how many effective decisions you have. Comparing this with the actual number of decisions tells you if any can be targeted for removal. Because getting rid of code is the best possible kind of test,* removing potentially redundant code is good testing at its best.

One of the most common and most troublesome sources of correlated decisions is directly related to the reprehensible practice of "saving code." Link d in the above example is typical. The designer had thought to save some common code by doing the initial processing that followed the first decision, merging to execute the common code, and then splitting again to do the different code based on the second decision. It's relatively harmless in this example. Most often, the second decision will be based on a flag which was set on the link appropriate to the predicate's value at the first decision. The second decision is based on the flag's value, but it is obviously correlated to the first. Think of these two pieces as being widely separated and embedded within a much larger and more complicated routine. Now the nature of the correlation is subtle and obscure. The way it's usually done, though, is not even this sensible. The programmer sees a previously written sequence of code that seems to correspond to part of the case that is yet to be programmed. He jumps into the middle of the old code to take advantage of the supposedly common code and puts in a subsequent test to avoid doing the wrong processing and to get him back onto the correct path. Maintaining such code can be a nightmare, especially because such "saved code" is rarely documented. This can lead to future bugs even though there may be no bugs at first.**

---

*Remember that the highest goal of testing is to prevent bugs. If bugs occur at 1% per source statement, then credit yourself with a bug "found" and "corrected" for every hundred lines of code you eliminate. Adjust this to the local bug rate. Bad routines tend to have a lot of superfluous code and a high bug rate—say, 3% to 4%: you can earn your pay on such routines.

**Frankly, while many programmers insist that they branched into a hunk of code to save space, we know that they really did it to save work—'fess up!

Correlated decisions on a path, especially those that prevent functionally sensible paths, should be suspected. At best they provide an opportunity for simplifying the routine's control structure and, therefore, for saving testing labor, or they may reveal a bug. It is rare that such correlated decisions (those that prevent functionally sensible paths) are due to a deep subtlety in the specification.

3.4.3. Dependent Predicates

Finding sensitizing values for dependent predicates may force you to "play computer." Usually, and thankfully, most of the routine's processing does not affect the control flow and consequently can be ignored. Simulate the computer only to the extent necessary to force paths. Loops are the most common kind of dependent predicates; the number of times a typical routine will iterate in the loop is usually determinable in a straightforward manner from the input variables' values. Consequently it is usually easy to work backwards to determine what input value is needed to force the loop a specified number of times.

3.4.4. The General Case

There is no simple procedure for the general case. It is easy to state the steps involved but much harder to accomplish them.

1. Select cases to provide coverage on the basis of functionally sensible paths. If the routine is well-structured, you should be able to force most of the paths without deep analysis. Any intractable path should be examined for potential bugs before investing a lot of time solving equations, or whatever you might have to do, to find input values that will force the path.
2. Tackle the path with the fewest decisions first. Give preference to non-looping paths over looping paths.
3. Start at the end of the path and not the beginning. Trace the path in reverse and list the predicates in the order in which they appear. The first predicate (the last on the path in the normal direction) imposes restrictions on subsequent predicates (previous when reckoned in the normal path direction). Determine the broadest possible range of values for the predicate that will satisfy the desired path direction.
4. Continue working backwards along the path to the next decision. The next decision may be restricted by the range of values you determined for the previous decision (in the backward direction). Pick a range of values

for the affected variables that is as broad as possible for the desired direction and is consistent with the set of values thus far determined.

5. Continue until you have reached the entrance and therefore have established a set of input conditions for the entire path.

Whatever manipulations you are doing can always be reduced to equivalent numerical operations. What you are doing in tracing the path backwards is building a set of numerical inequalities or a combination of numerical inequalities, equations, and logical statements. You are trying to find input values that satisfy all of them. These are the values that will force the path. If you cannot find such a solution, it may mean that the path is not achievable. Alternatively, it means that you couldn't solve the set of inequalities—most likely it means that you've found a bug.

An alternate approach to use when you are truly faced with functionally sensible paths that require equation solving to sensitize is a little easier. Instead of working backwards along the path, work forwards from the first decision to the last. To do this, though, you may have to drop your preconceived paths. Let's say that you have already sensitized some paths and all the rest seem to be dependent and/or correlated.

1. List all the decisions that have yet to be covered in the rough order in which you expect to traverse them. For each decision, write down the broadest possible range of input values that affect that decision.
2. Pick a direction at the first decision on the path that appears to go in the direction you wish to go. Adjust all input values—that is, the range of input values—that are affected by your choice. For example, A was restricted to positive integers at input and B was any letter between "D" and "G". The first decision restricted A to less than 10 and B to "E" or "F". This restricted set of input values is now used for the next decision.
3. Continue in this way, decision by decision, always picking a direction that gets you closer to the exit. Because the predicates are dependent and/or correlated, your earlier choices may force subsequent directions.
4. Assuming that the procedure does not lead to impossible or contradictory input values (which means that the attempted path is not achievable), start a new path, using the last decision at which you had a choice, assuming that such a path will provide additional coverage.

The advantage of the forward method over the backward method is that it's usually less work to get the input values because you are solving the simultaneous inequalities as you go. The disadvantage is that you don't quite know where you're going. The routine is the master and not you.

3.5. Desk Checking

Desk checking is often an indeterminate and interminable process. Too often the programmer is expected to do desk checking by simulating the computer's behavior. This is unfair and inhuman, and because people are such bad computers, ineffectual. Test cases, when all is said and done, fall into two main categories: 1) structure-based test cases which are dominated by path testing, and 2) function-based test cases in which it is possible to specify the output for a given input. The functional test cases can usually be derived from a specification that directly or indirectly provides the expected outputs for specific inputs. Mathematical routines are an obvious exception to this although it may still be possible to use tabulated values or simple special cases that are trivially solvable. Let's consider the typical routine in which the functional requirements can be converted into a listing of required outputs for given inputs. It is clearly not effective to manually simulate the computer's behavior for such cases. It is much easier to use the best possible simulator, the computer itself. Run the program through those test cases and see if it works. So, checking out that kind of case should not be part of desk checking. There are some routines, however, in which it may be necessary to "play computer." For such routines, use a trace or insert trace statements that will dump the important values at each step. Desk checking for such cases consists of following the trace and making sure you understand what the computer did at every step. The computer is not going to make mistakes and it's less work to follow what it did than to simulate its doing it. So again, these cases should not be part of normal desk checking.

The objective of desk checking should be to do things which humans can do, preferably well, and computers can't, and not to do things which computers can do exquisitely and humans poorly, if at all. Here are a few examples:

1. *Syntax Checking*—If humans could do syntax checking, we wouldn't have so many syntax errors. If you do syntax checking well, you probably don't have many syntax errors, and it's not likely that a desk check for syntax errors will reveal anything. If you do have syntax errors, it proves that you're no good at syntax checking, so what do you expect to catch by manual syntax checking?
2. *Cross Reference Checks*—The program must be checked for undeclared variables, unreferenced labels, unitialized values, and so on. This should be done by the source language processor. Unfortunately, some assemblers are notoriously poor in this respect. Do it only under protest. Humans aren't terrible at this job, but it's a terrible job. If you must do it,

do it systematically. Use index cards, or better yet, a rotary card file (one card for every object of interest), and write down the cross references by hand as you go through each statement or instruction.

3. *Convention Violations*—All well-run projects establish conventions for naming variables, labels, subroutines, and so on. These conventions may specify the first five letters of an eight-letter mnemonic and leave the last three to the programmer. Similarly, there may be additional conventions for the length of the mnemonic, use of numerics, and so on. Additional stylistic conventions may prohibit certain kinds of constructs. Checking for style violations is a form of syntax checking and consequently should be automated but often isn't. Agitate for language features and preprocessors that permit the formal declaration of stylistic conventions and the subsequent automatic checking thereof. If such facilities are not available, protect yourself by further cutting down stylistic freedom within your own routine. Use very regular label assignments and conventions. Name things in such a way that it will be possible to tell at a glance that something is awry. If automatic facilities are not available, you will have to check it yourself (or better yet, get someone else to check for you—while you check that person's code) as part of desk checking. Go through the program one convention at a time, rather than trying to check all conventions simultaneously. It's actually faster and more thorough to methodically read the program 10 times for 10 different conventions than to attempt to read it once for all 10 conventions simultaneously.

4. *Detailed Comparison*—The source code (the coding sheet, say) must be compared, character-by-character to the actual code produced by keypunching. This should be done only after all automated checks have been done and after you have done the manual checks of steps 2 and 3 (assuming they were necessary. It is an ugly and tedious job but essential. Again, it is better to get someone else to do it for you, It's really unavoidable. Say you wrote the code on a coding sheet. There's no character-recognition equipment available that will read your handwritten code as reliably as a human keypunch operator. Say you typed the code on the coding sheet or directly into the computer or at a terminal. Then there are typing errors to pick up. It's amazing how persistent tygopraphical errors are. This book was proofread ten times by professional proofreaders and editors, who are really excellent at it, and yet, tygopraphical errors remain. How many did you find so far? Do this check with a ruler. Expose only one line at a time. Do it a word at a time, a character at a time, and say the letters, and move your lips as you read. This is no place for glancing or speed-reading. Try it on this paragraph,

5. *The Flowchart*—Recreate the flowchart or PDL specification from the

keypunched and compiled or assembled code (after the above checks have been done) and compare it to the design flowchart. Better yet, have someone else recreate the flowchart and a third person do the comparison. The computer can't do the original flowchart or read it, so it can't do this comparison. Furthermore, the comparison of design intentions as expressed in the original flowchart, to what was coded and to the flowchart produced from the code entails notions of equivalence between flowchart and code constructs that are presently beyond the ken of computers.

6. *Path Sensitizing*—The final step in desk checking should be path sensitizing. Design the paths from the design flowchart or PDL specification but attempt to sensitize them from the code. If you can force all the paths you intended, it may prove nothing, but if there are paths or segments in the coded version which appeared to be reasonable in the design but which you cannot force from the code, then you've probably found a bug. Simulate only that part of the processing that you must to sensitize the paths. Once you have successfully found sensitizing values for all the test paths, you have perforce desk checked every line of code involved in the control flow and every decision. That is, your desk checking has achieved coverage and you're not likely to learn anything more from desk checking; get to work running your test cases.

As usual, I've prescribed a procedure that entails a lot of work. It's a trade. Either you do the work now, in a systematic, unpressured way, or you or someone else does it later on the test floor. Or worse, you may have to get up in the middle of the night, when the snow is piled a foot high, battle your way to the airport so that you can catch the last plane out to Frittersville. Remember, "There's never enough time to do it right, but there's always enough time to do it over." Tedious as this desk-checking procedure might seem, it does maximize the effective utilization of human resources. It is humane, and it does work.

Meticulous desk checking appears to be capable of catching 30% of all bugs, and it is particularly effective against wild cards. Unstructured desk checking, which is typically dominated by a futile attempt to simulate the computer, actually does not take any less time. What usually happens is that you start out and do a few cases in detail, possibly correctly. Then the cases get tougher and the mind wanders and gets confused. So another case is attempted, but because the whole procedure is unstructured, chances are that this case has already been covered, although it doesn't appear to have been. This kind of desk checking stops not when it's done but when someone (thankfully) tells you to stop or when you can no longer stand the strain, pain, and frustration.

To reiterate desk checking:

1. Do a detailed comparison of the original (handwritten, say) code to the keypunched version for anything that cannot be caught by the computer.
2. Recreate the flowchart or PDL specification based on the code and compare it to the design flowchart or source PDL specification.
3. Select test paths based on the design flowchart or PDL specification but sensitize the paths based on the code.
4. Simulate no more of the computer than you must to sensitize the paths.
5. Whenever possible, get others to do this work for your routine and reciprocate by doing it for theirs.

4. TEST CASE GENERATION AND INSTRUMENTATION

4.1. Automatic Test Case Generation

There is no simple way to automatically generate test cases. Research in this area continues, and it is expected that eventually useful test tools will result (CICU75, MILL75, MILL77C, RAMA75A, RAMA76, VOGE80). The basic problem of all automatically derived test cases is in their effective limitation to static analysis. The basic limitation to automatically generated test cases is that the test case generator software does not understand the program, and if it were given (and could use) sufficient data to approach understanding, such data, which would have to be provided in a formal language, might also have bugs. There is one relatively simple way to generate test cases that does not rely on a deep analysis of the program's structure, either automated or manual: by using random test data. There are however, several difficulties and weaknesses in random test data, especially if that is the only kind of test that's done.

1. Random data produces a statistically insignificant sample of the possible paths through most routines (HUAN75, MORA78). Because it may be difficult to determine how many feasible paths there are, even copious tests based on random data may not allow you to produce a statistically valid prediction of the routine's reliability.
2. There is no assurance of coverage. Running the generator to the point of 100% coverage could take centuries.
3. If the data are generated in accordance with statistics that reflect expected data characteristics, the test cases will be biased to the normal paths—the very paths that are least likely to have bugs.

4. It may be difficult or impossible to predict the desired outputs and therefore to verify that the routine is working properly; all you might learn is that it did not blowup but not whether what it did made sense or not. In many cases, the only way to produce the output against which to make a comparison is to run the equivalent of the routine; which equivalence is as likely to have bugs as the routine being tested.

If random path generation is to be used, instead of generating test cases in accordance with the probability of traversals at decisions, the test cases should be generated in accordance with the complementary probability. That is, if the probability of branching in a given direction is P, test paths should be generated so that the probability of branching for the test cases is 1-P at that decision. This would, at least, bias the paths away from the normal cases and toward the weird cases that are more likely to have bugs.

As a supplementary method of generating test cases, particularly when applied at a system level, using random test data is not a bad idea. This is assuming that it is possible to run the system on a test bed with a test data generator and then to force the system through thousands and millions of cases. If done as part of system-level stress testing (BEIZ83), random test data is more effective yet.

4.2. Instrumentation

4.2.1. The Problem

You could fall into the trap of designing excellent tests for a routine or system that has no bugs. Let's say you design a set of tests that corresponds to what you believe is a covering set of paths. If you run those test cases, can you be sure that you have traversed every link and taken every branch? Absolutely not! You can make that claim only if you are sure that the routine has no bugs, in which case, why are you testing? Similarly, relying on an automated test data generator that produces a covering path set does not solve the problem. The test system will cover something alright, but what it covers is what it is working on and not necessarily what you intended. As long as there is the possibility of discrepancy between what you intended and what you have, between your concept of the routine's behavior and its actual behavior, there is a possibility that the best planned set of tests will not achieve coverage or, if it does, that what was covered was not what you expected. It is therefore, necessary to **instrument** the program with probes that measure or identify the paths traversed. The instrumentation can, of course, have bugs of its own.

4.2.2. General Strategy

There are methods for automating the optimizing of the placement of instrumentation probes. Ramamoorthy (RAMA75B) shows that automated methods can do slightly better than heuristic methods in identifying the best places for probes. This is significant in the design of automated test aids. The general strategy for manual placement of probes follows. We want to assure coverage. In principle, we have to place a probe on every link. At its simplest, a probe consists of a counter which is incremented every time it is passed. Here's a tentative set of rules:

1. Put a counter as close as possible to each exit of a decision.
2. Put a counter as close as possible to the entry point of each link leading into a junction; that is, just prior to any **GOTO** or equivalent statement.

This rule applied to loops leads to:

3. Put a counter just after the loop-determining decision.
4. Put a counter just before the loop-back point.

Execute the tests as planned. Prior to the test, calculate the value that each counter should have at the conclusion of the test. When two counters exist on the same link, they should have exactly the same predicted value. If the counts are not as expected, there is a bug or some other problem, possibly conceptual. This strategy, while helpful, does not guarantee a bug-free program. The situation shown in Figure 3-9 is a case in point:

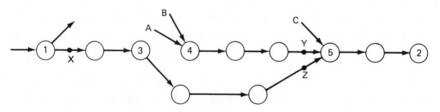

Figure 3-9. Instrumentation with Bugs.

The counters are named A, B, C, X, Y, and Z. The program should have gone directly from node 3 to node 4. A counter at X will read correctly. Node 4 has been instrumented with counters A and B and what you believe is counter Z, which should have been at the input link to node 4 but is actually at the input to node 5. The counters will provide the right values, but the bug will not be caught by this technique alone. This problem can be resolved by insisting on another counter just after each junction node. The entire pre-scription then becomes equivalent to the simpler rule of:

Put a counter as close as possible to the beginning and to the end of each link.

The checkout procedure then consists of answering the following questions:

1. Does the begin-link counter value equal the end-link counter value for all links?
2. Does the input-link count of every decision equal the sum of the link counts of the output links from that decision?
3. Does the sum of the input-link counts for a junction equal the output-link count for that junction?
4. Do the counts match the values you predicted when you designed the test?

4.2.3. Traversal Markers and Traces

A more elaborate form of instrumentation (RAMA75B) is called a **traversal marker**. Say that you named every link with a lowercase letter. Instrument all links so that the corresponding letter is recorded when that link is executed. The succession of letters produced in going from the routine's entry to its exit should, if there are no bugs, exactly correspond to the path name (i.e., the "name" you get when you concatenate the link names traversed on the path—e.g., *abcde*). Because links can be chewed open by bugs, it's wise to install two markers—one at the beginning of each link and one at the end. The test criteria now are:

1. Does every link name appear twice in succession (e.g., *aabbccddee*)?
2. Does the succession of link names correspond exactly to the expected path name?

In practice, you would be more likely to use numbers rather than letters. That is, number each link. Then you would have to store this succession of numbers in a push-down list or buffer, or something of the sort. I use the following method for small routines. I use a single counter and "name" each link by a prime number, starting with 2. The proper path should result in an unique number that I can easily calculate. For example, if the path is

(2,3,5,11,13,7), the corresponding number is (2 × 2 × 3 × 3 × 5 × 5 × 11 × 11 × 13 × 13 × 7 × 7) = 901,800,900. A wrong number tells me that something is wrong, and factoring it into its prime factors tells me what went wrong. Note that this is not strictly equivalent to traversal markers, because some information, particularly the order in which the links were traversed, is lost.* I'm betting that bugs that interchange link orders are very improbable—it's a good bet.

You can use a bit-mapping technique if there aren't too many links. Assign a unique bit for each link on the path. Set the bit when the link is entered, and set the corresponding bit in another word when the link is exited. Again you've lost order information, but the essential fact that the link was traversed, in some order, has been recorded. You can increase counters and traversal markers and augment them with storage of critical or interesting values. Eventually, if you put enough of this stuff in, you will effectively achieve a full interpretive trace of the routine. The variations are endless and limited only by your imagination and budget.

4.3. Implementation

The introduction of probes, especially if you have to put them in by hand, provides new opportunities for bugs. Automatically inserted probes are less bug prone, but can only be inserted in terms of the real rather than the intended structure. This discrepancy can be great, especially if control is affected by what goes on in lower-level routines that are called by the routine under test. Instrumentation is relatively more important when path testing is used at the higher levels of program structure, such as with transaction flows (see Chapter 4), than when it is used at the unit level. Furthermore, at the higher levels, the possibility of discrepancies between actual and intended structure is greater; but instrumentation overhead is relatively smaller.

It is simplest and most effective to install probes when programming in a language that permits **conditional assembly** or **compilation**. The probes are written in the source code and tagged into categories. Both counters and traversal markers can be implemented, and one need not be parsimonious with the number and placement of probes because only those that are activated for that test will be compiled or assembled. For any test or small set of tests, only some of the probes will be active. Only rarely would you compile with all probes activated and then only when all else failed.

---

*This is just a primitive Gödel numbering of paths. You could get more elaborate with your coding scheme and not lose the sequence information. Unfortunately, the resulting numbers get big fast and the additional overhead required for multiple-precision multiplication soon outweighs the advantage—to the point where straightforward storage of link names is simpler.

Conditional assembly and compilation must be used with caution, however, particularly as one progresses from unit to system levels. A unit may take just a few seconds to compile or assemble. But, (and this is language and language processor dependent), the same routine, if compiled or assembled in the context of a full system, could take many hours—thereby canceling many of the advantages of conditional assembly and compilation.

If conditional assembly or compilation are not available, use macros or function calls for each category of probe to be implemented. The probe can be turned on or off by modifying the macro or function definition or by setting ON/OFF parameters within the functions or macros. Use of macros or functions will also reduce bugs in the probes themselves. A general purpose routine can be written to store the outputs of traversal markers. Because efficiency is not really an issue, you can afford the overhead and can use a piece of standard code to record things.

Plan your instrumentation in levels of ever increasing detail so that when all probes are active at the most detailed level, they will serve as a diagnostic tool. Remember that path testing based on structure should comprise only half of all the tests that are to be done, and while the instrumentation may be installed to verify path testing, it will be useful in other tests as well.

4.4. Limitations

Every probe you activate gives you more information, but with each probe the information is further removed from reality. The ultimate "probe," a full interpretive trace, gives you the most information possible but so distorts timing relations that timing and race-condition bugs will hide under your probes. Location-dependent bugs also hide under probes. If, for example, someone made an absolute assumption regarding the location of something in the data base, the presence or absence of probes could modify things so that the bug could be seen only when the probe was inactive and not with the probe in place. In other words, the very probe that is designed to reveal bugs may hide them. Such "peek-a-boo bugs" are really tough.

5. SUMMARY

1. Path testing based on structure is a powerful tool at the unit level. With suitable interpretation, it can be used for functional tests at the system level (see Chapter 4).
2. The objective of path testing is to execute a sufficient number of tests to assure that, as a minimum, all decisions have been taken in all directions

and that all instructions have been executed at least once. Both criteria are necessary.

3. Select paths as deviations from the normal paths, starting with the simplest, most familiar, most direct paths from the entry to the exit. More paths should be added to provide full coverage.

4. Add paths to cover extreme cases for loops and combinations of loops: no looping, once, twice, one less than the maximum, the maximum. Attempt forbidden cases.

5. Determine the path sensitizing input-data sets for each selected path. If a path is impossible, choose another path that will also achieve coverage. But first ask yourself why seemingly sensible cases lead to unachievable paths.

6. Plan instrumentation that can verify path and decision coverage. Take advantage of conditional compilation or assembly if available.

7. Plan desk checking as a structured activity that follows all available automated checking and precedes test case running. Design test cases and path from the design flowchart or PDL specification but sensitize paths from the code as part of desk checking.

8. Document all tests and expected test results as copiously as you would document code. Treat each path like a subroutine. Predict and document the output for the stated input, the path trace (or name by links), and for branch and decision counts. Also document any significant environmental factors and preconditions. Your tests must be reproducible so that they can serve a diagnostic purpose if they reveal a bug. An undocumented test cannot be reproduced.

9. Be creatively stupid when conducting tests. Every deviation from the predicted path must be explained. Every deviation must lead to either a test change, a code change, or a conceptual change.

10. A test that reveals a bug has succeeded, not failed (MYER79).

4

PATH TESTING AND
TRANSACTION FLOWS

1. SYNOPSIS

Transaction flows are introduced as a representation of a system's functions. The same methods that were applied to process flowcharts can then be used for functional testing.

2. GENERALIZATIONS

While the primary use of flowcharts is to represent the control flow of a program or routine, the same graphical elements can be used to represent higher-level control flows or the flow of data modifications in a data base (FOSD76A). There are many different ways to represent software. Peters (PETE76) summarizes the most useful ones. And conversely, most models can be used to represent more than one aspect of program or system behavior. The flowchart was introduced as a model of a program's control flow—a distinctly structural concept. In this chapter, the same representation is used as a model of a program's functional behavior—a model, if you will, of the structure of the system's functions.

3. TRANSACTION FLOWS

3.1. Definitions

A **transaction** is a unit of work seen from a system user's point of view. A transaction consists of a set of operations, some of which are performed by a system, persons, or devices that are outside of the system. A transaction typically consists of a set of operations that begins with an input and ends with one or more outputs. At the conclusion of the transaction's processing, the transaction is no longer in the system, except perhaps in the form of historical records. A transaction for an online information retrieval system might consist of the following steps or **tasks**:

1. Accept input.
2. Validate input.
3. Transmit acknowledgement to requester.
4. Do input processing.
5. Search file.
6. Request additional directions from user.
7. Accept input.
8. Validate input.
9. Process request.
10. Update file.
11. Transmit output.
12. Record transaction in log.

The user sees this scenario as a single transaction. From the system's point of view, the transaction consists of twelve steps and ten different kinds of subsidiary tasks.

Most online systems process several different kinds of transactions. For example, a money machine can be used for withdrawals, deposits, bill payments, and money transfers. Furthermore, these operations can be done for a checking account, savings account, vacation account, and so on. While the sequence of operations may differ from transaction to transaction, most transactions have operations in common. For example, the money machine begins every transaction by validating the user's card and password number. Tasks in a transaction-flow diagram correspond to processing steps in a control flowchart. As with control flows, there can be conditional branches, unconditional branches, and junctions.

3.2. Example

Figure 4-1 shows part of a transaction flow. A microcomputer is used as a terminal controller for several VDU terminals. The terminals are used to process orders for parts, say. The order forms are complicated. The user specifies the wanted action, and the terminal controller requests the proper form from a remotely located central computer. The forms may be several pages long and may have many fields on each page. The form is transmitted by the central computer in a code designed to minimize communication-line usage. The form is then translated by the terminal controller for the user's

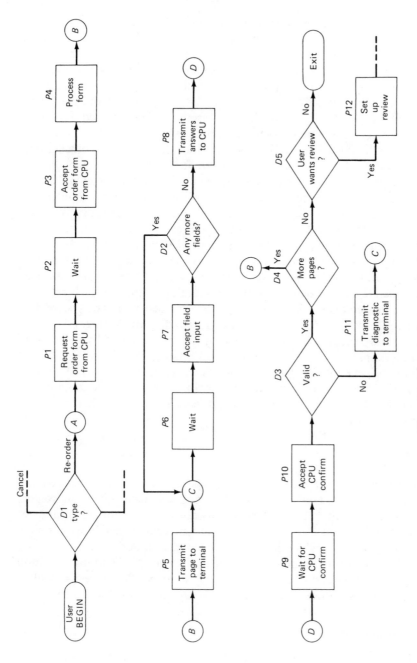

Figure 4-1. Example of a Transaction Flow.

benefit. The terminal controller only transmits the answers (i.e., the contents of the blanks) back to the central computer. As each page of the form is completed, the terminal controller transmits the answers to the central computer, which either accepts or rejects them. If the answers are not valid, a diagnostic code is transmitted by the central computer to the terminal controller which, in turn, translates the code and informs the user at the terminal. Finally, the terminal allows the user to review the filled-out form.

Decision D1 in Figure 4-1 is not part of the process as such—it is really a characteristic of the kinds of transactions that the terminal controller handles. However, there is a decision like this somewhere in the program. Process P1 probably consists of several subsidiary processes that are completed by the transmission of the request for an order from the central computer. The next step is "process P2," which involves no real processing. What the terminal controller will do here depends on the software's structure. Typically, transactions for some other terminal will be processed. Process P3 is a real processing step, as is P4, which does the translation. Process P6 is another wait for input. This has no direct correspondence to a program step. Decisions D2 and D4 depend on the structure of the form. Which branch is taken at decision D3 is determined by the user's behavior. The system does not necessarily have actual decisions corresponding to D1, D2, D3, D4, or D5. D1 and D5 could be implemented by interrupts caused by special keys on the terminal.

The most general case of a transaction flow, then, represents by a flowchart a scenario between people and computers. In a more restricted example, the transaction flow can represent an internal sequence of events that may occur in processing a transaction.

3.3. Usage

Transaction flows are indispensable for specifying the functional requirements of complicated systems, particularly online systems. A very big system, such as an air traffic control system, has not hundreds, but thousands of different transaction flows. The flows are represented by relatively simple flowcharts, many of which have a single straight-through path. Loops are relatively infrequent compared to ordinary flowcharts. The most common loop is used to request a retry after user-input errors. The system will allow the user to try, say three times, and will take the card away the fourth time.

3.4. Implementation

The implementation of a transaction flow is usually implicit in the design of the system's control structure and associated data base. That is, there is no direct, one-for-one correspondence between the "processes" and "decisions" of the transaction flows and corresponding program elements. A transaction flow is a representation of a path taken by a transaction through a succession of processing modules. Think of each transaction as represented by a **token**—such as a transaction-control block which is passed from routine to routine as it progresses through its flow. The transaction diagram is a pictorial representation of what happens to the tokens; it is *not* the control structure of the program that manipulates those tokens.

Figure 4-2 shows another transaction flow and the corresponding implementation of a program that creates that flow. This transaction goes through input processing, which classifies it as to type, and then passes through process A, followed by B. The result of process B may force the transaction to pass back to process A. The transaction then goes to process C, then to either D or E, and finally to output processing.

Figure 4-2b is a diagrammatic representation of a software architecture that might implement this and many other transactions. The system is controlled by an executive/scheduler/dispatcher/operating-system—call it what you will. In this diagram, the boxes represent processes and the links represent processing queues. The transaction enters (that is, it is created by) an input processing module in response to inputs received, for example, at a terminal. The transaction is "created" by the act of filling out a transaction-control block and placing that token on an input queue. The scheduler then examines the transaction and places it on the work queue for process A. But this does not necessarily mean that process A will be activated immediately. When a process has finished working on the transaction, it places the transaction-control block back on a scheduler queue. The scheduler then examines the transaction-control block and routes it to the next process based on information stored in the block. The scheduler contains tables or code that routes the transaction to its next process. In systems that handle hundreds of transaction types, this information is usually stored in tables rather than as explicit code. Alternatively, the dispatcher may contain no transaction-control data or code: the information could be implemented as code in each transaction processing module.

Figure 4-2c shows a possible implementation of this transaction processing system (highly simplified). Let's say that while there could be many different transaction flows in the system, they all used only processes A, B, C, D, E and disc and tape reads and writes, in various combinations. Just because the flow is A, B, C, D, E is no reason to invoke the processes in that order. For other transactions, not shown, the processing order might be B, C, A, E, D. A fixed invocation order based on one transaction flow might not be optimum for another. Furthermore, different transactions have different priorities that may require some to wait for higher-priority transactions to be

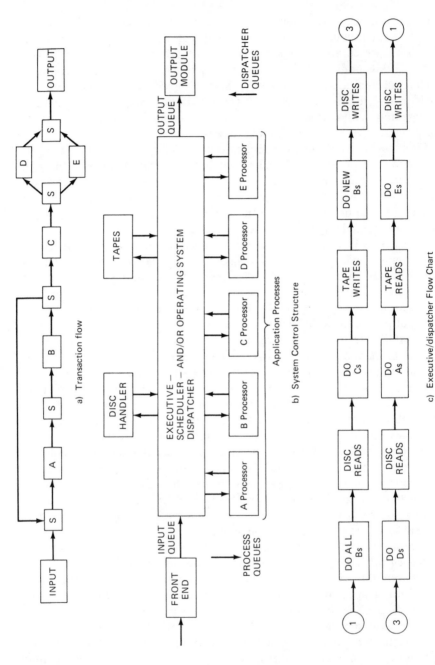

a) Transaction flow

b) System Control Structure

c) Executive/dispatcher Flow Chart

Figure 4-2. A Transaction Flow and Its Implementation.

processed. Similarly, one would not shut processing down for all transactions while waiting for a specific transaction to complete a necessary disc-read operation. In general, in multiprocessing, multiprogramming systems, there is no direct correspondence between the order in which processes are invoked and transaction flows. A given transaction will, of course, receive processing attention from the appropriate processing modules in the strict order required, but there could be many other things going on between the instances in which that transaction was being processed. I have left out the scheduler calls in Figure 4-2c to simplify things. Assume that there is a return of control to the scheduler after each process box. The whole program is organized as a simple loop. First, the scheduler invokes processing module B, which cleans up all transactions that are waiting for B processing at that moment. Then the disc reads are initiated and the scheduler turns control over to module C, which clears up all of its tasks. After the tape writes are done, module B is invoked again to take care of any additional work that may have accumulated for it. The process continues, and finally the entire loop starts over again. A cyclic structure like this is common in process control and communications systems, among many others. Alternatively, a more complex control structure can be used in which the processing modules are not invoked in fixed order but in an order determined by the length of the queues for those modules, the priority of the tasks, the priority of the active modules, and the state of the system with respect to I/O operations. A queue-driven approach is more common in commercial operating systems. The reasons for choosing one control structure over another is not germane to testing. It is a performance and resource-optimization question. For more information, see BEIZ78.

3.5. Complications

While in simple cases, transactions have a unique identity from the time they are created to the time they are completed, in many systems, one transaction can create several others, and transactions can also merge. The simple flowchart is inadequate to represent transaction flows that split and merge: a Petri-net model (PETE76) can be used. However, the available methodology for test case design based on Petri nets is not as well developed as that based on flowcharts. Most such problems can be reduced to a set of flows that can be represented by flowcharts. If a transaction splits at some point, say into two parts that then go on independently, treat it as three different transactions—one transaction type that starts at the beginning and ends at the split and two more that start at the split and end at their ends. Treat merging transactions the same way: from the point where they were created to the merger, and from the merger to the end. Document the split or merger to keep track of the test cases and to assure that the correlation of the merged and split components are kept correct.

4. TRANSACTION-FLOW TESTING

4.1. Get The Transaction Flows

Complicated systems that process a lot of different, complicated transactions should have explicit representations of the transaction flows, or the equivalent, documented. If transaction flows are part of the system's functional specification, half the battle is won. Don't expect to get pure transaction flows and don't insist on only that form of representing the system's processing requirements. There are other, equivalent representations, such as HIPO charts and Petri nets, that can serve the same purpose (PETE76). If these representations are available and if they are done correctly, it will be easy to create the transaction flows from them. The objective is to have a very high-level trace of what happens to transactions—a trace of the progression of actions, which, as we have seen, may not correspond to the design of the system executive or to the relation between the various processing modules that work on the transaction. Transaction flows are like flowcharts and consequently, we should expect to have them in increasing levels of detail. It is correct and effective to have subflows that are analogous to subroutines in normal flowcharts, although there may not be any processing module that corresponds to such subflows.

Designers ought to understand what they're doing. And it's obvious that if they don't, they are not likely to do it right. I've made it a practice to ask for transaction flows for the, say, ten most important transactions that a system is to process, preparatory to designing the system's functional test. I hope that that information is in the specification. If it isn't, it's likely that there will be some disagreement as to what the system is supposed to be doing. More important, the system's design documentation should contain an overview section that details the main transaction flows (all of them, it is hoped). If I can't find that or the equivalent, then I don't need a lot of complicated tests to know that the system will have a lot of complicated bugs. Detailed transaction flows are a mandatory prerequisite to the rational design of a system's functional test.

Like so much in testing, the act of getting the information on which to base tests can be more effective at catching and exterminating bugs than the tests that result from that information. Insisting on getting transaction flows or the equivalent is sometimes a gentle way of convincing an inept design group that they don't know what they're doing. These are harsh words, but let's face it: superb code and testing at the unit level is useless if the overall design is poor. And how can there be a rational, effective design if no one on the high-level design team can walk you through the more important transactions, step-by-step, alternative by alternative. I'm sure that mine is a biased sample, but every system I've ever seen that was in serious trouble had no transaction flows documented, nor had the designers anything that approximated that kind of functional representation; I'm sure it's possible to have a bad design even with transaction flows, though.*

To reiterate: the first step in using transaction flows as a basis for system-level functional testing is to get the transaction flows. Often, that's the hardest step. Occasionally, it's the only step before the project's canceled.

4.2. Test Design

Once you have a complete set of transaction flows, test design proceeds exactly as it does for ordinary flowcharts. You must test every link, every decision's outcome, every process. Links now encompass actual processes and the queues on which transactions wait for processing. Decisions and case statements are actions taken by the scheduler or dispatcher and do not necessarily correspond directly to instructions. In some systems, all queues may not go via a central dispatcher but may be linked directly from one process to the next. This is not necessarily bad, but it should be reckoned with. Coverage is essential and usually easy to achieve with functionally sensible paths. Loops are relatively rare, and when they do occur, there is usually some mechanism that limits the maximum number of iterations. However, poorly structured flows are relatively more common than they are in program flows.

4.3. Path Selection

Path selection for system-level functional testing based on transaction flows should have a distinctly different flavor than path selection done for unit-level tests based on flowcharts. Forbidden paths caused by correlated decisions were a bother at the unit-level and made path sensitizing difficult. Each

---

*I needed transaction flows to do a throughput model of a large system. It was another one of those bad projects on which I was consulted. Timing flows only represent high-probability paths, and the detailed order in which processing occurs within a link does not generally affect the timing analysis. I was having such poor luck getting the designers to create the transaction flows that in desperation, I sent them simplified versions suitable only to timing analysis and asked for a confirmation or a correction—hoping thereby to stir them into action. You guessed it—my model flows appeared in the next monthly design release as *the* design flows. Thankfully, my name wasn't on them.

forbidden path was suspected because a more structured approach might have eliminated the correlation that caused the path to be unachievable. In transaction-flow testing, in addition to coverage, you must look for achievable paths that should be forbidden. I wrote harsh words about unit-level programmers who jumped into the middle of code to save a few instructions. At the system level, however, we expect to merge transaction flows, use common parts, and do various things that we would condemn at the unit level. It is more justified at the system level, because the alternatives could mean large increases in program and data space, increased control complexity, a badly tuned system, and a host of other things. Consequently, it is not unusual to have paths deliberately blocked in order to use a common part for several different kinds of transactions. Furthermore, because the operation of the transaction flow is not localized to a single program but is distributed over several programs and results from their interaction, and because many more person-to-person interfaces are involved, it is more likely that essential interlocks that prevent various paths, will be missing, abused, or misunderstood. Finally, because some of the conditional branches in the transaction flows may be executed by humans whose actions are unpredictable, even though they are represented in the transaction flows, it may be impossible to guarantee decent structure for those flows.

Select a covering set of paths based on functionally sensible transactions as you would for ordinary flowcharts. Confirm these with the designers.* Now do exactly the opposite of what you would have done for unit-level tests. Try to find the most tortuous, longest, strangest path from the entry to the exit of the transaction flow. Create a catalog of these weird paths. Go over them not just with the high-level designer who laid out the transaction flows, but with the next-level designers who are implementing the modules that will process the transaction. It can be a gratifying experience, even in a well-designed and well-managed system. The act of discussing the weird paths will expose missing interlocks, duplicated interlocks, interface problems, programs working at cross purposes, duplicated processing—a whole lot of stuff that would otherwise have shown up only during the final acceptance tests, or worse, after the system was operating. The entire cost of independent testing can be paid for by a few such paths for a few well-chosen transactions. This is best done early in the game, while the system design is still in progress, before processing modules have been coded. I try to do it just after the internal design specifications for the processing modules are done and just before those modules are coded. Any earlier than that, you'll get a lot of "I don't

---

*In system-level functional testing it is more likely that the tester and designer are different persons—and far more effective if they are.

know yet" answers to your questions, which is a waste of both yours and the designer's time. Any later, it's already cast into code and correction has become expensive.

This process has diminishing returns. Most competent designers won't be caught twice. You have only to show them one nasty case and they'll review all their interfaces and interlocks and you're not likely to find any new bugs from that module—but you can catch most modules and their designers once. Eventually the blatant bugs have been removed, and those that remain are due to implementation errors and wild cards. Bringing up a weird path after a few rounds of this will just make the designer smirk as she shows you just how neatly your weird cases, and several more that you hadn't thought of, are handled.

The covering set of paths belong in the system functional tests. I still try to cover with weird paths in preference to normal paths, if I possibly can. It gives everybody more confidence in the system and its test. I also keep weird paths in proportion to what I perceive to be the designer's lack of confidence. I suppose it's sadistic hitting a person who's down, but it's effective. Conversely, you do get fooled by supremely confident idiots and insecure geniuses.

4.4. Hidden Languages

At the system level, you can't expect to find neat decision boxes and junctions as in a low-level flowchart. The actual decision may be made (usually is) in a process module, and the central dispatcher is usually indifferent to the transaction flows. Alternatively, the dispatcher may direct the flows based on control codes contained in the transaction's control block or stored elsewhere in the data base. Such codes actually constitute an internal language. If an explicit mechanism of this kind does exist, the transaction flows are indeed implemented as "programs" in this internal language. A commercial operating system's job control language or the set of task control codes combined with execution files are examples of such "languages."

The trouble is that these languages are often undeclared, undefined, undocumented, and unrecognized. Furthermore, unlike formal higher-order languages and their associated compilers or interpreters, neither the language's syntax, semantics, nor processor has been debugged. The flow-control language evolves as a series of *ad hoc* agreements between module designers. Here are some of the things that can go wrong:

1. The language is rarely checked for self-consistency (assuming that it's existence has been recognized).

2. The language must be processed, usually one step at a time, by an interpreter that may be centralized in a single routine but is more often distributed in bits and pieces among all the processing modules. That interpreter, centralized or distributed, may have bugs.

3. The "program," i.e., the steps stored in a transaction-control table, may have bugs or may become corrupted by bugs far removed from the transaction under consideration. This is a nasty kind of bug to find. Just as a routine may pass its tests but foul the data base for another routine, a transaction may pass all of its tests but, in so doing, foul the transaction-control tables for other transactions.*

4. Finally, any module that processes the transaction can have bugs.

If transaction-control tables are used to direct the flow, it is effective to treat that mechanism as if an actual language has been implemented. Look for the basic components of any language—processing steps, conditional-branch instructions, unconditional branches, program labels, possibly sub-routines (i.e., the tables can direct processing to subtables which can be used in common for several different flows), loop control, and so on. Assuming you can identify all of these elements, document a "syntax" for this primitive, undeclared language and discuss this syntax with whoever is responsible for implementing the transaction-control structure and software. The pseudo-language approach was used to provide flexibility in implementing many different, complicated, transaction flows. Therefore, it is reasonable to expect that any syntactically valid "statement" in this language should make processing sense. A syntactically valid, arbitary statement might not provide a useful transaction, but at the very least, the system should not blow up if such a transaction were defined. Test the syntax and generate test cases as you would for any syntax-directed test, as discussed in Chapter 7.

4.5. Instrumentation

Instrumentation plays a larger role in transaction-flow testing than in unit-level path testing. Counters are not useful because the same module could appear in many different flows and the system could be simultaneously processing different transactions. The information of the path taken for a given transaction must be kept with that transaction. This can be recorded either by the dispatcher or by the individual processing modules. What is needed is a trace of all the processing steps for the transaction, the queues on

---

*Strict separation of code and data, as in capabilities based machines such as the Plessy PP-250 which detect and enforce separation violations does not help because this is code masquerading as data.

which it resided, and the entries and exits to and from the dispatcher. In some systems, such traces are provided by the operating system. In other systems, such as communications systems or most secure systems, a running log that contains exactly this information is maintained as part of normal processing. You can afford heavy instrumentation compared to unit-level testing instrumentation, because the overhead of such instrumentation is typically small compared to the processing.

5. SUMMARY

1. The methods discussed for path-based structural testing of units and programs can be applied with suitable interpretation to functional testing based on transaction flows.
2. The biggest problem and the biggest payoff may be getting the transaction flows in the first place.
3. Full coverage is required for all flows, but most is gained from attempting strange, meaningless, weird paths.
4. Transaction-flow control may be implemented by means of an undeclared, unrecognized, internal language. Get it recognized, get it declared, and then test its syntax using the methods of Chapter 7.
5. The acts of attempting to design tests based on transaction-flow representation of functional requirements and discussing those attempts with the designer can unearth more bugs than any tests you run.

5

GRAPHS, PATHS AND COMPLEXITY

1. SYNOPSIS

Graphs are introduced as a simpler model of programs. The idea of a basic path set leads to McCabe's complexity metric, which is then used to judge how many path tests might be needed and how difficult it might be to design or test a piece of code.

2. GRAPHS

2.1. Notation

You might have noticed that the flowcharts got simpler as Chapter 3 progressed. The first flowchart, on page 44, was relatively complete. In Figure 3-4, I dropped the details of internal processing and replaced them with a simple box and a lowercase letter. The processing boxes were dropped in Figure 3-5. They were replaced with a single line, and it was understood that processing that was not germane to the control flow took place there. I snuck in a notational change in the flowchart of Figure 3-5c. In the final loop (node 7), the diamond serves both as a junction for two incoming flows, which are represented by the incoming arrows, and as a decision node, which is represented by the two outgoing arrows. The final transformation took place in Figure 3-9 where the diamonds were dropped and only circles (**nodes**) and arrows (**links**) remained. The point of this increasing simplification is that when looking at control-flow structure, or the structure of functional requirements as in Chapter 4, the details can be dropped and a clearer notation that makes the structure as obvious as possible can be used. That notation is **graph** notation, whose elements are:

nodes used for junctions, decisions, or combinations of both.

and **links** or **arcs** used to indicate that something of interest, such as a process, connects or relates two nodes.

Here is a two-way branch in this notation:

This is a case statement:

The point at which several flows merge looks like this:

Here are some loops:

(M = 2)   (M = 2)   (M = 4)

Even the circles are superfluous. We can leave them out, and do at times, to yield the following graphs equivalent to the above:

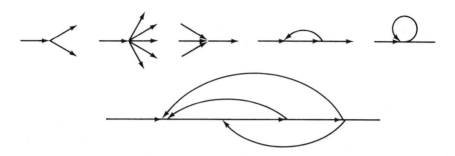

I don't remove the circles enthusiastically because they can be annotated with the actual program labels corresponding to that junction or decision. If you remove the circles and the labels that go with them, you may find it difficult to maintain correspondence between the graph and its program origin.

Subroutines are also represented by graphs. At the calling-program level, the subroutine is just another link. At its own structural level, it has its own graph. If it's important to see the interaction between the subroutine and its calling program, replace the link in the calling program by the graph of the subroutine—which is easy, if the subroutine has only one entry and one exit.

2.2. Names and Weights

Links and nodes need names. I use numerals to denote nodes and lowercase letters to name the links. This is convenient when working with the graphs, but it is a good idea to draw up a table of correspondences so that you know that "Node 3," say, corresponds to label "MXLDPRNT"; do the same for links. One more ingredient is needed to complete the notation—the **link weight**. Links are abstractions of something more complicated. That thing has properties. The property of interest of a graph is specified by the weights associated with the links. Here are some examples of what link weights can denote:

- The execution time for the link
- The probability that the link will be executed
- The number of memory references made in that link
- The number of instructions represented by the link

- The truth functional value (TRUE/FALSE) of a predicate that preceded the link—the A, $\overline{A}$ notation used earlier, for example
- The fact that the link or connection exists—1 if there is a link and 0 if there isn't
- Whether a resource was fetched or returned on that link
- The name of the subroutine called on that link
- The fact that the link has no interesting properties with respect to the question at hand

Links have as many properties and weights as there are sensible questions to ask about a routine. It is clearly not effective to list them all. Only one weight is usually used at a time—the weight best suited to express what it is the graph models. Graphs will be used in many different contexts in this book, not just as models of flowcharts and transaction flows. If the word "graph" is used in the sequel to refer to some property of graphs in general, you should understand that such properties apply to all graph representations and not just to the instance of a graph model, such as a flowchart, which is being discussed at the moment.

2.3. Path Bases (MCCA76, PAIG75A, PAIG77, PAIG78, SCHN79A, SCHN79B)

If a graph has k links, no path in that graph (including paths that do not necessarily start at entrances and end at exits) can be more than k links long without some link appearing at least twice. Consider all paths in a graph from any node to any other node. Such paths can be expressed as a succession of shorter paths or path segments. Suppose the links were named *a, b, c, d,* and *e.* Consider the set of all **path names** that can be constructed using these letters: *a, aa, ab, abc, aaaa, abcd, aebec, bcde,* and so on. Conceptually write this list down as a two-dimensional array—alphabetic in one direction and increasing length in the other. The first row is *a, b, c, d,* and *e.* The second row is *aa, ab, ac, ad, ae, ba,* and so on. The overwhelming majority of these path names do not correspond to paths of the graph—discard all such entries. It is clear that some paths, say *abcdabcd,* can be expressed in terms of shorter paths, in this case, *abcd.* What we are trying to do is to find a set of paths in terms of which it is possible to express all other paths. Such a set of paths is called a **base set** or **base.**

Because no path can be longer than k links without repeating some link, no path whose length is greater than k can be a member of a base-path set. Consequently, cut the table off for any entries longer than k. Start at the longest remaining entry and scan up the table. If you find a sequence of letters in a shorter entry that is part of the entry you are looking at, or if you can in any way express the longer entry as a concatenation of several shorter entries, the longer entry is obviously not a member of the base and should be struck out. Continuing in this way, we should achieve a base set, no? No! What will happen, if you think about it, is that we will be left with just *a, b, c, d* and *e*. Does this mean that our concept of base set is wrong or does it mean that there is no nontrivial base set?

2.4. Circuits

A **circuit** is any path in a graph (from any node to any other node) that starts and ends at the same node. While it is not possible to define a base set in terms of arbitrary path segments, it is possible to define a base in terms of circuits. However, one more concept is needed to do this. A graph is **strongly connected** (MAYE72) if there is a path between every two nodes (including the node and itself). It is obvious that most programs, for example, are *not* strongly connected because direct links between the exit and the entrance are usually forbidden. However, a program can be converted into a strongly connected graph by adding a fictitious link from the exit to the entry. If this is done, (and if every node were reachable from the entry, and if every node could reach the exit—both of which are essential in a bug-free routine) then, with the addition of this link, every node can be reached from every other node. A set of paths that can be used to define any path from any node to any node (perhaps by way of the fictitious exit-to-entry link that was added) is perforce capable of defining any path from the entry to the exit. Let's review the logic in this and then apply it in a few examples.

1. A set of paths from entry to exit, in terms of which any path in the graph can be expressed, is called a **base set** and should have interesting test-design implications.
2. Unfortunately, this simple notion breaks down and reduces to simple links. A more productive notion is to express the base set in terms of **circuits**—that is, paths from a node back to itself that include each link in it no more than once.
3. To do this, all nodes must be reachable from any other node. To assure this **strong connection** property, the graph must be augmented by a fictitious link from the exit to the entry, if one does not already exist.
4. A base set can now be defined in terms of circuits—that is, a set of circuits in terms of which it is possible to express any other circuit.
5. In particular, every path from entry to exit in the original graph is part of a circuit that might include the fictitious exit-to-entry link. Any set of

circuits that can express all other circuits perforce includes the set of all entry-to-exit paths.

The examples shown in Figure 5-1 show several important things:

1. The number of circuits in the base.
2. The value of the mysterious "M," first introduced in Chapter 3, which will be explained in the next section, and which is equal to the number of circuits in the base.
3. The circuits that make up the base (the "x" is put in parentheses to remind us that the x link is fictitious).
4. The number of paths and the paths required to cover the graph. This number is also equal to M.

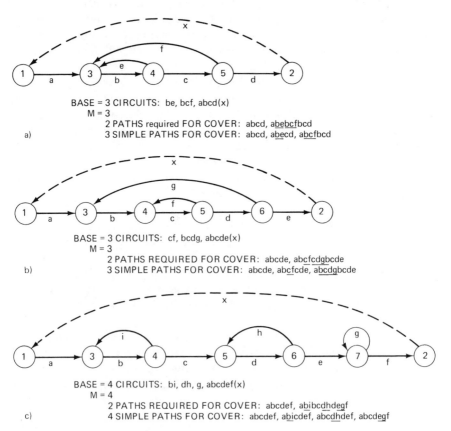

Figure 5-1. Paths and Bases.

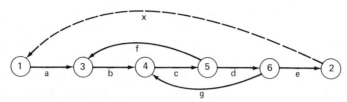

BASE = 3 CIRCUITS: bcf, cdg, abcde(x)
M = 3
1 PATH REQUIRED TO COVER: abcfbcdgcde
d)   3 SIMPLE PATHS FOR COVER: abcde, abcfcde, abcdgcde

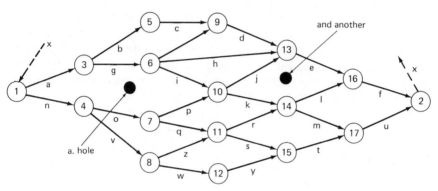

BASE = 11 CIRCUITS: abcdef(x), aghef(x), etc. mvwytu(x)
M = 11
e)   11 PATHS, SIMPLE OR COMPLEX FOR COVERAGE.

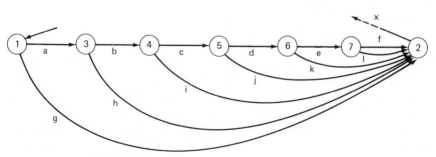

BASE = 7 CIRCUITS,
M = 7
f)   7 PATHS REQUIRED TO COVER

The actual circuits in a base are not very important to the design of tests, because in most cases the paths used for testing will be based on what makes sense, will be a simple as they can be, and, since they must start at an entry and end at the exit, may not correspond to the circuits of the base. Although it is possible to cover the graph in the first example of Figure 5-1 with only two paths, or Figure 5-1(d), with only one path, it is better to use short, functionally sensible paths rather than paths that achieve coverage in a minimum number of paths. Note however, that the number of simple paths— paths which we would have taken prior to knowing that there was such a thing as a base, is also equal to M (and will be, in most realistic cases). Example (e) has an important property—a graph can have more than one base. That is, there can be many different but equivalent ways of selecting circuits in terms of which all other circuits can be expressed. Note also that in examples (e) and (f) the number of circuits in the base, the number of paths required to cover, and the number of simple paths are all the same.

The question of bases and the minimum number of paths required to cover a graph, both with and without strong connectivity is theoretically important in the design of automated test tools that create covering path sets (NTAF78). However, the most important thing about bases in the pragmatic design of tests is that the number of circuits in a base should be used as a measure of software complexity and therefore of test and debug labor.

3. McCABE'S METRIC

3.1. What is a Metric?

A **metric** is any number used to measure an interesting property of something. There are as many different metrics as there are writers about metrics. In fact, Gilb (GILB77) has written a book on software metrics in which he lists more than fifty measures related to software quality, testing, reliability, maintainability, performance, and other subjects. As with all models of software, metrics examine one or a few aspects of a program and ignore everything else. Thus, stating that the mean processing time of a routine is 54.04 milliseconds says nothing about how the routine is structured, how difficult it might be to test, what it does, or how it works; it just says how long it takes to do whatever it is that it does. Similarly, a metric that measures the expected "time to the discovery of the next bug" tells us something about the expected reliability and little else. Metrics can be elaborated and combined with other metrics to yield ever more detailed numerical characterizations of programs that are ever more incomprehensible. An "everything" metric would tell us more about a routine than we wanted to know at any instant. A useful metric is simple and easy to evaluate, understand, and reconcile with intuition and measurements. McCabe's complexity metric is such a one, Halstead's (HALS75) metric, discussed in BEIZ83, is another.

3.2. Structural Complexity

McCabe's complexity metric (MCCA76) is closely related to the number of circuits required to cover a graph. It is defined as:

M	=	$L - N + 2P$ where:
L	=	the number of links in the graph
N	=	the number of nodes in the graph
P	=	the number of disconnected parts of the graph (e.g., a calling program and a subroutine)

The number M that appeared alongside the flowcharts in Chapter 3 was McCabe's metric for that flowchart. In all the examples, except for the one on page 45, there was only one connected part, and consequently, the value of P was 1. Figure 5-2 shows some more examples and their associated M values:

This metric has the intuitively satisfying property that the complexity of several graphs considered as a group is equal to the sum of the individual graphs' complexities. You can see this by analyzing Figure 5-3. Two disconnected graphs (say, flowcharts), having N1, L1 and N2, L2 nodes and links respectively, are combined and treated as a single entity with N1 + N2 nodes and L1 + L2 links. The arithmetic shows directly that the complexity of the sum is equal to the sum of the complexities.

This metric can also be calculated in two other ways. The value is also equal to the number of binary decisions in a program plus one. If all decisions are not binary, count a three-way decision as two binary decisions and N-way case statements as N-1 binary decisions. Similarly, the iteration test in a DO or other looping statement is counted as a binary decision. The rationale behind this counting of N-way decisions is that it would take a string of N-binary decisions to implement an N-way case statement.

The third way to evaluate M is to count "holes" (or connected regions for the topologically inclined). The example of Figure 5-1a has three "holes", if you include the fictitious link from the exit to the entry. Similarly for Example 5-1b. Example 5-1c has four holes. The real payoff for this method of evaluating M is in graphs such as Figure 5-1e. It's much easier to count eleven holes than the nodes and links.

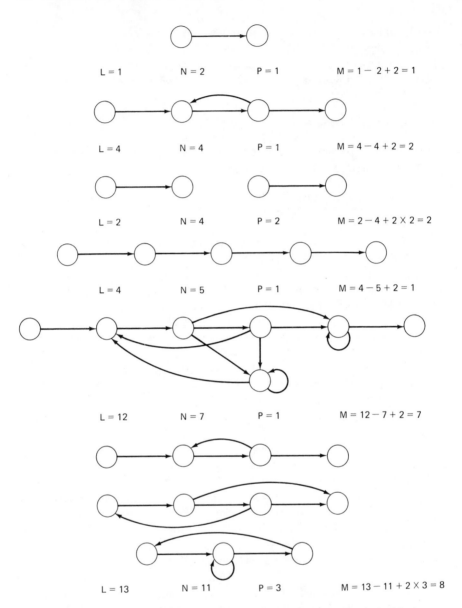

Figure 5-2. Examples of Graphs and Calculations of McCabe's Complexity Metric.

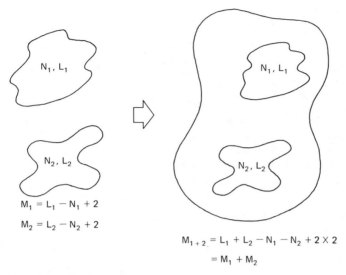

$$M_1 = L_1 - N_1 + 2$$

$$M_2 = L_2 - N_2 + 2$$

$$M_{1+2} = L_1 + L_2 - N_1 - N_2 + 2 \times 2$$

$$= M_1 + M_2$$

Figure 5-3. Complexity Sum and Sum of Complexities.

All three methods of figuring the complexity are useful. It's sometimes easier to count decision nodes, sometimes links and nodes, and sometimes holes. The intuitive relation between the three methods can be seen from the following flowchart:

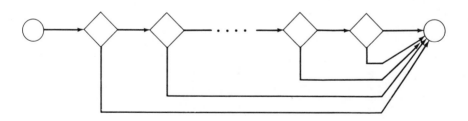

If the program had only one decision and a single entry and a single exit, it would have two links and two nodes and its complexity would be two. Looking at it another way, it has one binary decision and, consequently, its complexity is two. Each decision added increases the complexity by one, no matter which of the three alternate methods of looking at it you use: 1) one binary decision, 2) one additional node and two additional links, or 3) one hole.

3.3. Applications

3.3.1. Test Plan Completeness and Desk Checking

Evaluate the structural complexity of the program's design by the simplest means possible. As part of desk checking, reevaluate the complexity by counting decisions in the code. Any significant difference should be explained, because it's more likely that the difference is due to a missing path, an extra path, or an unplanned deviation from the design than to something else. Having verified the code's complexity, compare the number of test cases in the test plan to the code's complexity. In particular, count how many test cases are intended to provide coverage. If the number of covering test cases does not equal the structural complexity, there is reason for caution, because one of the following may be true:

1. You haven't calculated the complexity correctly. Did you miss a decision?
2. The cover is not really complete; there's a link that hasn't been covered.
3. The cover is complete, but it can be done with a few more but simpler paths.
4. It might be possible to simplify the routine.

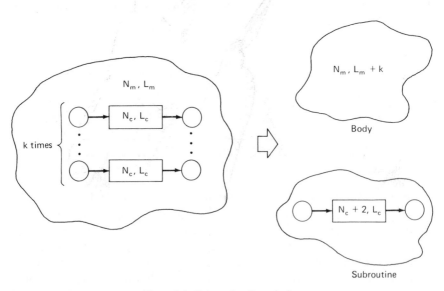

Figure 5-4. Subroutine Complexity.

3.3.2. When To Subroutine

McCabe's metric can be used to help decide if it pays to make a piece of code which is common to two or more links into a subroutine. Consider the graph of Figure 5-4.

The program has a common part that consists of N_c nodes and L_c links. This is the part being considered for conversion to a subroutine. This common part recurs k times in the body of the main program. The main program has N_m nodes and L_m links over and above the common part. The total number of links and nodes for the main program, therefore, is $L_m + kL_c$ and $N_m + kN_c$. When the common parts are removed, an additional link must be added to the main program to replace the code by a subroutine call. The subroutine's code must be augmented with an additional entry node and exit node. This table summarizes the transformation:

	EMBEDDED COMMON PART	SUBROUTINE FOR COMMON PART
Main nodes	$N_m + kN_c$	N_m
Main links	$L_m + kL_c$	$L_m + k$
Subnodes	0	$N_c + 2$
Sublinks	0	L_c
Main complexity	$L_m + kL_c - N_m + kN_c + 2$	$L_m + k - N_m + 2$
Subcomplexity	0	$L_c - N_c - 2 + 2 = L_c - N_c = M_c$
Total Complexity +2	$L_m + kL_c - N_m + kN_c + 2$	$L_m + L_c - N_m - N_c + k + 2$

The break-even point occurs when the total complexities are equal. A little algebra shows that this is independent of the main routine's complexity and is equal to: $M_c = k/(k - 1)$. For one call (k = 1), the total complexity must increase no matter how complex the subroutine itself is. For two calls, the crossover occurs at a complexity of 2 for the subroutine. For more calls, the crossover complexity decreases and is asymptotic to 1. In general, then, creating subroutines out of straight line code (complexity of 1) tends to increase net complexity rather than reduce it, if one takes into account the complexity of the calls and the fact that there are separate routines. Of course, you would not use this analysis as the sole criterion for deciding whether or not to make a subroutine out of common code.

One of the popular fads of the '70s was blind modularization. Rules such as "No subroutine shall contain more than 100 statements" were used in the hope of significantly reducing the frequency of bugs. Presumably, if all programmers followed such rules, the resulting programs would be simpler, easier to debug, more reliable, and so on. This rule was, unfortunately, put into a number of government specifications. The statistics (discussed below) show that McCabe's metric is a better measure of complexity than just the number of lines of code in a routine. It's intuitively better because it takes into account the increase in complexity due to subdividing a routine—something which a lines-of-code metric does not do. If anything, McCabe's metric underestimates the impact of subdividing code, because it says that the complexity of the whole is equal to the sum of the complexities of its parts—which is neat, but is likely to be an underestimate because complexity increases nonlinearly with more parts. The above analysis warns us that complexity can increase, rather than decrease, with modularization—as the following experience with my favorite bad project shows:*

The system was a multicomputer, distributed processing, distributed data base kind of thing—a tough proposition at best. Of all the silly rules that this benighted project adopted in the interest of improving programmer productivity and software reliability, the silliest was an absolute, nonappealable restriction of all modules to under fifty object-code instructions. Because the program was written in a higher-order language, and because the call/return sequence took up about half of the object code, what resulted were thousands of tiny subroutines and modules hardly more than ten source statements long. The typical number of calls per module was 1.1 (k = 1.1), which meant that the subroutines would have had to have a complexity of 10 or greater, if net complexity was to be reduced. However, the fifty-object-statement rule kept the average complexity down to about 1.01. This hypermodularity increased the predicted test and debug effort to several times that which had been estimated for unit design, test, and debugging. Because the hyperfine modularity and the other rules adopted were supposed to eliminate *all* bugs, the labor estimated for system integration and test was an order of magnitude less than it should have been. My estimates of the labor needed to integrate this vast horde of tiny, gnat-like subroutines was about thirty or forty times higher than the project's management expected. My predictions were not politely received, to say the least, and my association with the project ended soon after. They eventually dropped that rule (so I heard) very quietly when they redesigned the entire system for the version that did (eventually, and after a fashion) work.

I do not advocate great complicated unwashed masses of overly verbose code that ramble on and on and on and on and on, page after page after page,

---

*It was really a bad project, but it had its good sides—I will never again witness so many bad design practices and such lack of testing discipline (which supplied ample material for this book) under one roof. It was a real project, and it was rotten from keelson to hounds. Obviously, I can't identify it without risking a libel suit. As for discussing bad projects and what appears to be an uncommon frequency of them in my experience—it's not that I've had bad luck, but that consultants aren't usually called in for good projects. As for discussing bad projects at all—there's more to be learned from our mistakes than from our triumphs.

beyond the scope of human minds and ken. Programs like that are also untestable. But consider this when setting modularity rules: in addition to the net increase in complexity due to breaking a function up, there is a further increase due to additional code in a calling sequence, and possibly additional declarations. All of these add to the incidence of bugs and to the testing labor. Furthermore, each subdivision creates a new interface between the calling routine and called routine, and all interfaces breed bugs. Partition cannot be dictated by an arbitrary rule but must result from a trade analysis whose resulting optimum value is unlikely to exist at either extreme of the range.

3.3.3. A Refinement

Myers (MYER77) points out a weakness of McCabe's metric and suggests the use of a refinement thereto. A decision statement in languages such as FORTRAN can contain a compound predicate of the form: IF A & B & C THEN . . . A statement such as this could be implemented as a string of IF's, resulting in a different complexity measure. Figure 5-5 shows three alternate,

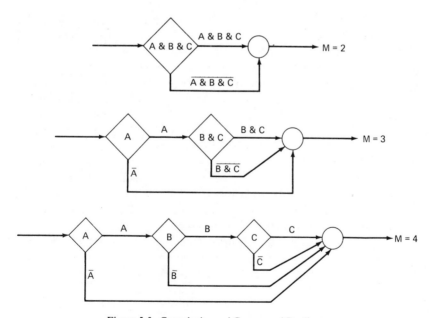

Figure 5-5. Complexity and Compound Predicates.

equivalent, representations of the same IF-THEN-ELSE statement. If the compound predicate is used in a single statement as in the first case, the complexity of the construct is only two, but if it is broken down into its constituent parts, the complexity increases to four. However, intuitively, all three constructs should have the same complexity. The refinement consists of accounting for each term of the predicate expression separately. For a predicate expression of the form A&B&C . . ., each predicate should be counted as if it were a decision. In more complicated expressions, such as "A&B&C OR D&E . . . ", again count each predicate. If a predicate appears more than once in an expression, you can take a pessimistic point of view and count each appearance or a slightly optimistic point of view and count only the first appearance.

3.3.4. How Good a Measure

Statistics on how well McCabe's metric correlates with design, test, and debugging difficulty are scarce, but the few reports we have are encouraging (BELF79, CHEN78A, CURT79A, ENDR75, FEUE79A, FEUE79B, SCHN79A, SCHN79B, SCHN79D, SHEP79C, THAY77, WALS79, ZOLN77).* The reported results confirm the utility of McCabe's metric as a convenient rule of thumb that is significantly superior to a raw instruction or statement count.

McCabe advises partitioning routines whose metric exceeds 10. Walsh confirms this advice (WALS79) by citing a military software project to which the metric was applied. They found that 23% of the routines with a metric value greater than 10 accounted for 53% of the bugs. Walsh further states, that in the same study of 276 procedures, the routines with M greater than 10 had 21% more errors per line of code than those with metric values below 10. Feuer (FEUE79A, FEUE79B) cites mixed results but provides strong correlation between the metric (actually, decision counts) and error rates for large programs. Curtis (CURT79A) also shows fair predictability.

It is too early to tell if this metric will eventually serve as a true bug predictor. It's not likely. There are other metrics, such as Halstead's (see BEIZ83), which, while harder to evaluate and apply, have been shown to be excellent aids to the prediction of test effort and bugs. The main appeal of M is its simplicity. People have long used program length as the main criterion for judging software complexity. Simple measures are inherently inaccurate, but they can provide useful rules of thumb. McCabe's metric should be used in combination with length to get a quick measure of complexity.

---

*Not all of these references provide direct information for McCabe's metric. Some provide correlations to decision counts and similar metrics that can be converted to McCabe's metric. For example, THAY77 and ENDR75.

Manzo (MANZ80) reports an innovative use of McCabe's metric. He uses it as a partial measure of programmer productivity. Recognizing that the higher the value of M, the more difficult the program is per line of code, he allocates additional time for design, coding, and testing of such routines. He also uses it as a warning device. Routines whose M is greater than 10 are given close scrutiny in recognition of the demonstrated nonlinearity in bug incidence above 10. However, there is no imposition of an arbitrary rule such as, "No program shall have a complexity greater than 10," because such a rule would be as ineffectual as arbitrary length limitations. For one thing, it would discourage the use of case statements or make them impossible in many situations. It would also force complicated but organized logic to be arbitrarily subdivided.

McCabe's metric has some additional weaknesses. It makes no real distinction as to the direction of flow. For example, an IF-THEN-ELSE statement has the same complexity as a single loop. This is not intuitively satisfying because we know that loops are more troublesome than simple decision sequences. Case statements, which provide a nice, regular structure, are given a high complexity value which is also counterintuitive. It also tends to judge highly regular, repetitive control structures unfairly. Conversely, if these weaknesses were to be rectified, it could only be done by increasing the complexity of the metric itself and taking it out of the realm of an easy-to-use measure of complexity.

4. SUMMARY

McCabe's structural complexity metric provides some useful rules of thumb:

1. Bugs per line of code increase discontinuously for M greater than 10.
2. Arbitrary modularity rules based on length, when applied to straight-line code that has few calls or only one call, increase rather than reduce complexity
3. The amount of design, code, test design, and test effort is better judged by structural complexity than by code length. A combination, in which logic and control are judged by McCabe's metric and processing by length, is useful.
4. Routines with high complexity, say 40 or more, should be given close scrutiny, especially if that complexity is not due to the use of case statements or other very regular control structures. If the complexity is due to loops and raw logic, consideration should be given to subdividing the routine into smaller, less complex segments, in order to avoid the nonlinear increase in effort associated with high complexity.

5. The complexity measure establishes a reasonable lower bound on the number of cases required to achieve cover—especially when based on simple predicate counts rather than raw decision counts (i.e., use the number of simple predicates plus 1). If fewer test cases than M are proposed, look for missing cases or the possibility of simplifying the logic or using tests that are less complicated.

Additional references and contributions related to structural complexity, McCabe's metric, bases, and related subjects can be found in BAKE79A, BAKE80, PAIG75A, PAIG77, PAIG78, SCHN79B and WOOD78.

6

PATHS, PATH PRODUCTS, AND REGULAR EXPRESSIONS

1. SYNOPSIS

Path expressions are introduced as algebraic representations of sets of paths in a graph. With suitable arithmetic laws (BRZO62, BRZO63, MCNA60) and weights, path expressions are converted into algebraic functions or **regular expressions** that can be used to examine structural properties of graphs or flowcharts, such as the number of paths, processing time, or whether a specified data access sequence can occur. These expressions are then applied to problems in test design and debugging.

2. PATH PRODUCTS AND PATH EXPRESSIONS

2.1. Basic Concepts

Every link of a graph can be given a name; this will be denoted by italics lowercase letters. In tracing a path or path segment through a flowchart or graph, you traverse a succession of link names. The name of the path or the path segment that corresponds to those links is expressed naturally by concatenating those link names. Thus if you traversed links *a, b, c,* and *d* along some path, the corresponding name for that path or path segment would be *abcd.* Alternatively, this path name is also called a **path product**. Figure 6-1 shows some examples.

Consider a pair of nodes in a graph and the set of paths between those nodes. That set of paths can be denoted by uppercase letters such as X or Y. The members of that set can be listed as follows for Figure 6-1c:

ac, abc, abbc, abbbc, and so on.

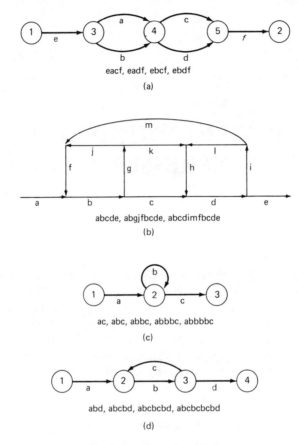

Figure 6-1. Examples of Paths.

Alternatively, that same set of paths can be denoted by:

$$ac + abc + abbc + abbbc + \text{and so on.}$$

The "+" sign is understood to mean "or." That is, between the two nodes of interest, paths *ac*, or *abc*, or *abbc*, and so on can be taken. Any expression that consists of path names and "ORs" and which denotes a set of paths (not necessarily the set of all paths) between two nodes is called a **path expression**.

2.2. Path Products

The name of a path that consists of two successive path segments is conveniently and naturally expressed by the concatenation or **path product** of the segment names. For example, if X and Y are defined as:

$$X = abcde$$
$$Y = fghij$$

then the path corresponding to X followed by Y is denoted by:

$$XY = abcdefghij$$

Similarly:

$$YX = fghijabcde$$
$$aX = aabcde$$
$$Xa = abcdea$$
$$XaX = abcdeaabcde$$

Furthermore, if X and Y represent sets of paths or path expressions, their product represents the set of paths that can be obtained by following every element of X by any element of Y in all possible ways. For example:

$$X = abc + def + ghi$$
$$Y = uvw + z$$

Then: $\quad XY = abcuvw + defuvw + ghiuvw + abcz + defz + ghiz$

If a link or segment name is repeated, that fact is denoted by using an exponent. The exponent's value denotes the number of repetitions:

$$a^1 = a;\ a^2 = aa;\ a^3 = aaa;\ a^n = aaaa \ldots \text{n times.}$$

Similarly if:

$$X = abcde$$

then:

$$
\begin{aligned}
X^1 &= abcde \\
X^2 &= abcdeabcde &&= (abcde)^2 \\
X^3 &= abcdeabcdeabcde &&= (abcde)^2 abcde \\
&= abcde(abcde)^2 &&= (abcde)^3
\end{aligned}
$$

In general, the path product is not commutative, although expressions derived from it may be commutative. That is, in general $XY \neq YX$. The path product is associative, but expressions derived from it may not be. That is:

R1)   A(BC) = (AB)C = ABC

where A, B, and C are path names, sets of path names, or, path expressions.
    The zeroth power of a link name, path product, or path expression is also
needed for completeness. It is denoted by the Greek letter lambda (λ) and
denotes the fact that there is no path.

$$a^0 = \lambda$$
$$X^0 = \lambda$$

2.3. Path Sums

The "+" sign was used to denote the fact that path names were part of the
same set of paths. In particular, consider the set of paths that can lie between
two arbitrary nodes of a graph. Even though these paths can traverse
intermediate nodes, they can be considered as "parallel" paths between the
two nodes. The **path sum** denotes paths in parallel between two nodes. Links
a and b in Figure 6-1a are parallel paths and are denoted by $a + b$. Similarly,
links c and d are parallel paths between the next two nodes and are denoted
by $c + d$. The set of all paths between nodes 1 and 2 of Figure 6-1a can be
considered as a set of parallel paths between nodes 1 and 2 and can be
denoted by $eacf + eadf + ebcf + ebdf$. If X and Y are sets of paths that lie
between the same pair of nodes, then X + Y denotes the result of combining
those sets of paths. Consider the following example:

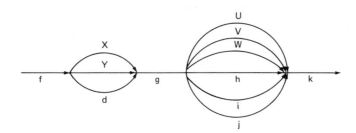

    The first set of parallel paths is denoted by X + Y + d and the second set
by U + V + W + h + i + j. The set of all paths in this flowchart or graph is
naturally expressed by:

$$f(X + Y + d)g(U + V + W + h + i + j)k$$

Keep in mind in the above example that the uppercase letters can represent individual segment names (*pqrst*, say) or sets of segment names, such as *pqrst + pqrsst + pqrssst, +. . . .* Because the path sum is just a set union operation, it is clear that it is commutative and associative:

R4) $X + Y = Y + X$

R3) $(X + Y) + Z = X + (Y + Z) = X + Y + Z$

2.4 Distributive Law

The product and sum operations are distributive, and the ordinary rules of multiplication apply. That is:

R4) $A(B + C) = AB + AC$ and $(B + C)D = BC + BD$

Applying these rules to Figure 6-1a yields:

$$e(a + b)(c + d)f \qquad = e(ac + ad + bc + bd)f$$
$$= eacf + eadf + ebcf + ebdf$$

for the set of all paths from node 1 to node 2 in that graph.

2.5. Absorption Rule

If X and Y denote the same set of paths, then the union of these sets is unchanged, consequently:

R5) $X + X = X$ (absorption rule)

Similarly, if a set consists of path names and a member of that set is added to it, the "new" name, which is already in that set of names, contributes nothing and can be ignored. For example, if:

$$X = a + aa + abc + abcd + def$$

then evidently:

$$X + a = X + aa = X + abc = X + abcd = X + def = X$$

It follows that any arbitrary sum of identical path expressions reduces to the same path expression.

2.6. Loops

Loops can be understood as an infinite set of parallel paths. Say that the loop consists of a single link b. Then the set of all paths through that loop point would be:

$$b^0 + b^1 + b^2 + b^3 + b^4 + b^5 \ldots$$

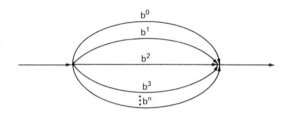

This potentially infinite sum is denoted by b^* for an individual link and by X^* when X is a path expression. If the loop must be taken at least once, then it is denoted by a^+ or X^+. The path expressions for Figure 6-1c and 6-1d respectively, as expressed by this notation, are:

$$ab^*c = ac + abc + abbc + abbbc + \ldots$$

and

$$a(bc)^*bd = abd + abcbd + abcbcbd + a(bc)^3bd + \ldots$$

Evidently:

$$aa^* = a^*a = a^+$$

and

$$XX^* = X^*X = X^+$$

It is sometimes convenient to denote the fact that a loop cannot be taken more than a certain, say n, number of times. A bar is used under the exponent to denote that fact as follows:

$$X^{\underline{n}} = X^0 + X + X^2 + X^3 + \ldots X^{n-1} + X^n$$

The following rules can be easily derived from the previous rules:

R6) $X^n + X^m$ $= X^n$ if n is bigger than m
                    $= X^m$ if m is bigger than n
R7) $X^n X^m$ $= X^{n+m}$
R8) $X^n X^*$ $= X^* X^n$ $= X^*$
R9) $X^n X^+$ $= X^+ X^n$ $= X^+$
R10) $X^* X^+$ $= X^+ X^*$ $= X^+$

2.7. Null Sets and NonPaths

Returning to the meaning of terms such as a^0 or X^0, which indicate no paths, the following rules, previously used without explanation, apply:

R11) $\lambda + \lambda = \lambda$
R12) $\lambda X + X\lambda = \lambda$ Following or preceding a set of paths by a nonpath nullifies all paths in that set.
R13) $\lambda^n = \lambda^n = \lambda^* = \lambda^+ = \lambda$ No matter how often you take a nonpath, it's still a nonpath.
R14) $\lambda^+ + \lambda = \lambda^*$

The final notation needed is the empty set or the set that contains no paths, not even the nonpath λ. The null set of paths is denoted by the Greek letter phi (Φ). The following rules apply:

R15) $X + \Phi = \Phi + X = X$
R16) $X\Phi = \Phi X = \Phi$ If you block the paths of a graph fore or aft by a graph that has no paths, there won't be any paths.
R17) $\Phi^* = \lambda + \Phi + \Phi^2 \ldots = \lambda$

3. A REDUCTION PROCEDURE

3.1. Overview

This section presents a reduction procedure for converting a graph, such as a flowchart, whose links are labeled with names into a path expression that denotes the set of all paths in that flowchart or graph. The procedure is a node-by-node removal algorithm. You follow these steps, which initialize the process:

1. Combine all serial links by multiplying their path expressions.
2. Combine all parallel links by adding their path expressions.

3. Remove all self loops (from any node to itself) by replacing them with a link of the form X*, where X is the path expression of the link in that loop.

The remaining steps are in the algorithm's loop:

4. Select any node for removal other than the initial or final node. Replace it with a set of equivalent links whose path expressions correspond to all the ways you can form a product of the set of incoming links with the set of outgoing links.
5. Combine any remaining serial links by multiplying their path expressions.
6. Combine all parallel links by adding their path expressions.
7. Remove all self-loops as in Step 3.
8. Does the graph consist of a single link between the entry node and the exit node? If yes, then the path expression for that link is a path expression for the original graph; otherwise, return to Step 4.

Each step will be illustrated and explained in further detail in the next sections. Note the use of the phrase "a path expression," rather than "the path expression." A flowchart or graph can have many equivalent path expressions between a given pair of nodes. That is, there are many different ways to generate the set of all paths between two nodes without affecting the content of that set. The appearance of the path expression depends, in general, on the order in which nodes are removed.

3.2. Cross-Term Step (Step 4)

The cross-term step is the fundamental step of the reduction algorithm. It removes a node, thereby reducing the number of nodes by one. Successive applications of this step is what eventually gets you down to one entry and one exit node. The following diagram shows the situation at an arbitrary node that has been selected for removal:

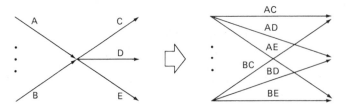

The rationale for this step is intuitively obvious. Whatever the set of paths represented by A and C say, there can be no other paths for the combination other than those represented by AC. Similarly, the removal of the node results in the AD, AE, BC, BD, and BE path expressions or path sets. If the path expressions are path names, it is clear that the resulting path names will be the names obtained by traversing the pair of links. If the path expressions denote sets of paths or path sums, using the definition of multiplication and the distributive rule produces every combination of incoming and outgoing path segments, as in:

$$(a + b)(c + d) = ac + ad + bc + bd$$

Applying this step to the graph of Figure 6-1b, we remove several nodes in order:

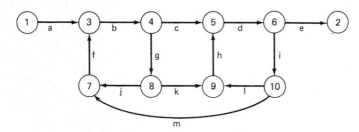

Remove node 10 by applying Step 4 and combine by Step 5 to yield:

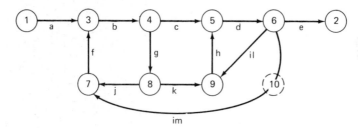

Remove node 9 by applying Steps 4 and 5 to yield:

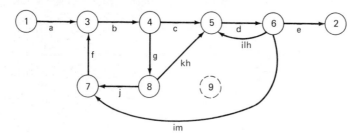

Remove node 7 by Steps 4 and 5:

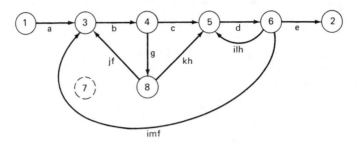

Remove node 8 by Steps 4 and 5:

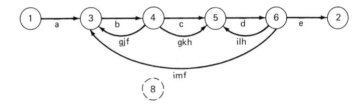

3.3. Parallel Term (Step 6)

Removal of node 8 in the previous step led to a pair of parallel links between nodes 4 and 5. Combine them to create a path expression for an equivalent link, $c + gkh$.

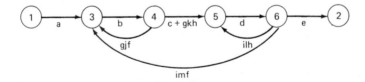

3.4. Loop Term (Step 7)

Removing node 4 leads to a loop term. The graph has now been replaced with the following equivalent, simpler graph:

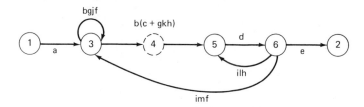

There are two ways of looking at the loop-removal operation:

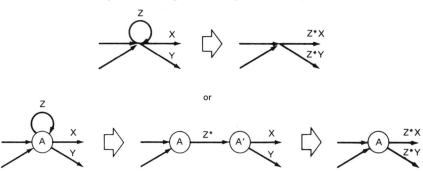

In the first way, we remove the self-loop and then multiply all outgoing links by Z*. The second way shows things in more detail. We split the node into two equivalent nodes, call them A and A′ and put in a link between them, whose path expression is Z*. Then we remove node A′ using the steps 4 and 5 rule for node removal to yield outgoing links whose path expressions are Z*X and Z*Y.

Continue the process by applying the loop removal step:

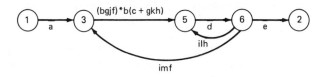

Removing node 5 produces:

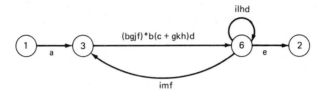

Remove the loop at node 6:

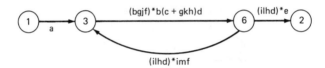

Remove node 3:

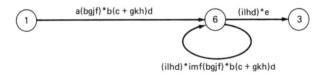

Removing the loop and then node 6 results in the following ugly expression:

$$a(bgjf)^*b(c + gkh)d((ilhd)^*imf(bgjf)^*b(c + gkh)d)^*(ilhd)^*e$$

We shouldn't blame the expression for being ugly because it was, after all, derived from an ugly, unstructured monster of a graph. With structured code, the path expressions are tamer. Figure 6-2 shows a few examples:

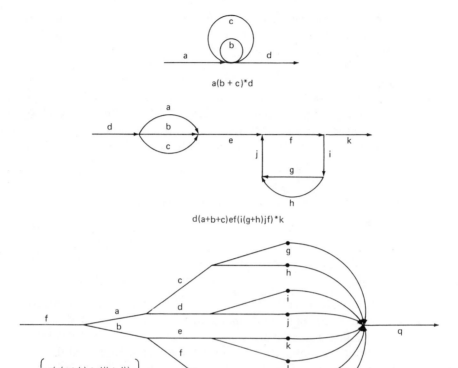

Figure 6-2. Some graphs and Their Path Expressions.

3.5. Comments, Identities, and Node-Removal Order

I said earlier that the order in which the operations are done affects the appearance of the path expressions. Such appearances of differences also result in identities that can sometimes be used to simplify path expressions.

I1)	$(A + B)^*$	=	$(A^* + B^*)^*$
I2)		=	$(A^*B^*)^*$
I3)		=	$(A^*B)^*A^*$
I4)		=	$(B^*A)^*B^*$
I5)		=	$(A^*B + A)^*$
I6)		=	$(B^*A + B)^*$
I7)	$(A + B + C \ldots)^*$	=	$(A^* + B^* + C^* + \ldots)^*$
I8)		=	$(A^*B^*C^* \ldots)^*$

These can be derived by considering different orders of node removals and then applying the series-parallel-loop rules. Each change in order can produce a different appearance for the path expression and therefore, a path expression identity. Don't make the mistake of applying these identities to finite exponents or +. These identities hold only because they denote infinite sets of paths. These identities are not very important anyhow, because we will rarely deal with path expressions as such but rather with other kinds of expressions that are derived from the path expressions by using link weights and link arithmetics. As an example of misapplying the identities, consider:

$$(A + B)^2 \neq (A^2 + B^2)^2 \neq (A^2B^2)^2$$

If A consists of the single link a and B is link b, the three expressions correspond to the following sets of paths:

$$
\begin{aligned}
(A + B)^2 &= aa + ab + bb + ba \\
(A^2 + B^2)^2 &= (a^4 + a^2b^2 + b^2a^2 + b^4) \\
(A^2B^2)^2 &= a^2b^2a^2b^2 = (a^2b^2)^2
\end{aligned}
$$

Keep in mind that this algorithm can be used to find a path expression between any two nodes in a graph, including a node and itself, and it is not restricted to finding a path expression between the entry and the exit of a flowchart, although this might be the most common and most useful application. The method is tedious and cumbersome, what with having to constantly redraw all the graphs. However, in Chapter 12, a more powerful version of the same algorithm which can find a path expression between every pair of nodes with less work than this graphical method requires is presented.

4. APPLICATIONS

4.1. General

The previous sections of this chapter are more abstract than I and most readers are apt to like. They are, I admit, remote from the substantive problems of testing and test design. The purpose of all that abstraction, however, was to present one very generalized concept—the path expression, and one very generalized way of getting it, the node-removal algorithm, so that the same concepts would not have to be discussed over and over again as one variation on a theme after another. Every application follows this common pattern:

1. Convert the program or graph into a path expression.
2. Identify a property of interest and derive an appropriate set of "arithmetic" rules that characterizes the property.

3. Replace the link names by the **link weights** (remember them?) for the property of interest. The path expression has now been converted to an expression in some algebra, such as ordinary algebra, regular expression theory, or boolean algebra. This algebraic expression summarizes the property of interest over the set of all paths.
4. Simplify or evaluate the resulting "algebraic" expression to answer the question you asked.

If it seems that the above algorithm requires you to invent a new form of arithmetic for each application, that's true, but it's far less formidable than it seems. In practice you don't do it as outlined above. You substitute the weights (the properties associated with the links) first and simplify as you develop the path expression, using the right kind of arithmetic as you remove the nodes. This is apt to be hazy in the abstract, so let's get to the first application.

4.2. How Many Paths in a Program?

4.2.1. The Question

The question is not simple. Here are a few different ways you could ask it:

1. What is the maximum number of different paths possible?
2. What is the fewest number of paths possible?
3. How many different paths are there really?
4. What is the average number of paths?

In all that follows, by "path" I mean paths from the entrance to the exit of a single-entry, single-exit routine.* The first question has a straightforward answer and constitutes the first application. The second question concerns the fewest number of paths and is inherently difficult. No satisfactory algorithm exists; however, I'll present a reasonable approximate solution for nicely structured flowcharts. If we know both of these numbers (maximum and minimum number of possible paths) we have a good idea of how complete our testing is. Suppose that the minimum number of possible paths is 15 and the maximum is 144 and that we had planned only 12 test cases. The discrepancy should warn us to look for incomplete coverage. Consider two routines with comparable structure and comparable testing requirements—one with a maximum path count of 1000 and the other with a maximum path count of 100. In both cases, say that coverage was achievable with 10 paths.

---

*Not a fundamental requirement. See Chapter 12 for paths from any node to any other node, including multientry and multiexit routines.

We should have more confidence in the routine with a lower maximum path count, because the 10 paths explore more of the possibilities for the 100-path routine than for the 1000-path routine.

Determining the actual number of different paths is an inherently difficult problem because there are unachievable paths due to correlated and dependent predicates. If all the predicates are uncorrelated and independent, not only does the flowchart have no loops, but the actual, minimum, and maximum numbers of paths are the same.

The "average" number of paths is a meaningless number. There is only one path through each time the routine is used, although it could be a different path each time. The questions one should ask are questions such as, "What is the length of the average path?," "What is the mean processing time considering all paths?," and "What is the most likely path?" These questions all involve a notion of probability. A model for that is also provided as an application in the next section. It should not require deep analysis to find the "typical" or normal path. It should be obvious: the one that runs straight through the program. That should be tested, of course, and tested first, even though it will probably be the least revealing path of all.

4.2.2. Maximum-Path Arithmetic

Label each link with a link weight that corresponds to the number of paths that that link represents. Typically, that's one. However, if the link represented a subroutine call, say, and you wanted to consider the paths through the subroutine in the path count, then you would put that number on the link. Also mark each loop with the maximum number of times that the loop can be taken. If the answer is infinite, you might as well stop the analysis because it's clear that the maximum number of paths will be infinite. There are three cases of interest: parallel links, serial links, and loops. In what follows, A and B are path expressions and W_A and W_B are algebraic expressions in the weights.

CASE	PATH EXPRESSION	WEIGHT EXPRESSION
PARALLELS*	A + B	$W_A + W_B$
SERIES	AB	$W_A W_B$
LOOP	$A^n = A^*$	$\displaystyle\sum_{j=0}^{n} W_A^{\,j}$

---

*Adjustments may be needed to avoid overcounting if both sets contain λ. i.e., if λεX and λεY with W_x and W_y respectively, then $W_{x+y} = W_x + W_y - 1$. Otherwise the null path would be counted twice.

The arithmetic is ordinary algebra. This is not a true upper bound for the number of paths, but a larger number because the model does not include paths that might be forbidden due to correlated and dependent predicates. The rationale behind the parallel rule is simple. The path expressions denote the paths in a set of paths corresponding to that expression. The weight is the number of paths in each set. Assuming that the path expressions were derived in the usual way, they would have no paths in common and consequently, the sum of the paths for the union of the sets would be the sum of the number of paths in each set. The serial rule is explained by noting that each term of the path expression (say the first one A) will be combined with each term of the second expression B, in all possible ways. If there are W_A paths in A and W_B paths in B, then there must be $W_A W_B$ paths in the combination. The loop rule follows from the combination of the serial and parallel rules, taking into account going through zero, once, twice, and so on. If you know for a fact that the minimum number of times through the loop is not zero but some other number, say j, then you would do the summation from j to n rather than from 0 to n.

4.2.3. A Concrete Example

Here is a reasonably well-structured program. Its path expression, with a little work, is shown below:

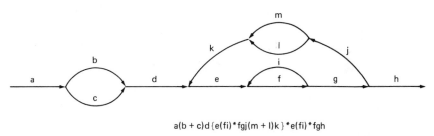

a(b + c)d{e(fi)*fgj(m + l)k}*e(fi)*fgh

Each link represents a single link and consequently is given a weight of "1" to start. Let's say that the outer loop will be taken exactly four times and the inner loop can be taken zero to three times. The steps in the reduction are:

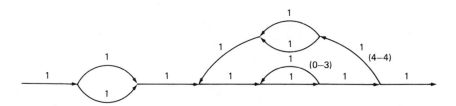

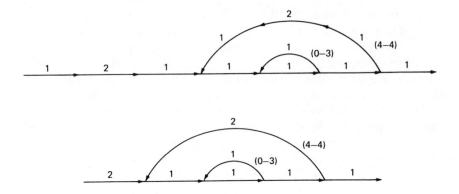

For the inner loop,

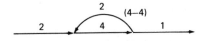

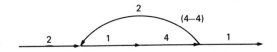

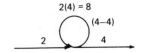

Alternatively, you could have substituted a "1" for each link in the path expression and then simplified, as follows:

$$1\,(1+1)\,1\,(1\,(1\,(1\times1)^{\underline{3}}\,1\times1\times1\,(1+1)\,1)^4\,1\,(1\times1)^{\underline{3}}\,1\times1\times1$$

$$\begin{aligned}
&= 2\,(1^{\underline{3}}1\times(2))^4\,1^{\underline{3}}\\
\text{but } 1^{\underline{3}} \quad &= 1+1^1+1^2+1^3 \quad = 4\\
&= 2\,(4\times2)^4\times4 \quad = 2\times8^4\times4\\
&= 32{,}768
\end{aligned}$$

This is the same result we got graphically. Reviewing the steps in the reduction, we:

1. Annotated the flowchart by replacing each link name with the maximum number of paths through that link (l) and also noted the number of possibilities for looping. The inner loop was indicated by the range (0-3) as specified, and the outer loop by the range (4-4).
2. Combined the first pair of parallels outside of the loop and also the pair corresponding to the IF-THEN-ELSE construct in the outer loop. Both yielded two possibilities.
3. Multiplied things out and removed nodes to clear the clutter.
4. Took care of the inner loop: there were four possibilities, leading to the four value. Then we multiplied by the link weight following (originally link *g*) whose weight was also 1.
5. Got rid of link *e*.
6. Used the cross-term to create the self-loop with a weight of $8 = 2 \times 4$ and passed the other 4 through.

We have here a test designer's bug. I've contradicted myself. I said that the outer loop would be taken exactly four times. That doesn't mean it will be taken *zero* or four times. Consequently, there is a superfluous "4" on the output leg in Step 6. Therefore the maximum number of different paths is 8,192 rather than 32,768.

4.3. Approximate Minimum Number of Paths

4.3.1. Structured Code

The node-by-node reduction procedure can also be used as a test for structured code. Structured code can be defined in several different ways that do not involve ad hoc rules such as not using GOTOs. A graph-based definition by Hecht (HECH77B) is:

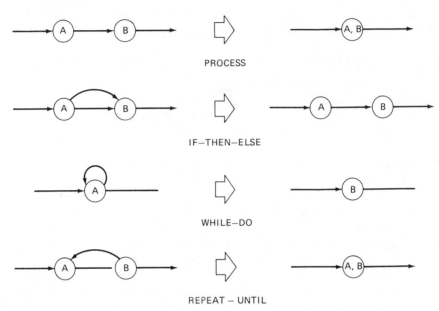

Figure 6-3. Structured Flowchart Transformations.

Definition: A structured flowchart is one that can be reduced to a single link by successive application of the transformations of Figure 6-3.

Note that the cross-term transformation is missing. An alternate characterization by McCabe (MCCA76) states that:

Definition: Flowcharts that do not contain one or more of the graphs shown in Figure 6-4 as subgraphs are structured.

4.3.2. Lower Path-Count Arithmetic

A lower bound on the number of paths in a routine can be approximated for structured flowcharts. It is not a true lower bound because again, forbidden paths could reduce the actual number of paths to a lower number yet. The appropriate arithmetic is:

CASE	PATH EXPRESSION	WEIGHT EXPRESSION
PARALLEL	$A + B$	$W_A + W_B$
SERIES	AB	$MAX (W_A , W_B)$
LOOP	$A^{\underline{n}}$	$1, W_1$

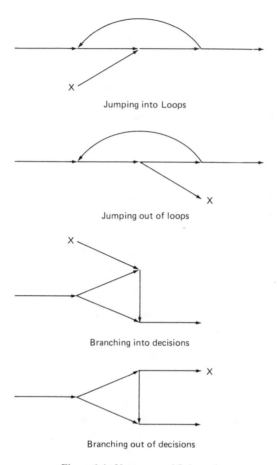

Figure 6-4. Unstructured Subgraphs.

The parallel case is the same as before. The values of the weights are the number of members in a set of paths. There could be an error here because both sets could contain the null path, but because of the way the loop expression is defined, this cannot happen. The series case is explained by noting that each term in the first set will combine with at least one term in the second set. The minimum number of combinations must be the greater of the number of possibilities in the first set and the second set. The loop case requires that you use the minimum number of loops—possibly zero. Loops are always problematic. If the loop can be bypassed, then you can ignore the term in the loop. I don't think that this is a meaningful lower bound, because what was the loop there for in the first place? By using a value of 1, we are asserting that we'll count the number of paths under the assumption that the loop will be taken once. Because in creating the self-loop, we used the cross-term expression, there will be a contribution to the links following the loop, which will take things into account.

Alternatively, you could get a higher lower bound by arguing that if the loop were to be taken once, then the path count should be multiplied by the loop weight. This however, would be equivalent to saying that the loop was assumed to be taken both zero and once, because again, the cross-term that created the self-loop was multiplied by the series term. Generally, if you ask for a minimum number of paths, it's more likely that the minimum is to be taken under the assumption that the routine will loop once—because this is consistent with coverage.

Applying this arithmetic to the earlier example gives us the identical steps until Step 3, where we pick it up:

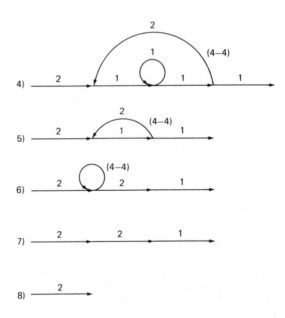

If you go back to the original graph on page 123 you'll see that it takes a minimum of two paths to cover, and it can be done in two paths. The reason for restricting the algorithm to structured graphs is that for nonstructured graphs the result can depend on the order in which nodes are removed. Structured or not, it's worth calculating this value to see if you have at least as many paths as the minimum number of paths calculated this way. If you have fewer paths in your test plan than this minimum you probably haven't covered. It's another check.

4.4. The Probability of Getting There

4.4.1. The Problem

I suggested in Chapter 3 that, if anything, path selection should be biased toward the low probability paths rather than the high probability paths. This raises an interesting question—just what is the probability of being at a certain point in a routine? This question can be answered under suitable assumptions, primarily that all probabilities involved are independent, which is to say that all decisions are independent and uncorrelated. This restriction can be removed but it's beyond the scope of this book. We'll apply the same algorithm as before—a node-by-node removal of all uninteresting nodes.

4.4.2. Weights, Notation, Arithmetic

Probabilities can come into the act only at decisions (including decisions associated with loops). Annotate each link that exits a decision with a weight equal to the probability of going in that direction. Evidently, the sum of the probabilities of the links that leave a node must equal 1. For a simple loop, if the loop will be taken an average of N times, the looping probability is $N/(N + 1)$ and the probability of not looping is $1/(N + 1)$. A link which is not part of a decision node has a probability of 1. The arithmetic rules are those of ordinary arithmetic.

CASE	PATH EXPRESSION	WEIGHT EXPRESSION
PARALLEL	A + B	$P_A + P_B$
SERIES	AB	$P_A P_B$
LOOP	A*	$P_A / (1 - P_L)$

Where P_A is the probability of the link leaving the loop and P_L is the probability of looping, the rules are those of ordinary probability theory. If you can do something either from column A with a probability of P_A or from column B with a probability P_B but not both, then the probability that you do either is $P_A + P_B$. For the series case, if you must do both things, and their probabilities are independent (as assumed), then the probability that you do both is the product of their probabilities.

$$P_A = 1 - P_L$$

$$P_{NEW} = \frac{P_A}{1 - P_L} = \frac{1 - P_L}{1 - P_L} = 1$$

A loop node has a looping probability of P_L and a probability of not looping of P_A, which is obviously equal to $1 - P_L$. Following the rule, all we've done is replace the outgoing probability with 1—so why the complicated rule? After a few steps in which you've removed nodes, combined parallel terms, removed loops and the like, you might find something like this:

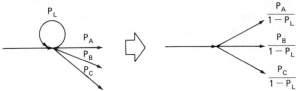

because $P_L + P_A + P_B + P_C = 1$, $1 - P_L = P_A + P_B + P_C$, and

$$\frac{P_A}{1 - P_L} + \frac{P_B}{1 - P_L} + \frac{P_C}{1 - P_L} = \frac{P_A + P_B + P_C}{1 - P_L} = 1$$

which is what we've postulated for any decision.

4.4.3. Example

Here is a complicated bit of logic. We want to know the probability associated with cases A, B, and C.

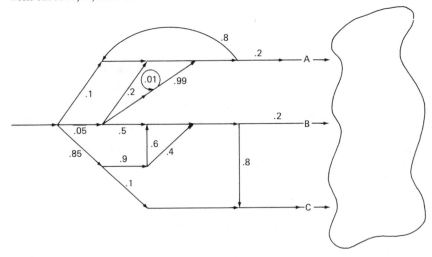

I'll do this in three parts, starting with case A. Note that the sum of the probabilities at each decision node is equal to 1. Start by throwing away anything that isn't on the way to case A, and then apply the reduction procedure. To avoid clutter, we usually leave out probabilities that are equal to 1—they're understood.

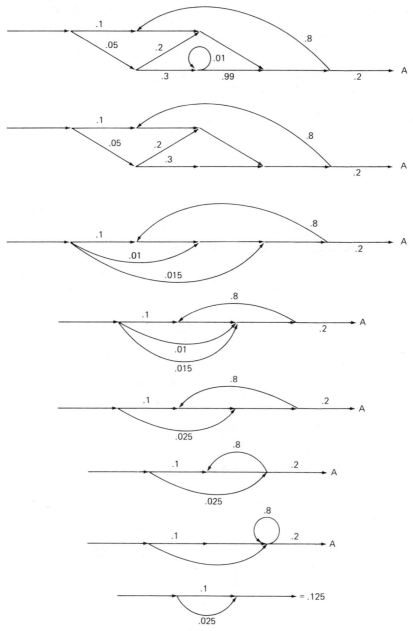

Case B is simpler:

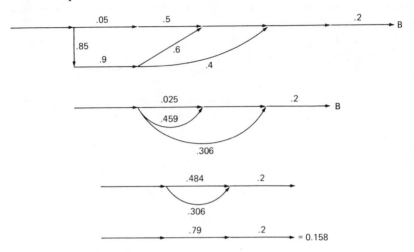

Case C is similar and should yield a probability of $1 - .125 - .158 = .717$:

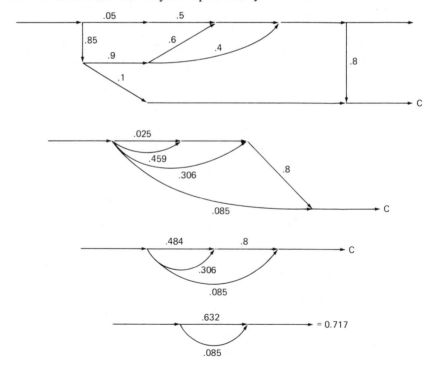

This does check. It's a good idea when doing this sort of thing to calculate all the probabilities and verify that the sum of the routine's exit probabilities does equal 1. If it doesn't, then you've made an error in calculation or, more likely, you've left out some branching probability. Calculating the probability of reaching a point in a routine is not completely trivial, as you can see. If the logic is convoluted, simplistic methods of estimating can be very far off. It's better to analyze it.

How about path probabilities? That's easy. Just trace the path of interest and multiply the probabilities as you go. Alternatively, write down the path name and do the indicated arithmetic operation. Say that a path consisted of links *a, b, c, d, e,* and the associated probabilities were .2, .5, 1., .01, and 1 respectively. Path *abcbcbcdeabddea* would have a probability of 5×10^{-10}. Long paths are usually improbable. Covering with short, simple paths is usually covering with high probability paths. If you're going to make an argument related to testing based on probabilities, be prepared to evaluate those probabilities. If someone refutes a test based on probabilities, be prepared to demand an evaluation thereof, rather than a haphazard guess.

Another good practice is to calculate the sum of the probabilities of the paths in the test set. A routine could have millions of paths but can be covered by ten or twenty. Calculate the sum of the probabilities for those paths and compare the sum with unity. Given two proposed sets of tests, the set whose path probability sum is greater provides a more complete test than the set whose path probability sum is smaller. Be careful how you apply this because:

1. Getting the probabilities can be very difficult.
2. Correlated and dependent predicates do not follow the simple rules of multiplication and addition. A comparison made in such cases could be misleading.
3. In most cases, the probabilities of the covering path set tend to be very small. Don't expect to compare test plan A with a probability sum of 0.9 to test plan B with a sum of 0.8—it's more likely to be a comparison of 10^{-9} to 10^{-10}.

4.5. The Mean Processing Time of a Routine

4.5.1. The Problem

Given the execution time of all statements or instructions for every link in a graph and the probability for each direction for all decisions, find the mean processing time for the routine as a whole. Under suitable assumptions, specifically that the decisions are uncorrelated and independent, the following algorithm gives you the results. In practice, getting the probabilities is half the work. Data dependencies and correlated decisions can be handled with modifications of the algorithm. Furthermore, the standard deviation and higher moments can also be calculated. For further information, see BEIZ78.

4.5.2. The Arithmetic

The model has *two* weights associated with every link: the processing time for that link, denoted by T, and the probability of that link. The rules for the probabilities are identical to those discussed in Section 4.4. The rules for the mean processing times are:

CASE	PATH EXPRESSION	WEIGHT EXPRESSION	
PARALLEL	A + B	T_{A+B}	$= (P_A T_A + P_B T_B)/(P_A + P_B)$
		P_{A+B}	$= P_A + P_B$
SERIES	AB	T_{AB}	$= T_A + T_B$
		P_{AB}	$= P_A P_B$
LOOP	A*	T_A	$= T_A + T_L P_L/(1 - P_L)$
		P_A	$= P_A/(1 - P_L)$

The parallel term is just the average of the processing time over all the links that were in parallel. Because the first node could have links that do not terminate on the second node of the parallels, we must divide by the sum of the parallel probabilities to get the proper mean. The serial term is intuitively obvious as the sum of the two processing times. The probability portion of the loop term is the same as before. The processing-time component consists of two parts. The part that was on the link leaving the loop (T_A) and the contribution of the loop. The loop contribution is most easily understood by substituting the value $N/(N + 1)$ for the probability of looping, under the assumption that the routine was expected to loop N times. The $P_L/(1 - P_L)$ term then reduces to just N. If the routine is expected to loop N times, and each time takes T_L seconds, and thereafter it does T_A seconds worth of work, then the mean time through the entire process is $T_A + NT_L$.

4.5.3. An Example

As an example, we'll use our old standby now annotated with branch probabilities, loop probabilities, and processing times for each link. The probabilities are given in parentheses. The node-removal order will be as in the previous use of this graph. It helps to remove nodes from the inside of loops to the outside.

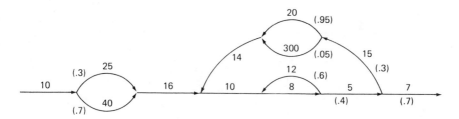

1. Start with the original graph properly annotated with probabilities and processing time in microseconds or in instructions or in whatever else is meaningful and convenient.

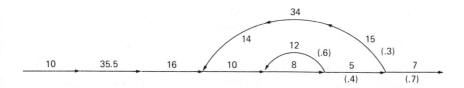

2. Combine the parallel links of the outer loop. The result is just the average of the processing times for the links because there aren't any other links leaving the first node. Also combine the pair of links at the beginning of the graph.

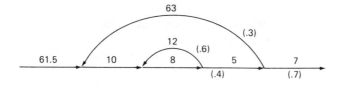

3. Combine all the serial links you can.

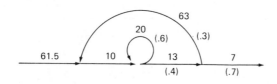

4. Use the cross-term step to eliminate a node and to create the inner self-loop.

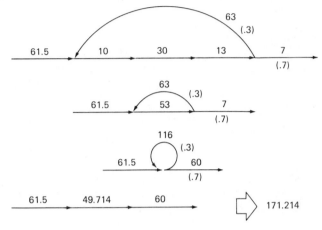

4.6. Push/Pop, Get/Return, Set/Reset

4.6.1. The Problem

This model can be used to answer several different questions that can turn up in debugging. It can also help decide which test cases to design. The question is: given a pair of complementary operations such as PUSH (the stack) and POP (the stack), considering the set of all possible paths through the routine, what is the net effect of the routine PUSH or POP? How many times?, and under what conditions? Here are some other examples of complementary operations to which this model applies:

> SET/RESET a flag.
> GET/RETURN a resource block.
> OPEN/CLOSE a file.
> START/STOP a device or process.

4.6.2. Push/Pop Arithmetic

CASE	PATH EXPRESSION	WEIGHT EXPRESSION
PARALLEL	A + B	$W_A + W_B$
SERIES	AB	$W_A W_B$
LOOP	A*	W_A*

An arithmetic table is needed to interpret the weight addition and multiplication operations. Typically, the exponent for loops will be the normal exponent. As before, we must be careful with the loop case: if a specific number of loops will be taken, the nonlooping term is not multiplied for the links following the loop. The Greek letter lambda (λ) is used to indicate that nothing of interest (neither PUSH nor POP) occurs on a given link. "H" will denote PUSH and "P" will denote POP. The operations are commutative, associative, and distributive.

PUSH/POP MULTIPLICATION TABLE

X	H PUSH	P POP	λ NONE
H	H^2	λ	H
P	λ	P^2	P
λ	H	P	λ

PUSH/POP ADDITION TABLE

+	H PUSH	P POP	λ NONE
H	H	P + H	H + λ
P	P + H	P	P + λ
λ	H + λ	P + λ	λ

Example:

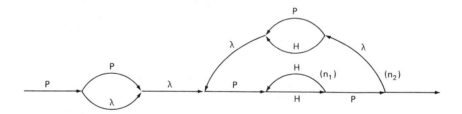

$$P(P + \lambda)\lambda\{P(HH)^{n_1} HP\lambda(P + H)\lambda\}^{n_2} P(HH)^{n_1} HP$$

Simplifying by using the arithmetic tables:

$$(P^2 + P)\{P(HH)^{n_1}(P + H)\}\ ^{n_2}(HH)^{n_1}$$
$$(P^2 + P)\{H^{2n_1}(P^2 + \lambda)\}^{n_2} H^{2n_1}$$

The circumstances under which the stack will be pushed, popped, or left alone by the routine can now be determined. Table 6-1 shows several combinations of values for the two looping terms—n_1 is the number of times the inner loop will be taken and n_2 the number of times the outer loop will be taken.

N_1	N_2	PUSH/POP
0	0	$P + P^2$
0	1	$P + P^2 + P^3 + P^4$
0	2	$\displaystyle\sum_{1}^{6} P^i$
0	3	$\displaystyle\sum_{1}^{8} P^i$
1	0	$\lambda + H$
1	1	$\displaystyle\sum_{0}^{3} H^i$
1	2	$\displaystyle\sum_{0}^{5} H^i$
1	3	$\displaystyle\sum_{0}^{7} H^i$
2	0	$H^2 + H^3$
2	1	$\displaystyle\sum_{4}^{7} H^i$
2	2	$\displaystyle\sum_{6}^{11} H^i$
2	3	$\displaystyle\sum_{8}^{15} H^i$

Table 6.1. Results of the PUSH/POP Graph Analysis.

These expressions state that the stack will be popped only if the inner loop is not taken. The stack will be left alone only if the inner loop is iterated once, but it may also be pushed. For all other values of the inner loop, the stack will only be pushed.

Exactly the same arithmetic tables are used for GET/RETURN a buffer block or resource, or in fact, for any pair of complementary operations in which the total number of operations in either direction is cumulative. As another example, consider INCREMENT/DECREMENT of a counter. The question of interest would be: for various loop counts, considering the set of all possible paths, is the net result a positive or negative count and what are the values? The arithmetic tables for GET/RETURN are:

X	G	R	λ
G	G^2	λ	G
R	λ	R^2	R
λ	G	R	λ

+	G	R	λ
G	G	G + R	G + λ
R	G + R	R	R + λ
λ	G + λ	R + λ	λ

Example:

$$G(G + R)G(GR)^*GGR^*R$$
$$= G(G+R)G^3R^*R$$
$$= (G + R)G^3R^*$$
$$= (G^4 + G^2)R^*$$

This expression specifies the conditions under which the resources will be balanced on leaving the routine. If the upper branch is taken at the first decision, the second loop must be taken four times. If the lower branch is taken at the first decision, the second loop must be taken twice. For any other values, the routine will not balance. Therefore, the first loop does not have to be instrumented to verify this behavior because it's impact should be nil. The first decision and the second loop should be instrumented.

4.6.3. Set/Reset Arithmetic

This application is a little trickier because the operations are not associative. If a flag is SET when already set, then it will remain set. Similarly for reset. The arithmetic tables are:

X	S	R	λ
S	S	λ	S
R	λ	R	R
λ	S	R	λ

+	S	R	λ
S	S	S + R	S + λ
R	S + R	R	R + λ
λ	S + λ	R + λ	λ

Also: S*S = S   R*R = R

But: (RS)S = λS = S

R(SS) = R(S) = λ

Putting in explicit parentheses helps keep track of things.

Example:

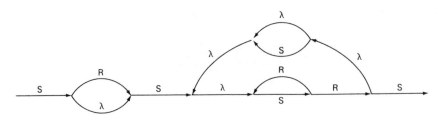

S(R + λ)S{λ(SR)*SR(λ(λ + S)λ)}*(λ(SR)*SR)S
But SR = RS = λ

= S(R + λ)S{λ + S}*S
= (SR + Sλ)S{λ + S}*S
= (λ + S)S{λ + S}*S
= S(λ + S)*S
= S

Therefore, no matter what path is taken, and how many times the loops are traversed, the net effect of the routine is always a SET operation. The same arithmetic tables will apply to any complementary pair of operations that are absorptive (SS = S), nonassociative, but commutative.

4.7. Limitations and Solutions.

The main limitation to these applications is the problem of excluded paths, which arise principally from correlated predicates. The node-by-node reduction procedure, and most graph-theory-based algorithms work well when all paths are possible, but may provide misleading results when some paths are excluded. The approach to handling excluded paths (for any application) is to partition the graph into subgraphs so that all paths in each of the subgraphs are possible. The resulting subgraphs may overlap, because one path may be common to several different subgraphs. Each predicate's truth-functional value potentially splits the graph into two subgraphs. For n predicates, there could be as many as 2^n subgraphs. Here's the algorithm for one predicate:

1. Set the value of the predicate to TRUE and strike out all FALSE links for that predicate.
2. Discard any node, other than an entry or exit node, that has no incoming links. Discard all links that leave such nodes. If there is no exit node, the routine probably has a bug because there is a predicate value that forces an endless loop or the equivalent.
3. Repeat Step 2 until there are no more links or nodes to discard. The resulting graph is the subgraph corresponding to a TRUE predicate value.
4. Change "TRUE" to "FALSE" in the above steps and repeat. The resulting graph is the subgraph that corresponds to a FALSE predicate value.

Only correlated predicates whose values exclude paths should be included in this analysis—not all predicates that may control the program flow. You can usually pick out the subgraphs by inspection because only one or two predicates, that each appear in only a few places, are the source of the excluded paths. If it isn't that simple, the routine is probably more complicated than it should be. A side benefit of the partitioning is that it may suggest a simpler, cleaner, and easier to test routine. The cost of this simplicity is probably a modest increase in the number of statements, which is partially paid for by an improvement in running time. However, ask yourself why the routine is hard to analyze and why a formal analysis was required to see how various sets of paths were mutually exclusive. More often it's because the routine's a murky pit than because it's deep and elegant.

5. REGULAR EXPRESSIONS, INITIALIZATION, AND SEQUENCE PROBLEMS

5.1. The Problem

One of the more common data-related problems is improper initialization or inadvertent destruction of a value prior to its use. Some of these problems can be caught by static analysis done by a compiler if the source code is written in a higher-order language. But if the dirty work is done in the body of an assembly language routine, a static analysis may not help. Furthermore, the number of such problems is incredible and may be highly application dependent. Consequently, you should not expect built-in test tools for these problems.

The generic problem is that of looking for a specific sequence of operations considering all possible paths through a routine. Let's say the operations are SET and RESET, denoted by s and r respectively, and we want to know if there is a SET followed immediately by a SET or a RESET followed immediately by a RESET (i.e., an ss or an rr sequence). Unlike the previous examples, we will not take advantage of a possible arithmetic over the various operations, because we are interested in knowing if a specific sequence occurred, not what the net effect of the routine is. Here are some additional application examples:

1. A file can be opened (o), closed (c), read (r), or written (w). If the file is read or written to after it's been closed, the sequence is nonsensical. Therefore, cr and cw are forbidden. Similarly, if the file is read before it's been written, just after opening, we may have a bug. Therefore, or is also a forbidden sequence. Furthermore, oo and cc, while not actual bugs, are a waste of time and therefore should also be examined.
2. A tape transport can do a rewind (d), fast-forward (f), read (r), write (w), stop (p), and skip (k). There are rules concerning the use of the transport, such as, you cannot go from a rewind to a fast-forward without an intervening stop or from a rewind or fast-forward to a read or write without an intervening stop. The following sequences are forbidden: $df,$ $dr, dw, fd, fr,$ and so on. Does the flowchart lead to forbidden sequences on any path, and if so, what sequences and under what circumstances?
3. A FORTRAN routine can initialize a variable or define it by an assign-

ment statement. The variable can also be undefined by doing an operation, such as exiting a DO, in which case the iteration variable is no longer available. Reference (reading or using in an assignment or operational statement) prior to definition or after undefinition is clearly a bug. Is there a path that will lead to this kind of bug?

4. You suspect a bug that could occur only if two operations, *a* and *b* occurred in the order *aba* or *bab*. Is there a path along which this is possible?

5.2. The Method

Annotate each link in the graph with the appropriate operator or the null operator λ. Simplify things to the extent possible, using the fact that $a + a = a$ and $\lambda^2 = \lambda$. Other combinations must be handled with care, because it may not be the case that a null operation can be combined with another operation. For example, λa may not be the same thing as a alone. You now have a **regular expression** that denotes all the possible sequences of operators in that graph. You can now examine that regular expression for the sequences of interest. A useful theorem by Huang (HUAN79) helps simplify things. The theorem is:

Let A, B, C, be nonempty sets of character sequences whose smallest string is at least one character long. Let T be a two-character string. Then if T is a substring (i.e., if T appears within) of AB^nC, then T will appear in AB^2C.

As an example, let:

$$A = pp$$
$$B = srr$$
$$C = rp$$
$$T = ss$$

The theorem states that *ss* will appear in $pp(srr)^n rp$ if it appears in $pp(srr)^2 rp$. We don't need the theorem to see that *ss* does not appear in the given string. However, let:

$$A = p + pp + ps$$
$$B = psr + ps(r + ps)$$
$$C = rp$$
$$T = p^4$$

Is it obvious that there is a p^4 sequence in AB^nC? The theorem states that we have only to look at:

$$(p + pp + ps)(psr + ps(r + ps))^2rp$$

Multiplying out the expression and simplifying shows that there is no p^4 sequence.

A further point of Huang's theorem is directly useful in test design. He shows that if you substitute $\lambda + X^2$ for every expression of the form X^*, the paths that result from this substitution are sufficient to determine if a given two-character sequence exists or not.

5.3. An Example (HUAN79)

A variable can be referred to (r), defined (d), undefined (u), or nothing need be done to it (λ). Consider the following two-character operator sequences:

rr—quite reasonable. The variable was referred to twice in succession.
ru—not a bug. The variable was accessed and then discarded.
rd—not a bug. The variable was accessed and then redefined.
ur—clearly a bug. The variable was made inaccessible and then accessed. This is an initialization error.
uu—not clearly a bug, but suspicious.
ud—not a bug. The variable was destroyed and then defined.
dr—the normal initialization sequence.
dd—suspicious. Why modify the variable or initialize it and the do it again without an intermediate reference?
du—also suspicious. The variable was defined and then thrown away without reference.

Of the nine possible two-character sequences, *ur* is clearly a bug and *uu, dd,* and *du* are suspicious. Here is a flowchart that has been annotated with the operators at the links that correspond to the variables of interest:

The *ur* bug is clear from the regular expression. It will occur whenever the first loop is not taken. The second part of Huang's theorem states that the following expression is sufficient to detect any two-character sequence:

$$d(r + \lambda)r(\lambda + (udr)^2)ur(\lambda + d^2)ru$$

This makes the *dd* bug obvious. A *uu* bug cannot occur because there is no left-hand term that ends in *u*. Similarly, a *du* bug cannot occur because the only left-hand term ending in *d* is the last parenthesis, which is followed by *ru*.

$$(drr + dr)(\lambda + udrudr)(urru + urd^2\,ru)$$

There's no point in following through because the bugs have been found. Generally, you would have to do this for every variable of interest. Also, the weights used with any link will change from variable to variable, because different things are being done with each variable. For this reason, it's best to write down the path expression and to substitute the operators later. That way, you don't have to constantly redraw the graph and redo the path expression.

A better way to do this is to subscript the operator with the link name. Doing it this way, you don't lose the valuable path information. When two or more links or operators are combined, combine the link names. Here's the problem done over again with this feature added:

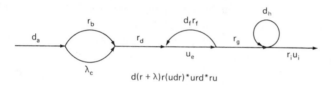

$$d(r + \lambda)r(udr)^*urd^*ru$$

The path expression is:

$$a(b + c)d(ef)^*egh^*i$$

The regular expression is:

$$d_a(r_b + \lambda_c)r_d(u_e d_f r_f)^*u_e r_g d_h^*r_i u_i$$

Applying Huang's Theorem:

$$d_a(r_b + \lambda_c)r_d(\lambda + (u_e d_f r_f)^2)u_e r_g(\lambda + d_h^2)r_i u_i$$

$$(d_a r_b r_d + d_{ac} r_d)(u_e r_g + u_e d_f r_f u_e d_f r_f u_e r_g)(r_i u_i d_h^2 r_i u_i)$$

The resulting expression tells us the same thing and preserves the path names so that we can work back to see what paths are potentially responsible for the bug, or alternatively, what paths must be tested to assure detection of the problem.

5.4. Generalizations, Limitations, and Comments

Huang's theorem can be easily generalized to cover sequences of greater length than two characters. Beyond three characters, though, things get complex and this method has probably reached its utilitarian limit.

If A, B, and C are nonempty sets of strings of one or more characters, and if T is a string of k characters, and if T is a substring of AB^nC, where n is greater than or equal to k, then T is a substring of AB^kC. A sufficient test for strings of length k can be obtained by substituting P^k for every appearance of P^* (or P^n where n is greater than or equal to k). Recall that:

$$P^k = \lambda + P + P^2 + P^3 + \ldots P^k.$$

There's a warning to be issued concerning the use of regular expressions. There are almost no other useful identities beyond those shown earlier for the path expressions. There are some nice theorems for finding sequences that occur at the beginnings and ends of strings (BRZO63) but no nice algorithms for finding strings buried in an expression. The mathematics for finding initial and terminal substrings is not very nice—it's analogous to taking derivatives of algebraic expressions, and things tend to get abstract fast. Because you can usually see if a sequence starts or ends a regular expression by inspection, the additional mathematics hardly seem worthwhile. The main use of regular expressions is as a convenient notation and method of keeping book on paths and sets of paths. Once you get used to it, doing the algebra and manipulating the expression is easier than tracing (and perhaps missing) paths on a flowchart.

6. SUMMARY

1. A flowchart annotated with link names for every link can be converted into a path expression that represents the set of all paths in that flowchart. A node-by-node reduction procedure is used.
2. By substituting link weights for all links, and using the appropriate arithmetic rules, the path expression is converted into an algebraic expression that can be used to determine: the minimum and maximum number of possible paths in a flowchart, the probability that a given node will be reached, the mean processing time of a routine, and other models.
3. With different, suitable arithmetic rules, by using complementary operators as weights for the links, the path expression can be converted into an expression that denotes, over the set of all possible paths, what the net effect of the routine is.

4. With links annotated with the appropriate weights, the path expression is converted into a regular expression that denotes the set of all operator sequences over the set of all paths in a routine. Rules for determining if a given sequence of operations are possible are given.

7

DATA VALIDATION AND SYNTAX TESTING

1. SYNOPSIS

System inputs and data must be validated. Internal and external inputs conform to formats which can usually be expressed in **Backus-Naur form** (a specification which can be mechanically converted into more input-data validation tests than anyone could reasonably want to execute).

2. GARBAGE

2.1. A Protest

I think one of the worst cop-outs ever invented by the computer industry is "garbage-in equals garbage-out." We know when to use that one! When a program of ours screws up in a nasty way. People are inconvenienced by the host of subsidiary problems that result. A big investigation is launched and it's discovered that an operator made a mistake, an improper tape was mounted, or the source data was inconsistent, or something like that. That's the time to put on the Guru's mantle, shake your head from side to side, disclaim all guilt, and mutter, "What do you expect? Garbage-in equals garbage-out."

Do we have the right to say that to the families of the passengers on an airliner that crashes? Will you offer that explanation for the failure of the intensive care unit's monitor system? How about a nuclear reactor meltdown, a supertanker run aground, or a war? GIGO is no explanation for anything except our failure to install good data-validation checks, or worse, our failure to test the system's tolerance for bad data. The point is that garbage shouldn't get in at all—not in the first place or in the last place. Every system must contend with a bewildering array of internal and external garbage, and if you don't think the world is hostile, how do you plan to cope with alpha particles?

2.2. Casual and Malicious Users

Systems that interface with casual, nontechnical users must be especially robust and consequently must have prolific validation checks. It's not that the users of cash machines, say, are willfully hostile but that there are so many of them; so many of them and so few of us. Call it the million-monkey phenomenon, if you want to. A million monkeys sit at a million typewriters for a million years and eventually one of them types Hamlet. The more users, the less knowledgeable they are, the more likely that eventually, on pure chance, they'll hit every spot at which the system's vulnerable to bad inputs.

There are a few malicious users in every population—infuriating people, professional Blue Meanies who delight in doing strange things to the systems they use. Years ago they'd pound the sides of vending machines for free sodas. Their sons and daughters invented the blue-box used to get free long-distance and international telephone calls. Now they're tired of probing the nuances of their home video games and they're out to attack computers. They're out to get *you*. Some of them are even programmers. They are persistent and systematic. A few hours of attack by one of *them* is worse than years of ordinary use and bugs found by chance. And there are so many of them; so many of them and so few of us.

Then there is crime. It's estimated that computer criminals (using mostly hokey inputs) are raking in hundreds of millions of dollars annually. Some criminals could be doing it from a telephone booth in Arkansas with an acoustic coupled programmable calculator. Every piece of bad data unknowingly accepted by a system, every crash-causing input sequence, is a chink in the system's armor that knowledgeable criminals can use to penetrate, corrupt, and eventually suborn the system to their own purposes (LEIB74). And don't think the system's too complicated for them. They have your listings, and your documentation, and the data dictionary, and whatever else they need.* There aren't many of them, but they are smart, highly motivated, and possibly organized.

2.3. Operators

Roger and I were talking about operators and the dirty things they can do, and the scenarios were getting a bit farfetched. Who would think of mounting a tape with a write ring installed, writing a few blocks, stopping, carefully opening the transport's door, dismounting the tape reel without unloading the buffers, removing the ring, remounting the tape without telling the

---

*Remember, the best embezzler is always a trained accountant—why shouldn't the best computer criminal be a skilled programmer?

system, and then attempting to write a new block? The potential malice we ascribed to the operators was embarrassing me. I said to Roger (who was one of the designers concerned with the impact of operator shenanigans), "What the operators have done to these systems in the past is bad enough—just imagine how they would act if they knew how we talked about them."

To which he snapped, "If they knew how we talked about them, they'd probably act the way we expect them to!"

I'm not against operators and I don't intend to put them down. They're our final defense against the bugs we've left in the system. Too often they manage, by intuition, common sense, and brilliance, to snatch a mere catastrophe from the jaws of annihilation. Operators make mistakes and when they do, it's often serious. It's right that they probe the system's defenses, categorize its weaknesses and idiosyncrasies, and prepare themselves for all the eventualities we didn't think of.

2.4. The Internal World

Large systems have to contend not only with a hostile external environment but also a hostile internal environment. Malice doesn't play a role here, but oversight, miscommunication, and chance can be just as deadly. Any large system is subdivided into relatively independent subsystems and consequently, there are many internal interfaces. Each such interface presents another opportunity for data corruption and may require explicit internal-data validation. Furthermore, hardware can fail in bizarre ways that will cause it to pump streams of bad data into memory, into another computer, across channels, and so on. Another piece of software may fail and do the same. Finally, if none of the above gets to you, there're always alpha particles.

2.5. What To Do

Data validation is the first line of defense against a hostile world. Good designers will design their system so that it just doesn't accept garbage—good testers will subject their systems to the most creative garbage possible. Input-tolerance testing is usually done at the system level, such as in a formal function test or in a final acceptance test, and consequently, the tester is usually distinct from the designer.

This kind of testing and test design is more fun than any other kind I know of. This is the place where you can be an Incredible Hulk's Incredible Hulk. It's great therapy and they pay you for it. My family and pets love it when I'm designing or running this kind of test; after I'm through kicking and stomping the programmers around, there's not a mean bone left in my body.

However, to be really aggravating takes organization, structure, discipline, and method—random potshots and waiting for vicious inspirations with which to victimize the programmer just won't do the job.

3. A GRAMMAR FOR FORMATS

3.1. Objectives

Every input must conform to a format. That format may be formally specified or "just understood," but it does exist. Data validation consists of testing the input for conformance to that format. It's best when the format is defined in a formal language—best for the system designer and the test designer. Whether the designer creates the data-validation software from a formal specification or not is not important to the test designer, but the test designer needs a formal specification to create useful garbage. That specification is conveniently expressed in **Backus-Naur form**; any similarity to regular expressions is deliberate.

3.2. BNF Notation (BACK59)

3.2.1. The Components

Every input to a system or routine can be considered as if it were a string of characters. The system accepts valid strings and rejects invalid ones. If the system fails on an invalid string, we've really got it. If it accepts an invalid string, then it's guilty of GIGO. There's nothing we can do about syntactically valid strings, all of whose values are reasonable but just plain wrong—that kind of garbage we have to accept. The definition of a valid format must be formal, starting with the most elementary components, the characters themselves. Here is a sample definition:

alpha:characters	::= A/B/C/D/E/F/G/H/I/J/K/L/M/N/O/P/Q/ R/S/T/U/V/W/X/Y/Z
numerals	::= 1/2/3/4/5/6/7/8/9
zero	::= 0
signs	::= !/#/$/%/&/*(/)/−/+/=/;/:/"/'/,/./?/ /
space	::= / sp

The left-hand side of each definition is the name given to the collection of objects that appear on the right-hand side of the definition. The symbol

"::=" is to be taken as a single symbol which means "is defined as." The slash "/" means "or." We could have used the plus sign for that purpose, but that wouldn't be in keeping with the way BNF is usually defined. The next-to-the-last slash means "*or*" in the "*signs*" definition, while the last slash is a slash which is one of the signs. We are using BNF to define a miniature language. The "::=" is part of the language in which we talk about the mini-language, called the "**metalanguage**." Similary, the last slash is part of the language we're defining, and the previous slash is part of the metalanguage. Spaces and blanks are always confusing because we can't display them on paper. We use the b symbol or *sp* to mean a space. The actual spaces on this page have no meaning. Similarly, an underlined symbol is used for anything else that can't conveniently be printed, such as *null, end-of-text, clear screen, carriage return, line feed, tab, shift up, shift down, index, backspace,* and so on.

3.2.2. Operators and Operations

The operators are the same as those used in path expressions and regular expressions: "or," concatenate (which doesn't need a special symbol), " *,* " and "+." Exponents, such as A^n will have the same meaning as before—n repetitions of the strings denoted by the letter A. A format is defined in BNF as a set of definitions. Each definition may in turn refer to other definitions or to itself in such a way that eventually it gets down to object characters that form the input to the routine. It's simpler than it sounds. Here's an example:

$$word ::= alpha:character\ alpha:character\ /\ numeral\ sp\ numeral$$

I've defined an input string called *word* as a pair of *alpha:characters* or a pair of *numerals* separated by a space. Here are examples of *words* and *nonwords,* by this definition:

words	: AB, DE, XY, 3 4, 6 7, 9 9, 1 2
nonwords	: AAA, A A1, A), 11, 111, WORD, NOT WORD, +

There are 722 possible *words* in this primitive format and an infinite number of non*words*. If the strings are restricted to four characters, there are more than a million non*words*. The designer wants to detect and accept *words* and reject non*words*; the tester wants to generate non*words* and force the program to deal with them.

As before, something like *object*$_1^3$ means one to three *objects, object** means zero or more repetitions of *object* without limit, and *object*$^+$ means one or more repetitions of *object*.

3.2.3. Examples

This is an example and not a real-world definition of a telephone number:

special:digit	::=	1/2/5
zero	::=	0
other:digit	::=	3/4/6/7/8/9
ordinary:digit	::=	*special:digit / zero / other:digit*
exchange:part	::=	*other:digit^2 ordinary:digit*
number:part	::=	*ordinary:digit^4*
phone:number	::=	*exchange:part number:part*

According to this definition, the following are *phone:numbers,*

$$3469900, 9904567, 3300000$$

and these are not:

$$5551212, 5510000, 123, 8, ABCDEFG, WA5\text{-}9550, 665\text{-}6088.$$

Another example:

$$\textit{operator:command} \quad ::= \quad \textit{mnemonic field:unit}_1^8\ +$$

An *operator:command* consists of a *mnemonic* followed by one to eight field:units and a plus sign.

field:unit	::=	*field delimiter*
mnemonic	::=	*first:part second:part*
delimiter	::=	*sp / , / . / $ / *sp$_1^{42}$*
field	::=	*numeral / alpha / mixed / control*
first:part	::=	*a:vowel a:consonant*
second:part	::=	*b:consonant alpha*
a:vowel	::=	A/E/I/O/U
a:consonant	::=	B/D/F/G/H/J/K/L/M/N/P/Q/R/S/T/V/X/Z
b:consonant	::=	B/G/X/Y/Z/W/M/R/C
alpha	::=	*a:vowel / a:consonant / b:consonant*
numeral	::=	1/2/3/4/5/6/7/8/9/0
control	::=	$/*/%/sp/@
mixed	::=	*control alpha control / control numeral control / control control control*

Here are some valid *operator:commands*:

ABXW   A.   B.   C.   7.   +
UTMA   W   *sp*   *sp*   *sp*   *sp*   +

And the following are not *operator:commands:*

ABC *sp* +
A *sp* BCDEFGHIJKLMNOPQR *sp*[47] +

The telephone number example and the operator command example are different. The telephone number started with recognizable symbols and constructed the more complicated components from them, while the command example started at the top and worked down to the real characters. These two ways of defining things are equivalent—it's only a matter of the order in which the definition lines are printed. The top-down order is generally more useful and it's the usual form for formal language design. Looking at the definition from the top down leads you to some tests and looking from the bottom up can lead to different tests.

As a final notational convenience, it's sometimes useful to be able to enclose an expression in parentheses to reduce the number of steps in the definition. For example, the definition step for *field:unit* could have been simplified as follows:

$$operator:command ::= mnemonic \ (field \ delimiter)_1^8 \ +$$

This is fine if you don't have parentheses that can confuse you in the definitions. The notation can also be expanded to identify optional fields, conditional fields, and the like. In most realistic formats of any complexity, you won't be able to get everything expressed in this notation—nor is it essential that you do so; additional narrative descriptions may be needed.

4. TEST CASE GENERATION

4.1. Generators, Recognizers, and Approach

A data-validation routine is designed to recognize strings that have been explicitly or implicitly defined in accordance with a formally specified input format. It either accepts the string, because it has recognized it as a valid string, or rejects it and takes appropriate corrective action. The routine is said to be a **string recognizer**. Conversely, the test designer attempts to generate strings and is said to be a **string generator**. There are three possible kinds of incorrect actions :

1. The recognizer does not recognize a good string.
2. It accepts a bad string.
3. It may accept or reject a good string or a bad string, but in so doing, it fails.

Even small specifications lead to many good strings and far more bad strings. There is neither time nor need to test them all. Strings' errors can be subdivided as follows:

1. *High-level syntax errors.* The strings have violations of the topmost level in a top-down BNF syntax specification.
2. *Intermediate-level syntax errors.* Syntax errors at any level other than the top or bottom.
3. *Field-syntax errors.* Syntax errors associated with an individual field, where a field is defined as a string of characters that has no subsidiary syntax specification other than the identification of characters that compose it. A field is the lowest level at which it is productive to think in terms of syntax testing.
4. *Delimiter errors.* Violation of the rules governing the placement and the type of characters that must appear as separators between fields.
5. *Field-value errors.* Not syntax errors, but errors associated with the contents of a field.
6. *Syntax-context errors.* When the syntax of one field depends on values of other fields, there is a possibility of an interaction between a field-value error and a syntax error. For example, when the contents of a control field dictate the syntax of subsequent fields.
7. *Field-value correlation errors.* The contents of two or more fields are correlated by a functional relation between them. There is not full freedom in picking their values. The value of one field is restricted by another field's value.
8. *State-dependency errors.* The permissible syntax and/or field values is conditional on the state of the system or the routine. A command used for startup, say, may not be allowed when the system is running.

4.2. Where Does the BNF Specification Come From?

Format tests appear mostly as system-level functional tests. Little or no use is made of the structure of the routine that processes the inputs. Consequently, it's more likely that the designer and the tester are separate persons. If there is no formal BNF specification, I try to get the designers to create one—at least the first version of one. In some programs this is not a problem because input formats are usually formally defined—communications systems or language processors, for example. Realistically, though, if a formal BNF specification does not exist, the designers will have to create a document that can be easily converted into one. If you get the designer to create the first version of the BNF specification, you may find that it is neither consistent nor complete. Test design begins with requests for clarification of that preliminary specification. Many serious bugs can be avoided this way. If you can't get the designers to create the first version of the BNF specification, you do it yourself. It doesn't really matter if it's complete or correct, as long as it's down on paper and formal. Present that version of the specification to the designers and state that tests will be defined accordingly. There may be objections, but the result should be a reasonably correct version in short order.

Using a BNF specification or something close to it is the easiest way to design test cases for format validation. It is also the easiest way for designers to organize their work, but unfortunately, they don't always recognize that. You can't begin to design tests unless you have a clear agreement as to what is right or wrong. If you attempt to design cases without a formal syntax specification, you'll find that you're throwing test cases out, both good and bad, as the designers change the rules in response to the test cases you show them. If you can't get a formal agreement on format syntax early in the project, put off that kind of test design and concentrate on some other area. Alternatively, and more productively, participate in the design, even though you're responsible for testing, under the guise of getting a specification tied down. You'll clear up a lot of bugs that way.

It can boomerang, though. I pushed for a BNF specification of operator command formats on one system. The formats had been adapted from a previous system in the same family whose formats were clearly specified. This designer fell in love with BNF specifications and created a monster that was slightly more complicated than a combination of PL1, Algol, and COBOL— and mostly wrong. To make matters worse, the first version of the operator's manual was written in this pseudo-BNF, so that an operator would have had to plow through several levels of abstract syntax to determine which keys to hit. Good human engineering will dictate relatively simple, clean, easy-to-understand BNF specifications for user and operator interfaces. Similarly, internal formats for interprocess communications should also be simple. There's usually a topmost syntax level, several field options, and occasionally, some syntax-dependent subfields. Be suspicious if it gets so complicated that it looks like the specification of a new programming language. That's not a reasonable kind of thing to expect a casual user or operator to employ.

4.3. Test Case Design

4.3.1. General Principles

I've divided the kinds of errors that can occur in an input string into eight broad categories. The strategy is to create one error at a time, while keeping all other components of the input string correct. That is, in the absence of the single error, the string would have been accepted. Once a complete set of tests has been specified for single errors, do the same for double errors and then triple errors. However, if there are of the order of N single-error cases, there will be of the order of N^2 double-error and N^3 triple-error cases. Once past the single errors, it takes a lot of judicious pruning to keep the number of tests reasonable. This is almost impossible to do without looking at the implementation details.

4.3.2. Top, Intermediate, and Field-Level Syntax Errors

Say that the topmost syntax level is defined as:

$$item ::= atype \mid btype \mid ctype \mid dtype \, etype$$

Here are some obvious test cases:

1. *Do it wrong.* Use an element which is correct at some other lower syntax level, but not at this level.
2. *Wrong combination.* The last element is a combination of two other elements in a specified order. Mess up the order and combine the wrong things:
   dtype atype / btype etype / etype dtype / etype etype / dtype dtype
3. *Don't do enough.*
   dtype / etype
4. *Don't do nothing.* No input, just the end-of-command signal or carriage return. Amazing how many bugs you catch this way.
5. *Do too much.*
   atype btype ctype dtype etype / atype atype atype / dtype etype atype / dtype etype etype / dtype etype[128]

Focus on one level at a time and keep the level above and below as correct as you can. It may help to draw the **definition tree**. Using the telephone number example:

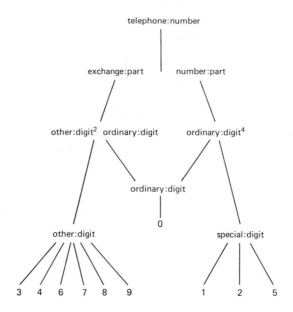

The test cases practically design themselves now:

TOP LEVEL
1. Do nothing.
2. An *exchange:part* by itself.
3. A *number:part* by itself.
4. Two *exchange:parts.*
5. Two *number:parts.*
6. An *exchange:part* and two *number:parts.*
7. Two *exchange:parts* and one *number:part.*
NEXT LEVEL
8. Bad *exchange:part*
    8.1-do nothing—covered by Test 3 above.
    8.2-no *other:digit.*
    8.3-two *special:digits.*
    8.3-three *special:digits.*
    8.4-et cetera.

9. Bad *number:part*
    9.1-not enough *digits.*
    9.2-too many *digits.*
    9.3-et cetera.
THIRD LEVEL
10. Bad *ordinary:digit*
    10.1-not a *digit*—use an alphabetic.
    10.2-not a *digit*—use a control character.
    10.3-not a *digit*—use a delimiter.
    10.4 -not a *digit*—leave it out.
    10.5-and so on.
FOURTH LEVEL
11. Bad *other:digit*—as with bad *ordinary:digit.*
12. Bad *special:digit*—as with bad *ordinary:digit.*
13. Et cetera.

You must keep checking back to the previous levels and downward to the next levels as you generate cases. Not everything generated by this procedure produces bad cases, and the procedure may lead to the same test case by two different paths. The corruption of one format element could lead to a correct but different format. Such tests are useful because logic errors in the format recognizer might miscategorize the string. Similarly, if a test case (either good or bad) can be generated via two different paths, it is an especially good case because there is a potential for confusion in the routine. I'm fond of test cases that are difficult to design and difficult to recognize as either good or bad— not because I want to retain a case in which I've invested a lot of labor, but because if I'm confused, it's likely that the designer will also be confused.

It's not that the designer is dumb and the tester smart, but the designer has much more to do than the tester. To design and test format-validation tests takes 5% to 10% of the effort required to design, code, test, validate, and integrate a format-validation routine. The designer has ten to twenty times as much work to do as does the tester. Given equal competence, if the tester gets confused with so little to do by comparison, it's a safe bet that the overloaded designer will be more confused by the same case.

4.3.3. Delimiter Errors

Delimiters are characters or strings of characters placed between two fields to denote where one ends and the other begins. Delimiter problems are an excellent source of test cases. Therefore, it pays to identify the delimiters and the rules governing their syntax.

1. *Missing Delimiter*—This kind of error causes adjacent fields to merge. This may result in a different, but valid, field or may be covered by another kind of syntax error.
2. *Wrong Delimiter*—It's nice when several different delimiters are used and there are rules that specify which can be used where. Mix them up and use them in the wrong places.
3. *Not a Delimiter*—Includes any character or string that is not a delimiter but could be put into that position. Note the possibility of changing adjacent field types as a result.
4. *Too Many Delimiters*—The number of delimiters appearing at a field boundary may be variable. This is typical for spaces, which can serve as delimiters. If the number of delimiters is specified as 1 to N, it pays to try 0, 1, 2, N−1, N, N+1, and also an absurd number of delimiters, such as 127, 128, 255, 256, 1024, and so on.
5. *Paired Delimiters*—Another juicy source of test cases. Parentheses are the archetypal paired delimiters. There could be several kinds of paired delimiters appearing within a format. If paired delimiters can nest, as in "(() ())," there are a whole set of new evils to perpetrate. For example, "BEGIN,BEGIN,END," "BEGIN,END,END." Nested paired delimiters provide opportunities for matching ambiguities. For example, "((()(( )))" has a matching ambiguity and it's not clear where the missing parenthesis belongs.
6. *Tolerant Delimiters*—The delimiter may be optional or several alternate formats may be acceptable. In communications systems, for example, the start of message is defined as ZCZC, but many systems allow any one of the four characters to be corrupted. Therefore, #CZC, Z#ZC, ZC#C, and ZCZ# (where "#" denotes any character) are all acceptable; there are a lot of nice confusing ways to put in a bad character here:
   a. A blank.
   b. Z or C in the wrong place—CCZC,ZZZC,ZCCC,ZCZZ (catches them every time!).
   c. Something off-the-wall—especially important control characters in some other context.

Tolerance is most often provided for delimiters but can also be provided for individual fields and higher levels of syntax. It's a sword of many edges— more than two for sure—all of them dangerous. Syntax tolerance is provided for user and operator convenience and in the interest of making the system humane and robust. But it also makes the format-validation design job and testing-format validation designs more complicated. Format tolerance is sophisticated and takes sophisticated designs to implement and consequently, many more and more complicated tests to validate. If you can't do the whole job from design to thorough validation, there's no point in providing the tolerance. Most users and operators prefer a solid system with rigid format rules to a system with tolerant format rules that don't always work.

4.3.4. Field-Value Errors

We've been able to keep away from any notion of meaning up to this point. None of the test cases described above took into account what the fields meant. Fields do have meaning and that meaning is not normally part of the field-syntax specification. Fields are treated like loops. Every field should have a specification for the range of permissible values. We can consider the field as if its contents are numbers. Nothing is lost by this assumption because we can convert everything to equivalent numerical values if we choose to.

1. *Boundary Values*—Bugs congregate at the edges of fields just as they do at the ends of loops. The obvious cases to try are: minimum -1, minimum, minimum $+1$, typical good value, maximum -1, maximum, maximum $+$ 1, a whole lot more than the maximum.
2. *Excluded Values*—Test excluded field values like excluded values for loops. Break the range up into allowed and excluded ranges and do boundary checks on each range.
3. *Troublesome Values*—Dig into the implementation and particularly into the data base and see how the field is stored. The boundary values for the storage element are excellent choices for tests. For example: 0, 15, 16, 31, 32, 63, 64, 127, 128.
4. *Type Changes and Conversions*—You can't spot the potential for this kind of error without looking at the data base or the code. If an object's type is changed (see Chapter 2, Section 3.5.4), new cases may be worth trying. For example, if a character field is also used as an integer or as a set of bit flags, the binary-limit values, such as 1,2,3,4,7,8,15,16,31,32 become more interesting.

4.3.5. Context-Dependent Format Errors

Components of the syntax may be interrelated and may be related by field values of other fields. The first field could be a format option code that specifies the syntax of subsequent fields. As an example:

command	::= *pilot:field syntax:option*
pilot:field	::= 1/2/3/4/5/6/7/8/9
syntax:option	::= *option1 / option2 / option3 / . . .*

The specification further states that option1 must be preceded by "1" as the value of the *pilot:field.* Actually, it would have been better had the specification be written as:

command	::= 1 *option1 / 2 option2 / 3 option3 . . .*

but that's not always easy to do. The test cases to use are clearly invalid combinations of syntactically valid field values and syntactically valid options. If you can rewrite the specification, as in the above example, to avoid such field value dependencies, then it's better you do so. However, if doing so requires vast increases in formalism, which could be handled more clearly with a side-bar notation that specifies the relation, then it's better to stick to the original form of the specification. The object is to make things as clear as possible to the designer and to yourself, and excessive formalism can destroy clarity just as easily as modest formalism can enhance it.

4.3.6. Correlated Field Values

This is analogous to correlated predicates or correlated values in testing a routine. In fact, correlated field values may be a source of input-variable predicate correlation. When variables are numerical and correlated by an equation or inequality, you can plot the valid domains of two variables, as in Figure 7-1:

The shaded part of the figure corresponds to the forbidden combinations. As usual, test cases should be derived from the boundary points, particularly where two or more variables become illegal simultaneously. Effective test areas are shown by the circles. Hit the corners with A good, B bad, A bad, B good, both good, both bad—with values just at the boundaries. For more than two correlated fields (or input-data values) handle it two variables at a time. You've done all the single-error cases for correlated variables. Say that three variables are correlated—call them A, B, and C. Keep C valid and draw a figure such as the above for A's relation to B. Design appropriate boundary cases. Then make B valid and do the interaction between A and C. Then make A valid and do the B to C interactions. Finally, take a small sample of the boundaries for three variables simultaneously. You may find that it is very difficult to find such points and, worse, to verify that the cases are indeed correct or incorrect. Don't agonize about it. If it's difficult for you to decide

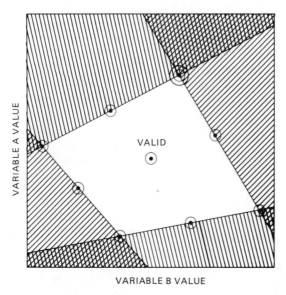

Figure 7-1. Test Cases and Variable Domains.

if a combination of values is correct or not, have faith that it will also be difficult for the routine's designer. Design the test, but leave the result unspecified. What you should be looking for is not so much that the routine accepts or rejects the combination of field values, but that it doesn't blow when given such a combination.

If the variables are combinations of logical values, case values, alphabetic and numerical values, then simple numerical inequalities will not help. Use lists and tables to specify the correlated combinations and the conditions under which they're valid or invalid.

4.3.7. State-Dependency Errors

The format or field value that may be acceptable at one instant may not be acceptable at the next, because validity depends on the transaction's or the system's state. As an example, say that the operator's command-input protocol requires confirmation of all commands. After every command the system expects either an acknowledgement or a cancellation, but not another command. A valid command at that point should be rejected, even though it is completely correct in all other respects. As another example, the system may permit, as part of a startup procedure, commands which are forbidden after the system has been started, or it may forbid otherwise normal commands during a startup procedure. A classical example occurs in communications systems. The start of message sequence ZCZC is allowed tolerance (see page 160) when it occurs at the beginning of a message. However, because the system has to handle Polish language words such as: "zczalny, jeszcze, deszcz, czerwiec, czesc, plaszcz, and zczotka" (BEIZ79), the rules state that any subsequent start-of-message sequence that occurs prior to a correct end-of-message sequence (NNNN) must be intolerant; the format is changed at that point and only an exact "ZCZC" will be accepted.

I divide state-dependency errors into simple and complicated. The simple ones are those that can be described by at most two states. All the rest are complicated and best handled by the methods of Chapter 11. The simple ones take two format specifications—or two field-value specifications—and require at worst double the work.

4.4. The Source of the Syntax

Unless the syntax is that of a programming language or a communication format or is derived from a previous system that's in operation or from some other source that's been in use for a long time, it's not likely that the syntax of the formats you're testing will approach anything close to being valid. There will be inconsistencies. There will be valid cases that are rejected and other cases, valid or otherwise, for which the action will be unpredictable. I mean fundamental errors in the syntax itself and not in the implementation of the routines that analyze the format. If you have to create the formal syntax in order to design tests, you are in danger of creating the format you want rather than the one that's being implemented. That's not necessarily bad if what you want is a simpler, more reliable, and easier format to use, implement, and test.

Take advantage of every ambiguity and contradiction you detect in the format to push the format's design into something that has fewer exception conditions, fewer state dependencies, fewer field correlations, and fewer variations. Keep in close contact with the format's designer, who is often also the designer of the format-analysis routine. Maintain a constant pressure of weird cases, interactions, and combinations. Whenever you see an opportunity to simplify the format, communicate that observation to the format's designer—he'll have less to design and code, you'll have less to test, and the user will thank you both for a better system. It's true that flaws in the syntax may require a more elaborate syntax and a more complicated implementation. However, my experience has been that the number of instances in which the syntax can be simplified outnumber the instances in which it's necessary to complicate it by about ten to one.

Encourage a modular design that divides format analysis into discrete levels and that separates field-value checking from syntax checking. Encourage table-driven format analysis routines that can evaluate several different formats using the same basic software. Encourage designs that allow you to eliminate interactive tests and combinations wholesale. I've found it effective to use the threat of a test to turn the designer around to a simpler and more testable design.* The designer doesn't really know that you're not going to design 27,000 cases, and if you offer an alternative that has only 1000 ways to mess up the format, it's likely that the simpler approach will be taken, thereby eliminating the need for the test.

4.5. Where Did the Good Guys Go?

Syntax-directed test design is like a lot of other things that are hard to stop once you've started. A little practice with this kind of test design and you find that the most innocuous format leads to hundreds of tests. I use format test design as basic training for persons new to a test group. With little information and training they can churn out hundreds of good tests. It's a great confidence builder for people who have never done formal test design before and who may be intimidated by the prospect of subjecting a senior designer's masterpiece to a barrage of calculated heartburn. There are, however, several dangers to this kind of test design.

1. *It's easy to forget the normal cases.* I've done it often. You get so entangled in creative garbage that you forget that the system must also be subjected to good inputs. I've made it a practice to explicitly check every test area for the normal case.
2. *Don't go overboard with the combinations.* It takes iron nerves to do this. You have done all the single-error cases, and in your mind you know exactly how to go about creating the double- and triple-error cases. And there are so many of them that you can create an impressive mound of test cases in short order. "How can the test miss anything if I've tried 1000 input-format errors?," you think. Keep reminding yourself that any one test approach is inherently limited to discovering certain types of bugs. Keep reminding yourself that all those N^2 double-error cases and N^3 triple-error cases may be no more effective than trying every value from 1 to 1023 in testing a loop. Don't let the entire test become top-heavy with syntax errors at the expense of everything else just because syntax tests are so easy to design.

---

*A good threat can be more effective than a good test. It's like the instructor who gives you a list of 1000 questions and tells you that some portion thereof, say 50, will be on the final exam. You can characterize thousands of format test cases in a few pages—let the designer know exactly how you intend to design the cases, but don't let him know exactly which cases you will really use.

3. *Don't ignore structure.* Just because it's possible to design thousands of test cases without looking at the software that's going to handle those cases doesn't mean you should do it that way. Knowing the program's design may help you eliminate error combinations wholesale without sacrificing the integrity and thoroughness of the test. As an example, say that operator-command mnemonics are validated by a general-purpose preprocessor routine. The rest of the input-character string is passed to the appropriate handler for that operator command only after the mnemonic has been validated. There would be no point to designing test cases that deal with the interaction of command mnemonic errors, the delimiter between the mnemonic and the first field, and format errors in the first field. You don't have to know a whole lot about the implementation. Often, just knowing what parts of the format are handled by which routines is enough to avoid designing a lot of impressive but useless error combinations that won't prove a thing. The bug that could creep across that kind of interface would be so exotic that you would have to design it. If it takes several hours of work to postulate and "design" a bug that a test case is supposed to catch, you can safely consider that test case as too improbable to worry about—certainly in the context of syntax testing.

4. *There's more than one kind of test.* Did you forget that you had designed a bunch of path tests? that there are state-based tests to design (Chapter 11)? data-base tests (Chapter 8)? or decision-table-based tests (Chapter 9)? Each model of the system's behavior leads to tests designed from a different point of view, but many of these overlap. Although redundant tests are harmless, they cost money and little is learned from them.

5. *Don't make more of the syntax than there is.* You can increase or decrease the scope of the syntax by falsely making it more or less tolerant than it really is. This may lead to the false classification of some good input strings as bad and vice versa. Not a terrible problem, because if there is confusion in your mind, there may be confusion in the designer's mind. At worst, you'll have to reclassify the outcome of some cases from "accept" to "reject" or vice versa.

4.6. Running Syntax Tests

Syntax tests are easy to design but hard to run. Every character is important, every character must be documented, and every step in the test scenario must be documented. The difficulties are insidious. I touch-type reasonably well and consequently, I'm completely useless when it comes to inserting bad input strings. I forget what I'm doing and "correct" the input errors as I go. If it's at all possible, all input strings should be prepared in advance and recorded on some removable media. Old fashioned paper tape is the best. It's easy to see exactly which characters are where, including the characters that don't print or don't move the carriage. Cassettes are not nearly as convenient or legible. I feel so strongly about the virtues of paper tape for format testing that I think it's worth having at least one test terminal equipped with a tape reader and punch. Use the highest quality, fan-fold, mylar-laminated paper tape you can get; it's very expensive, about twice the price of magnetic tape (the 1980 price was $67/1000 feet). It's hard to get, must be specially ordered, but is well worth it. You will run those tapes hundreds of times before you're through, and ordinary paper tape will not stand up to being stomped on, kicked about on the floor, coffeed on and so on.

If you don't have a lot of syntax testing and/or if it's not possible to prerecord the scenarios, then you'll have to do it by hand. Use two, preferably three, persons to do it. The one at the terminal should be the most fumble-fingered person in the test group. The one with the test sheet should be semi-illiterate. The illiterate calls out one character at a time, using her fingers to point to it, and moving her lips as she reads. The fumble-fingered typist scans the keyboard (it helps if he's very myopic) and finally finds it.

"A" the illiterate calls out.

"A" the typist responds when he's got his finger on the key. He presses it and snatches it away in fear that it will bite him.

"Plus" the reader shouts.

"No dammit!" the third person, the referee, interrupts (the only one in the group who acts as if she had brains).

The idiot typist starts looking for the "dammit" key. . . .

Alright. I admit it's a fanciful scenario and I might be exaggerating a bit, but it is very hard to get knowledgeable, intelligent humans to do stupid things with anything that approaches consistency; syntax testing is dominated by stupid input errors that you've carefully designed. Don't you just hate it when a keypunch operator acts smart and "corrects" your "mistakes?"

4.7. Ad-Lib Tests

Whenever you run a formal system test there's always someone in the crowd who wants to try ad-lib tests. And almost always, the kind of test they want to ad-lib is an input-syntax error test. I used to object to ad-libbing, because it didn't prove anything—I thought. It doesn't prove anything substantive about the system, assuming you've done a good job of testing—which is why I used to object to it. It may save time to object to ad-lib tests, but it's not politic. Ad-libbing does prove you have confidence in the system and the test. Because a system wide functional demonstration should have been through a dry-run in advance, the actual test execution is largely ceremonial (or should be) and the ad-libbers are part of the ceremony, just as hecklers are part of the ball game—it adds color to the scene.

You should never object if the system's final recipient has cooked up a set of tests of his own. If they're carefully constructed, and well-documented, and all the rest, you should welcome yet another independent assault on the system's integrity. Ad-lib tests aren't like that. The customer has a hotshot operator who's earned a reputation for crashing any system in under two minutes, and she's itching to get her mitts on yours. There's no prepared set of tests, so you know it's going to be ad-libbed. Agree to the ad-libbing, but only after all other tests have been done. Here's what happens:

1. 90% to 95% of the ad-lib tests will be input strings with format violations, and the system will reject them as it should.
2. Most of the rest are good strings that look bad. The system will accept the strings and do as it was told to do, but the ad-lib tester won't recognize it. It will take a lot of explanation to satisfy the customer that it was a bona fide cockpit error.
3. A few seemingly good strings will be correctly rejected because of a correlation problem between two field values or a state dependency. These will also take a lot of explanation.
4. At least once, the ad-lib tester will shout "Aha!" and claim that the system was wrong. It will take days to dig out the documentation that shows that the way the system behaves for that case is precisely the way the customer insisted it behave—over the designer's objections.
5. Another time the ad-lib tester will shout "Aha!" but, because the inputs weren't documented and because nonprinting characters were used, it won't be possible to reproduce the effect. The ad-lib tester will be forever convinced that the system has a flaw.
6. There may be one problem, typically related to an interpretation of a specification ambiguity, whose resolution will probably be trivial.

This may be a bit harsh to the ad-lib testers of the world, but such testing proves little or nothing if the system is good, if it's been properly tested from unit level on up, and if there has been good in-house quality control. If ad-lib tests do prove something, then the system's so shaky and buggy that it deserves the worst that can be thrown at it.

5. HIGHER-ORDER FORMAT THINKING

Just as highly state-dependent formats and formats with many field interactions are not amenable to syntax-directed testing, there are opportunities for designing tests based on syntax thinking, even though the processing in question doesn't appear to have anything to do with formats or syntax. Here are a few examples:

1. The system uses an internal undeclared language for transaction control. The internal language has formats and syntax. Test the scheduler/executive and language interpreter as format processors whose "inputs" are steps in the transaction-control tables.
2. A system wide interprocess-communication convention has been established. Isn't that a mini-language? A preprocessor has been implemented to verify that the convention is followed. Test it by syntax-testing thinking.
4. An offline data-base generator package is used to create the data base. It has a lot of fields to look at and many rules to follow. More syntax to check.
5. Any internal format used for interprocess communications that does not consist of a simple, fixed-field format should be treated to a syntax test.

6. SUMMARY

1. Syntax testing begins with a validated format specification. That may be half the work of designing syntax tests.
2. Express the syntax in a formal language such as BNF.
3. Design syntax tests level by level from top to bottom making only one error at a time, one level at a time, leaving everything else as correct as possible.
4. Test the valid cases.
5. Concentrate on delimiters, especially paired delimiters, and delimiter errors that could cause syntactic ambiguities.
6. Test field-value errors and state dependencies.
7. Cut multiple-error conditions sharply at two and three simultaneous errors. Look for the bugs along the baseboards and in the corners.
8. Take advantage of the design to simplify the test.
9. Don't forget the valid cases.
10. Document copiously and prepare all inputs on paper tape if possible.
11. Give the ad-lib testers the attention they crave and deserve.
                         AND
12. Don't forget the valid cases.

8

DATA-BASE-DRIVEN TEST DESIGN

1. SYNOPSIS

The data-base documentation is a rich source of test ideas. It can be used to create tests and in support of quality assurance.

2. THE DATA BASE

2.1. Size and Scope

Systems are tending toward ever larger and more complicated data bases. As an example, a communication system might have 300 different kinds of tables. Each table has from 10 to 200 fields with an average of 20 fields per table. The fields range from single bits to multiple characters. Consider transaction-control blocks as an example. There may be a different version and interpretation of the fields for each transaction type and also fields that are common to all transactions. A data type need not have a physical existence until it is used. It is defined by data-base declarations but space is not allocated to it until needed. Examples of dynamically allocated tables include queue blocks, buffer blocks, and transaction-control blocks. Examples of statically allocated tables include device-status tables, processing-status tables, code-conversion tables, and transaction-definition tables. Some have only one copy, such as an equipment roster, while others, such as status-tables for individual devices, have many copies. Large complicated data bases have justifiably become the vogue because:

1. Low-cost main and mass memory has made online storage of large data bases feasible.
2. The high cost of software, which now dominates system costs, has led to the development of more generalized software, which is particularized through parameters and data stored in tables.

3. It has always been possible to trade processing code for data. Data-base maintenance is generally easier than code maintenance.
4. Shifting functions from code to tables provides a more flexible system, which is easier to modify and test.
5. The applications are getting more complicated. All other factors aside, this alone has made large data bases inevitable.

2.2. The Data Dictionary

We've assumed that the data base is centrally controlled, that there is at least one person on the project responsible for defining and distributing all data-base information. That information is documented in a **data dictionary**. It is a listing of all the tables in the system; the size of every table in characters, bits, words; the location and interpretation of every field, and if appropriate, every value of the field; the mnemonics by which each table and each field is accessed, and all aliases for those mnemonics; the field type, such as integer, bit, BCD, pointer, and so on; access restrictions for reading, writing, modification, and associated prerequisities; a cross reference to all routines that access the field and the table; and anything else that may help one to understand the use and meaning of every item in the data base. The data dictionary is maintained throughout the development cycle and beyond as carefully as the code's documentation is maintained. It is a *designed* structure. It is not allowed to just grow or accumulate.

One of the reasons that projects must have a data dictionary and data-base specialists to create it is that data declarations should be centrally controlled. If they are, many integration problems will be avoided. Also, in some programming languages, designing the data declarations is as difficult as designing the code. When the source language provides excellent facilities for data-base definition, it is inevitable that a significant part of the language's syntax will be related to data definition and initialization. Usually, the format and syntax of data declarations are different from that of normal code. Furthermore, it is unlikely that the typical programmer will ever use more than a few features of that part of the language. Consequently, only a data-base specialist is likely to become familiar with the full scope of the language's features with respect to data definitions.

Data-base driven tests can only be designed when there is a formal data dictionary. If the system is complicated and the project's scope comparable to that of our model project, and if there is no centralized data-base control, there will probably be so many bugs that a well-designed test will aggravate, rather than alleviate, the anxieties over the inevitable—that the system probably won't work and certainly not on time and certainly not within the projected budget.

2.3. Objective of Data-Base-Driven Test Design

Data-base-driven test design is not a test of the data base but rather the use of the data base as a source of ideas for testing the system. While derived from the technical details of the data base's structure, the test approach and objectives are distinctly functional. The tests derived by this approach are best suited to the verification of functional requirements as set down in a system specification. Furthermore, data-base-driven test design is more a quality assurance method, where the importance is in the doing, as contrasted to a pure test design method, where the importance is in the product (but is still, nevertheless, important for the doing). As a quality assurance method, it is a continuing process that begins early in the project's life and continues until the end. The peak of this activity occurs shortly after most of the system's tables and data structures have been designed and formally set down in a controlled document.

The data structures are a rich source of test design material at the unit level. The identification of correlated and dependent variables in conjunction with path testing is inherently related to testing based on data structures. Similarly, input-data-validation testing also has a data-base concern. However, where those kinds of tests tend to focus on a single routine, or a common front-end data-validation routine, the kinds of tests discussed in this chapter examine all routines in the system and their interactions—as do all function-based tests.

The principles of data-base driven testing are simple:*

1. Examine every item of functional significance in the data base for conformance to the system's functional objectives.
2. Find all contradictions in the data base and get them resolved by the designers.
3. Follow up to see that all such contradictions are resolved.
4. Design tests to confirm that the knottier contradictions have been properly resolved.

A comment about these objectives: if one intended to do the above completely, it would be a hopeless and endless task. You have to be

---

*There's an old proposal about how to solve the Soviet submarine menace—you boil the ocean, and all the submarines come up to cool off and are easily destroyed. This may sound like an ocean-boiling proposal, but it really isn't as hard to do as all that.

comfortable with the thought that the method will pay off statistically and that the greatest value is in bugs prevented rather than in bugs caught. It is possible to work in a functional area for weeks, postulate hundreds of test cases, catch dozens of problems, earn your pay several times over in prevented bugs, and yet not design a single actual test.

3. THE PROCESS

3.1. Overview and Prerequisites

The most important prerequisite is that there be at least one person on the test team with deep and broad knowledge of the application and sufficient knowledge of the substantive issues of programming to be able to talk intelligently with other programmers and designers. In short, the key person should be a senior designer. Furthermore, I don't think that this method can work too well if the test team is not to some extent independent of the design team. Because direct, open, informal access to the designers is also an essential prerequisite, the test team must also be resident; an independent, resident, competent, test team is the essential prerequisite to this approach. The approach consists of the following steps, each of which are discussed in further detail in the sequel:

1. Read the project's technical documentation and the functional specification, especially the data dictionary.
2. As you read, create a master file of cross-references among the various documents, their intentions, and their meanings.
3. Organize the file by splitting and merging functional areas, grouping problems and requirements in such a way as to make actual and potential contradictions obvious.
4. Discuss all apparent contradictions with the data-base designers and software designers.
5. Because most contradictions involve misconceptions between two or more persons, stage a friendly confrontation and act as referee.
6. When the contradiction has been resolved, follow it up and design tests that are intended to confirm the resolution of the contradiction.

3.2. Read The Documentation

Start by reading the functional specification in detail. As you read, create index cards (see Section 3.3. below for details) that correspond in tiny detail to each and every functional requirement that will be handled by software. It pays to have designed an overall structure for the tests that are to be created. If possible, let your test categories correspond to the specification sections. The time it takes to do this is about two to three times as long as it would take you to read the specification at a normal rate. If it took you a week to read, this effort would take three or four weeks. Dull work, but rewarding.

Most properly designed systems have a high-level internal technical specification that deals with the overall system architecture, the data-base structure, the identification of major subsystems and their roles, and so on. This document should also be read, just like the functional specification was read, meticulously, one item at a time. However, in reading this document, you are not interested in how the design is going to work but just in what the designers think the system is supposed to do, which may or may not match the specification—don't worry about that for now. Just read the design spec and make up cards for each point—another week or two of work. It's important at this stage not to get bogged down in how the system works and not to get involved in any form of technical critique—even if deserved, even if you believe that the technical approach hasn't a hope in hell of working. Contact the designers only to clarify technical points related to functions, possible differences in terminology from section to section, clarifications, and so on.

If you are tracking the design team correctly, a reasonable semblance of a useful data dictionary should exist by now. There's no point in starting this process until a few weeks before the first official version of the data dictionary is released. Read the data dictionary as you read the other documents. Read every table and every field and understand what it is. Each table in the data dictionary should have the identification of the designer who created it. Ignore any fields that are clearly of only internal significance. Create a card for every field that has obvious functional significance and mark those whose functional significance is tenuous or indirect. Talk to the table's designer to resolve the ambiguities. Don't worry if you make a mistake or two. As you do this, ideas will come to you concerning tests and scenarios—jot them down on a card. Section 4 has more details on how to get those ideas.

Finally, read the data declarations and the equate files. If you are lucky enough to be testing a software system in which the data dictionary is automatically maintained and results in the automated production of the data declarations, then much of this work is done for you. The main point of examining the equate files is that an object could have different names in different parts of the documentation and code. The equate files tell you which ones are actually identical (or are supposed to be). With such features, there is no need to manually check for structural contradictions between equated variables—the utility software or the source-language processor will do it for you.

3.3. The Master File

The master file is a card index of all items of functional interest in the specification, the designer's version of the specification (the primary design document), the data dictionary, and all other documentation of interest. I use a large rotary card file that holds about 3000 "3 × 5" cards. You can get rotary card files for larger or smaller cards. If they're smaller, you won't be able to get enough information on the card. If they're bigger (such as "5 × 7"), you'll be tempted to write a dissertation on each one. A small computer can be very helpful with the mechanics, but don't be trapped into the design of a special-purpose data management system. Keep it flexible. Having gone through this process a few times, I've also found it convenient to use form-feed cards. These are available in single-card versions (one card per row), double cards, and triple cards. I use mostly the double-card version, because as you'll see, you almost always want to make up two cards per item of interest. The form-feed cards are important. You will have to fill out many many cards. Each time you have to load a new card into your typewriter, you lose a few seconds, and more important, the thought you had is gone and lost forever. Form-feed cards also prevent backaches, and it's hard to concentrate on deep functional issues when your back hurts—I mean real backaches, not metaphorical ones—surprising how tiring it can be to reach for a new card every few seconds. Naturally, you're lost if you can't touch-type, so I should have made that a prerequisite also—as is a very good, new, correcting typewriter or alternatively a high quality personal computer such as an HP-85. It may seem strange to spend so much verbiage on nitty-gritty details like the kind of card to use, how to type them, and all that—however, it is a gruesome job, this job of creating the master file. It is a job no machine can do, and if not done to the requisite level of detail, it might as well not be done. It also takes several weeks of hard work. A discouraging several weeks in which you feel sure that it's useless work, can't possibly be of any benefit, and it hurts my shoulders like the dickens. If you don't have the right tools, and the right environment, easy-to-use cards and all that, you won't do it—you'll find some reason not to, in which case, you might as well skip to Chapter 9.

Still with me? Good! As you read the documents, point by point, make up a card for each point—one card per point—and keep the points small, not something like "process input transaction," or "validate format," but all steps involved in input transaction processing and every field in that format and just what it is that the user wants validated. Almost everything you read will, or should, raise questions. Consequently, you create not just one card for the item, but the following cards:

CARD 1—THE REQUIREMENTS CARD(S)

- Specification reference by paragraph, section, subsection, and so on., if derived from the specification. Design-document section reference if from the design document. Table and field identity if derived from the data dictionary or equate files.
- A very short, written statement of the requirement or the function or the values associated with that item—very short. For example: "Val no V's before Q's in FMT-7."
- Anything at all that pops into your head. Don't worry about whether or not it makes sense. Trust your intuition and get it down on paper.
- Any ideas you might get or any inspiration you might have for a test concerned with that item.

CARD 2—THE QUESTION CARDS

- Some convenient identifier to relate it back to card 1.
- Any question or issue that needs clarification because you don't understand the spec, or the data-base document, or because you're not sure if the item has direct functional significance.
- The name of the person most likely to give you a rational answer—first names are good—if you can't do this process on a first-name basis, you probably won't be able to do it at all. I put the name at the top of the card.
- If there's more than one question, make up a card for each question.

CARD 3—THE WHAT-IF CARDS

- These are also questions that are not intended to inform you, but that you intend to pose to the designers; they all begin with, "What if . . ." or "What happens when . . ." These are intended to be nasty questions.

Sometimes you may have to create up to 20 cards per item, but most of the time, it's just 2 cards. Wait until you've accumulated about 100 to 200 cards. Then pull the form out, fold it back and forth, and separate the cards. Then file them in the rotary card file by subject areas. Don't worry if they're not absolutely right. When in doubt, create another card and file it in the other subject area also. That'll happen quite often. You'll find that a given functional requirement or a data-base item cuts across 3 categories—good, make up 3 cards. And don't worry if you're wrong. It's better to create a few extra cards, some of which are wrong, than to miss a subtle interaction.

What you have done by this terrible process, is to create a crude, unsorted master cross-reference of the specification, to the design, to the data base, to the code, and to whatever else you put into the kettle. It's not a job that can be done by a nontechnical person, such as a secretary. It's not a job that can be done by junior personnel, who do not understand the full scope of the functional requirements and how one could go about designing your kind of system.

3.4. Data-Base Solitaire

I call it data-base solitaire because most of the cards come from the data base and organizing this crude index file is a solitary game. It can't be done by committees—they waste too much time over nonsubstantive differences of opinion and don't realize that the object of the game is to get the file organized and it doesn't really matter which organization you use, as long as it's reasonably consistent.

The file is organized into the following categories:

1. FUNCTIONAL—The major functional requirement categories are arranged so that each one is about the same size. I judge by the number of cards. If one of my earlier areas had 500 cards, I break it down into equal-size areas of 150 to 200 cards. If an area has only one or two cards, I drop the category altogether or dump the cards into a miscellaneous section.
2. TEST CARDS—These are cards that correspond to specific test ideas. This is a separate file (on the same rotary file) which corresponds to the functional cards. You can also keep these with the functional cards. I think it works equally well both ways.
3. CLARIFICATION QUESTIONS—Organize these by name of the person who is most likely to answer your questions.
4. WHAT-IF CARDS—Organized by the names of the persons most likely to be the targets of the "what if's."
5. TEST-ISSUE CARDS—These are cards concerning the design of tests. They usually start with "How in blazes can I test . . . ."
6. CONTRADICTION CARDS—Organized by the names of the persons most likely to resolve what you believe is a contradiction. There are always at least two cards here: one for each party to the contradiction. The specification, which represents the customer's interests, should also be a "person."
7. DON'T-KNOW CARDS—Where I put any cards that I can't find a place for.
8. PROCRASTINATION CARDS—Where I put cards that contain issues that I can't resolve at the moment, or that I'm too lazy to resolve at the

moment, but which I know can't be left unresolved indefinitely. Keep this file small. There are two ways to do this, both of them effective—resolve the issue yourself, or delegate to a subordinate.

When you first start to play data-base solitaire, you'll have mostly functional cards and clarification-question cards. As the process develops, you will have more test cards, what-if cards, and contradiction cards. This is a continuing process, and don't expect to get it finished all at once. Because at the beginning of the game you are still struggling to organize things, take the biggest batch of functional cards (I start by having all cards in the functional slot, and I move them to the other categories only later) or the functional area which you are most comfortable with and start subdividing. A system should be subdivided into about 10 to 20 areas, and each area into about 10 subareas. With 2000 cards initially, this will work out to about 10 to 20 cards per subarea. Once the major and minor functional categories are established, you can break out the clarification, what-if, and contradiction cards by name, in preparation for the next step—the interviews. But before the interviews, read the clarification-question cards. You'll find that many of them are now clear. Go back to the specification or the design or the data dictionary and attempt your own clarification. I find that about half of my technical questions answer themselves just by the fact that a bunch of clarification cards show up in the same subcategory as the specification reference and the data-dictionary entry. There's no point in wasting the designer's time with such questions.

3.5. The Interviews

There are two, possibly three, different interviews involved. The purpose of the first interview is to obtain a clarification of any unresolved questions you might have. The purpose of the second interview is to ask the what-if questions, and the purpose of the third interview is to get the material you need to set up a confrontation for contradictions.

The clarification interview is simple. I walk into the designer's office and ask him or her the questions, one at a time. I have the cards in my pocket and a batch of blank cards in another pocket. You'll never know what questions may be raised as a result of this conversation. The interviews are informal. If you get bogged down in memos and formal documentation, it's not going to work. I always conduct the first interview in the designer's office—it's a territorial issue. You are the novice coming to the guru for knowledge. We all like to talk about our work. You can't be harmful if you come in asking, "Please help me understand . . . ." This is *not* the time to bring up contradictions and what-if cards. A cooperative designer will give you an answer, an explanation, and will identify further references in the specification or design documentation that will help you understand. However, be careful. Some designers feel that if you don't understand all the gory technical details of their work, then to hell with you. Or they'll point you to some awesome document that would take you months to read. You are trying to relate things back to the functional requirements. If you get bogged down in a morass of technical details, the item's significance is probably internal and technical and the item doesn't relate in a useful way (from a test design point of view) to the functional requirements. You must control the interview so that it doesn't deteriorate into a learned discourse on the implementation. Keep steering back and back again to the functions. As soon as you see that it is not a direct functional issue, put the card in your pocket (you'll tear it up later out of the designer's sight) and go to the next card. Each of these sessions should take about an hour at most. If one person is the key to many areas, it's better to hold several sessions a few days apart than hit that person for hours at a time.

The second interview is totally different. This is the what-if interview. I think it's only fair to warn the designers about this one. I type each what-if on a separate card. I then drop the stack (not more than ten at a time) on the designers' desks when they're not looking or are out of the office. We've established an understanding and some ground rules. Each card corresponds to a nasty or tricky test case. The designer reads the cards and jots the answers down on the back. Most questions, about 90% in a good system, can be answered this way. I check back a few hours later to see if they've been answered. You must be a little bit of a pest in this phase. It's also understood that the cards *must* be answered and returned. Read the answers. Here are the kinds of answers you can get and what to do with them.

1. *A satisfactory answer.* Put the card into the test-card file if the issue seems important enough to test. Otherwise, leave the card in the functional file.
2. *No answer.* The issue remains to be answered and will be in the future. It's understood that there should be an approximate date when the issue is to be resolved. Get the date from the designer during the interview. Put it in an open-issue file which you check periodically for resolution.
3. *No answer. No future resolution.* Save the card for the interview.
4. *Unsatisfactory answer.* It seems to contradict the specification. Save the card for the interview.
5. *Contradictory answer.* It contradicts an answer or a statement you've marked for another designer. Create the contradiction cards and keep this one for the interview.
6. *You don't understand the answer.* Save the card for the interview.

You should have only a half-dozen cards for second interviews, and a few that concern questions that are too complicated to detail on a card. Take the contradiction cards along for this interview also. The first thing to do is to ask for a confirmation of the information on the contradiction cards. If a designer has made a statement, and you know there is a contradiction, don't confront the person with the contradiction just yet. Ask for clarification and confirmation. You'll probably hear something like:

"I told you that already,"

To which you can reply, "Yes, but I wasn't sure. Please say it again—dumb little me didn't understand it last time around."

You will get the confirmation, so mark the card as confirmed and hold it for the confrontation (discussed in Section 3.6). After all the contradictions have been confirmed, you're ready for the real part of the second interview.

You are no longer the meek acolyte seeking knowledge from the guru, but the devil incarnate, come to challenge, hassle, trouble, and destroy. Ask your what-if questions and *demand* satisfactory answers. "Show me how it works!" Force the programmer to cover the missing path in his mind. Push until both of you understand the problem, the issue, and the resolution. But because the designer is more expert than you, expect to "lose" 75% of the time. Expect to be wrong; expect to have raised a tempest in a teapot; expect to have misunderstood often, and don't be bothered by it. If you're usually right, it's an abominable design and probably doesn't need testing to prove it won't work.

The results of the second interview are interesting. Some programmers will thank you (assuming it's one of those 25% of cases when you're right) for having discovered the bug or deficiency. Some will invent a resolution on the spot, and it will hold water, but they'll not give you the satisfaction of letting you know you've caught a bug. Some will clam up and stop talking. And a few, a thankfully small few, will throw you out of their office. Don't be intimidated, give them a few days to cool off, and raise the question again (and again, and again, and again, if necessary). Eventually, they'll be convinced that you're not going to give up and they'll come around. In extreme cases, you may have to write an official memorandum concerning a design deficiency. Sometimes the programmer will admit that you're right, but the issue must be resolved at a higher administrative level. Then you may also need an official memo to point out a design deficiency.

Another variation on this game if you have the right kind of people, is to play the old policeman's game of good guy/bad guy. Good guy asks for information and education as well as confirmation of positions regarding contradictions from which bad guy constructs the nasty questions. Afterward good guy can go back and commiserate with the designer. If good guy/bad guy works for you, try switching roles around to keep the design team off guard as to who'll be who the next time. You can match the roles to the personalities involved. A woman may be the best bad guy for a certain man while for another, she would be better in the good guy role. Similarly, a man may work in some ways for a woman, or sex may have nothing to do with it. I use every psychological advantage I can because all bugs are inherently rooted in the human psyche and you need every trick you can use to exorcise them. Incidentally, don't bother keeping this method a secret from the designers. They eventually catch on to the game, but that doesn't seem to diminish its effectiveness at all.

3.6. The Confrontation

You have determined that there is a contradiction in the data base or in the minds of two or more programmers. It's time to arrange a confrontation. Time to switch roles again. This time, you play the part of a referee—an impartial, incorruptible officiator who does not care how the conflict is resolved, as long as it is resolved quickly and correctly. Do it now! Let's say there's a conflict and you've got one designer's version of it and have got it confirmed. Go back to the other designer and get an *immediate* reconfirmation (you've got the cards in your pocket). Get the two of them together as soon as possible. I like to use hallways for this. It's neutral territory. My office is too intimidating, and either designer's office gives one of them an advantage; do it in the halls. The conversation goes, "Bill says . . ., but you, Jane say not. . . . It doesn't seem to matter, from the point of view of functional requirements, which way it goes, and here's the specification reference, which is ambiguous or just doesn't say. I don't care how it's done, but get it done." Stick around long enough to get an answer or to be convinced that they are on their way to a resolution of the conflict. Put the cards with the date of the confrontation and a verbal statement of the resolution (if any, at that time) into a follow-up file. Follow it up and look for a change in the documentation. Resort to official memos and design deficiency notices only if it seems that the problem has been swept under the rug.

3.7. The Resolution

The result of the interviews or confrontations must be:

1. You understand the issue.
2. Both programmers in a conflict understand the issue.

3. A design change that will resolve the issue has been implemented or scheduled for implementation.

Design tests whose difficulty is proportional to the apparent conflict and the effort required to resolve the issue. If it is a simple issue, only simple tests are required, and no special tests are needed if the functional issue is covered elsewhere. If the resolution of the problem was protracted, if it required a lot of agonizing, redesign, memos, or even meetings, test the issue into the ground. Design functional tests that will confirm the proper resolution of the issue. Go over those tests with the designer as a final confirmation of everybody's understanding—especially if it involved a contradiction. Then both designers should confirm that the test will effectively demonstrate the effect.

3.8. Scope and Effort

Our model project will last two years and consume 40 man-years of labor. The total effort in independent functional test design and execution will take approximately five man-years. Unit testing, integration testing, and system testing are not included in independent testing but are part of the 40 man-years of effort. Creating the master file and all the cards, playing data-base solitaire, and setting up for the interviews will take on the order of two to three months for one person. The interviews, resolution of conflicts, and the rest will take an additional three to six man-months but can be divided among various members of the test team. The entire game gradually loses effectiveness as project emphasis shifts from design, to coding, to unit testing, and to integration testing. After one year on a two-year project, the game's practically useless. Once past the initial round of this kind of testing, you reach a point of diminishing returns, because integration testing will be more efficient at discovering the kind of bug that data-base-driven testing can discover.

4. SPECIFICS

4.1. Simple Fields and Parameters

These are fields which are not dependent on other fields, have individual meaning, and can be easily related back to functional requirements. All the checks which applied to data in individual-routine testing, such as in path sensitizing, or in data-validation testing apply here also. Because these fields relate to the functional requirements in a fairly direct way, given a field value, it should be straightforward to design a transaction or operation which will force that value to occur. In most cases, if the field has a range limit or excluded values, it should not be possible to create an input that will exceed the range or achieve the excluded values; data-validation checks should have eliminated the possibility. However, if it appears that an input value could force the field's value into a forbidden case, then the input should be tried, and the system should be expected to reject it. Here are some examples:

1. *Numerical Fields*—Boundary values as for all other data—minimum, less than minimum, one more than minimum, typical, one less than maximum, maximum, one more than maximum, excluded values, and boundaries near excluded values.
2. *Bit Fields*—All 2^n combinations are not needed. Typically, you only need one bit set at a time, one bit reset at a time, none set, and all set.
3. *Case Control Fields*—All cases.
4. *Boundary Checks*—What checks you use here depends on the way the computer accesses data. Assume that it's a 32-bit machine with word, half-word, and character addressing. Any field that doesn't fit on one of these natural boundaries should be given additional checks for values that come close, particularly for values that could cause overflow into another adjacent word. For example, a 16-bit numerical field spans two characters on two different words. While the range is 0 to 65,536, because of the boundary, 255 and 256 should also be tried. Variable-length fields should always be tested with values that force the minimum and maximum length. Also attempt to exceed the maximum length. If field-access macros are used or if the source language is strongly typed, this kind of check will prove little or nothing.

4.2. Semantic Shifts

A **semantic shift** occurs when the same item has different meanings to different people. This is a common source of bugs. You find this in the data-base check when a field has two different names and has been equated by an equate statement in the declarations. If the cards have been properly laid out, you should have created a card for the aliases that identified the cross-reference (therefore, the names should point to each other and also to different functions in the functional specification). For example, say that you have a security field and a priority field, and that they have been equated.

Because they refer to what appears to be different functional requirements, it is apparent that there is a difference of opinion regarding the field's meaning.*

Excavating semantic shifts is not a machine job because we have no computers that can say that "security" and "priority" are or are not the same. They might be in some systems or even in some parts of one system and not in another part of the same system. When you spot what appears to be a semantic shift, try to find a counterexample from the point of view of the user. A low-priority, high-security input, for example. Any combination that does not match the equated values must be explained by the designers. If the boundary values and excluded values do not match exactly, you can be sure that it is a real bug. Barring such obvious inconsistencies, the history of the semantic shift can give you insight into what kinds of tests to design. Most semantic shifts are not bugs but may become bugs in the future. Here are some possible histories for semantic shifts:

1. There was a time, earlier in the project, when the semantic shift did not exist, but the separation of the two functions occurred later. There should be two different fields. The counterexamples should spot that.
2. There were two fields originally and the designers knew it. They examined all combinations and came to the conclusion that they could equate the values, even though it didn't make functional sense. They could do it, but a routine here and there had to be "adjusted," "corrected," or "coerced" to make the match work. It's a bad idea. It'll be a hellish maintenance task in the future. Furthermore, there will be at least one programmer who's working under the assumption that the two fields are different. Test with counterexamples and supposedly forbidden combinations that "just can't happen."
3. The confusion is caused by a bad specification. For example, the specification discusses both input and output formats under the heading of "format" and assumes that you know that in this application they are not identical. Or else, the difference is referred to in a subsection under "Operator Training" which states: "Operators will receive training in the preparation of input formats and the interpretation of output formats, as specified in Appendix Q, and MIL-8977.098." Because neither the input- nor output-processing designer reads the section on operator training, it's

---

*The most dramatic semantic shift I ever saw caused a multimillion-dollar rocket and satellite to destroy themselves on the launch pad. A hardware designer saw two switches, the first was labeled "initiate final-stage separation sequence," while the other was labeled "initiate test of final-stage separation sequence." He wired them in parallel in an attempt to improve reliability. So during the countdown, they started the final-stage checkout, and the final-stage rockets ignited; the protective covers flew off the satellite, and it sprouted antennae and tried to go into orbit—a hundred feet off the ground. Semantic shifts can be like that.

no wonder the semantic shift gets in. However, the programmer who's doing the training-mode module never assumes that the two meanings are the same. A card that was generated from the "Operator Training" section should have ended up in the "Input-Processing" section and the "Output-Processing" section of the card index to bring the contradiction to your attention.

4. Not everybody speaks the same language. What does "vector," "array," "index," "pointer," "queue," "recovery," "checkpoint," "benchmark," "overlay," "executive," "file," "direct," "indirect," and "random" mean to you? I've run into at least two different meanings for each of these terms—sometimes on the same project. One person uses the phrase "indirect input vector pointer," another uses "indirect vector input pointer," a third person uses "indirect pointer input vector," or "input vector indirect pointer"—see what I mean? Then the data-base coordinator equates them all—glorious bug. It is hoped that most of these different meanings will be caught by structural differences that will prevent the equating of the two, three, four, or five fields.

The worst semantic shifts occur between specifications and designers. The resulting design is consistent, but wrong. Treat the specification as if it were written in a foreign language and translated into English by a person who understood neither the foreign language, nor English, nor the application. Distrust all jargon—it's far more likely to be local than universal. Translate technicalities into English (or your native language). Ask all parties to the equate what "indirect pointer vector input" really means in functional terms. Be *very* stupid and dense when you ask such questions. People may be impatient at first, but after a while, they'll realize that you're not so stupid after all.

Semantic shifts are not common but they deserve attention because they are very expensive. They tend to have ugly diffused implications, and correcting them may mean modifying many routines, the data base, or fundamental design assumptions. If you don't catch them now, they'll probably remain in the system until the customer's acceptance test is run.

4.3. Type Changes

Whenever a field is accessed in different ways, under different structural assumptions, there has been a type change (e.g., when a field is treated as a bit field, character field, or integer in several different parts of a program). Assembly language programs and older programming languages are vulnerable to this kind of shift. It's really a kind of semantic shift, but it merits separate consideration. Any type change is suspect, although it may not be a bug. The only nice thing about type changes is that usually you're able to spot them because two fields, which are described as different (e.g., bit versus character) but occupy the same space, are equated. Given these elementary kinds of type changes you should look for a more basic semantic shift behind it. Strongly typed languages such as Pascal solve this problem by spotting such inconsistencies.

4.4. Representation Changes

A functional element is represented in several different ways in the data base. For example, you could have a case variable that specified priority as high, medium, low, routine, ultra, and urgent. Elsewhere in the data base there is another priority field which is numerical, and priorities are listed as 1 to 12. In a third place, there is a binary field with four priority bits. They all appear to refer to "priority," but they appear to be incompatible. The following must be established:

1. Are the total number of distinct cases the same? If not, why not?
2. Are the excluded values the same?
3. Can you arrange them in a consistent manner, one for one, with the excluded values corresponding?
4. Do all the values correspond to functionally meaningful cases?

If you have three such fields, then you must check this three ways: A against B, B against C, and A against C. For four fields you would have to make six sets of comparisons.

Such representation changes do not necessarily imply bugs. The fourth question is the key. You might find that there are six external priorities, but sixteen internal priorities, some of which match the external ones and some of which don't. Furthermore, the internal priority of a transaction type might not be consistent with the external priority, but this does not mean there is a bug. For example, external priorities could be deliberately reversed for some phases of internal processing in the interest of processing efficiency or some other technical consideration. While there may be no bug, this kind of representation change must be confusing; consequently, it's likely that some programmers have made a mistake with respect to one representation or another. Use test cases that force apparent reversals, inconsistent boundary values, and inconsistent excluded values.

4.5. Splatters, Mergers, and Overlaps

Several fields are defined that cover the same physical space. There is clearly a semantic shift involved but also a structure change. Field A is the lower three bits of one word. Field B is the upper four bits of the adjacent word, and C is some field that includes all or part of both of them, and all of them appear to relate to things that have functional significance. Ask the following questions:

1. Are the ranges of the several fields consistent as to minimum, maximum, and excluded values?
2. Can you force cases that correspond to the inconsistencies?
3. Find functional cases that do not fit the overlap. What prevents these impossible transactions?

4.6. Access Changes

This applies primarily to tables that have multiple entries and multiple fields per entry. You can access such tables in one of two ways: use an offset that corresponds to the field location within the entry and increment by entry size, or go to the entry and then access the specific field. A routine that had to access a single field of all entries would use the first method, while a routine that had to access several fields in the same entry would probably use the second method. Such differences in access methods are usually not due to bugs. Furthermore, that kind of simple access change may be very difficult to spot in the data-base documentation. You can spot this sort of change, however, when the entries and fields are accessed by an index or by a combination of direct access and indexes. The key is to find all the indexes or pointers by which the field is accessed. This is documented explicitly in a proper data-base dictionary or is supplied automatically through the use of field-access macros. In a higher-order language, the method of documentation, if any, may be more difficult to spot. You play the same game with the index that you play with individual fields: minimum and maximum boundaries, excluded values, and so on. Boundary mismatches are not necessarily bugs, but they should be investigated.

4.7. Dynamic Resources

Data-base items, particularly dynamically allocated resources, are used for many different purposes. Each usage has an associated set of field definitions.

But some fields, such as link fields, status fields, corresponding disc addresses, and other administrative fields are common to all uses. Typically, for any one resource, it is possible to describe a tree of nested data structures. The top of the tree (we draw trees upside down) has only those fields which are common to all uses. The next level down has the first kind of split, and so on, as shown in Figure 8-1.

Most of the fields will correspond to internal things and are therefore not good sources of questions. Offhand, without looking into how these resources are used, you can't tell which routines will use a given format. However, it's a safe bet that formats that are close to one another on the tree will be used for similar, and possibly interactive, purposes. Look for the same functional item stored in different ways or in different places in nearby formats. For example, a priority field is always represented as a two-character field in a half-dozen different formats that are on the same tree branches; however, in several places it appears in a different part of the format. It would be better if they were in the same location throughout, but if they're not, there's a high likelihood of confusion over which version to use where. Explore the use of the resource for each such field with the designers and see if you can create a transaction that will pass through more than one of these formats. There is a possibility of initialization problems, failure to move the field as required, picking up the wrong field, and so on. Use this as a starting point and continue to investigate conflicting locations farther and farther away on the tree. If you find a conflicting location for a functional field, and you can create a transaction that uses both of the conflicting locations, then by all means, include that transaction in your test. What may happen is that the representation will change in the interest of simplicity—perhaps as a result of your questions—but not all routines will be changed to match.

4.8. Inconsistent Hooks and Changes

One common data-base-related problem is the inconsistent implementation of future enhancements. A given transaction has at present 8 cases which are represented by a 3-bit field. The designer, thinking of future enhancements, implements a 4-bit field. So far so good. However, in a different representation, which is related to the same functional area, a single-character numerical field is used to represent the cases—the expansion concept is inconsistent. We expect programmers to provide "hooks" for future enhancements that can be foreseen. Memory is so cheap that there's no point in strapping yourself to save a bit here and there. A good data-base dictionary lists all such "hooks" by identifying reserved values, reserved bits, reserved characters, reserved codes, and so on. However, the degree to which the enhance-

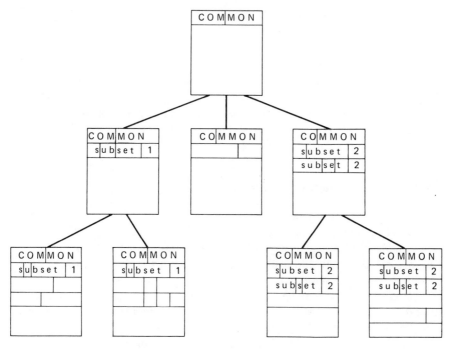

Figure 8-1. Dynamic Resource Structure.

ment is implemented is not usually controlled; the decision is left to the individual programmer, and that's the source of the problem.

A programmer may see how to implement the enhancement with respect to his routine. For that programmer, the hooks are real and there is no future enhancement to consider—it's already been implemented. No problem yet, but possibly a problem in the future. You should certainly try "reserved" cases, if they can be forced by a suitably structured transaction. The scenario, however, is not over. Later in the project, different hooks are put in or different functions are installed, which utilize the previously reserved space, and now the impossible case is possible, but wrong with respect to the program that had the hooks in early. A proper data dictionary management system will flag such changes, document them, and distribute them throughout the project. The individual designers should look at the data base to see if "their" fields were modified or used elsewhere or used in a different way, but they don't always do that. All changes in the data dictionary should be flagged from version to version. You cannot just look at the data dictionary once; like the programmers, you must check to see if any fields have changed in a way that is likely to cause trouble. Don't do this for all fields—only for those that have direct functional meaning. You should be tracking them anyhow to see if there have been any functional changes that would necessitate new test cases or obviate old ones. Read the data base and look for the changes. Compare the old version to the new and pay particular attention to reserved fields that are no longer reserved; to fields that were "to be determined" and have now been determined; to cases and values that are newly defined; and especially to cases, fields, and values that were defined and are no longer defined. If a new data-base dictionary comes out once a month, the entire scan can be done in about an hour.

5. OTHER USES AND OTHER SCOPES

It's not possible for one person or a small test group to do this process for a very large system. Luckily, large systems are subdivided into distinct subsystems and each of these has a data base. Do the data base test design for each subsystem separately and a high-level test design for only that part of the data base which is common to all subsystems.

The same principle can be used at lower levels, which are more closely tied to internal, technical issues. Within a program, say, there are data-base items that "belong" only to that program (whether or not they are in private space or in common space). That program has it's own functional specification, and consequently, has data items which have "functional" significance within that program's context. The same methodology can be applied, only the labor is less because the scope is smaller. At the lowest level, the individual programmers should ask themselves the same questions with respect to that part of the data base which is uniquely used by their programs.

6. SUMMARY

The data base of the typical system is a rich source of ideas that can lead you to test cases that would not be obvious either from a specification alone, a design document alone, or from purely structural considerations. A properly defined, designed, and maintained data dictionary is the principle source of the information needed to create such tests. The most important part of such test design, however, is the organization of the information into a copious and detailed cross-reference index, which if properly constructed, seems to expose potential contradictions by magic. Each contradiction must be investigated and resolved. The harder the resolution, the more important it is to construct system-level functional tests that probe the validity of the conflict's resolution.

9

DECISION TABLES AND
BOOLEAN ALGEBRA

1. SYNOPSIS

The functional requirements of some programs can be specified by a decision table. The decision-table representation is a useful basis for test design. The analysis of specification consistency and completeness can be done using boolean algebra. Boolean algebra can also be used as a basis for test design.

2. DECISION TABLES

2.1. Definitions and Notation

Table 9-1 is an example of a **limited-entry decision table**. It consists of four areas called the **condition stub**, the **condition entry**, the **action stub**, and the **action entry**. Each column of a decision table is a **rule** that specifies the conditions under which the actions named in the action stub will take place. The condition stub is a list of names of program decisions or tests. These could be direct decisions or the result of a more complicated process executed by a subroutine. Decisions are usually **binary**—that is, they can be reworded into questions that can be answered with a "YES" or "NO." Binary decisions are not a strict requirement, but things are generally simpler with binary decisions. A rule specifies the answer required of a decision for the rule to be satisfied. The required answer can be specified as "YES," "NO," or "I," which means that the result of the decision is **immaterial** to the satisfaction of the rule.

The **action stub** is a list of names of the actions the routine will take or initiate if the corresponding rule is satisfied. If the **action entry** is "YES," the action will take place; if "NO," the action will not take place. An immaterial entry (I) in the action stub is meaningless. Table 9-1 can be translated as follows:

CONDITION ENTRY

	RULE 1	RULE 2	RULE 3	RULE 4
DECISION 1	YES	YES	NO	NO
DECISION 2	YES	I	NO	I
DECISION 3	NO	YES	NO	I
DECISION 4	NO	YES	NO	YES
ACTION 1	YES	YES	NO	NO
ACTION 2	NO	NO	YES	NO
ACTION 3	NO	NO	NO	YES

CONDITION STUB (rows DECISION 1–4)
ACTION STUB (rows ACTION 1–3)

ACTION ENTRY

Table 9-1. An Example of a Decision Table.

a. Action 1 will take place if decisions 1 and 2 are satisfied and if decisions 3 and 4 are not satisfied (Rule 1), or if decisions 1, 3, and 4 are satisfied (Rule 2).

b. Action 2 will take place only if none of the decisions are satisfied (Rule 3).

c. Action 3 will take place if decision 1 is not satisfied and decision 4 is satisfied (Rule 4).

It is not obvious from looking at this specification whether or not all 16 possible combinations of the four decisions have been covered. In fact, they have not; a combination of YES, NO, NO, NO, for decisions 1 through 4 respectively, is not covered by these rules. In addition to the stated rules, therefore, an ELSE condition must be provided. The ELSE condition is a set of entries that specifies the default action when all other rules fail. The default case for Table 9-1 is shown in Table 9-2. Decision tables can be specified in specialized languages that will automatically create the default rules. Consequently, when programming in such languages, it is not necessary to make an explicit default specification. However, when decision tables are used as a tool for test case design and specification analysis, the default conditions must be explicitly specified or determined. If the set of rules covers all the combinations of YES/NO for the decisions, a default specification is not needed.

Decision tables are usually represented with only one action for each rule—although several rules could specify the same action. This can always

	RULE 5	RULE 6	RULE 7	RULE 8
DECISION 1	I	NO	YES	YES
DECISION 2	I	YES	I	NO
DECISION 3	YES	I	NO	NO
DECISION 4	NO	NO	YES	I
DEFAULT ACTION	YES	YES	YES	YES

Table 9-2. The Default Rules for Table 9-1.

be done. Suppose a rule specified two actions, say "1" and "2," you could then give the combination of actions a new name, say "4," and redraw the table. There is no need to force each rule to specify only one action in the use of decision tables; to do so could be confusing.

2.2. Decision-Table Processors and Implementation

Decision tables can be automatically translated into code and as such, constitute a higher-order language. The decision table's translator examines the specifications (given as a decision table) for consistency and completeness and fills in any default rules that may be required. The usual order of processing in the resulting object code is to first examine the first rule. If the rule is satisfied, the corresponding action takes place. Otherwise, the second rule is tried. This continues until either a satisfied rule results in an action or no rule is satisfied and the default action takes place. The actual code implemented could be complicated and could lead to an arrangement of decisions that does not correspond directly with the decision table, but which is more efficient of processing time and memory than a straightforward implementation might be.

Decision tables as a source language have the virtue of clarity, a direct correspondence to specified requirements, and maintainability. The principal deficiency is object-code inefficiency. There was a time when it was thought by some that the use of decision tables would herald a new era in programming. Their use, it was claimed, would eliminate most bugs and poor programming practices and would reduce testing to trivia. Such claims are rarely made now, but despite such former unrealistically high hopes, decision tables have become entrenched as a useful tool in the programmer's kit, particularly in business data processing.

2.3. Decision Tables as a Basis for Test Case Design

If a specification is given directly as a decision table, it follows that decision tables should be used for test case design. Similarly, if a program's logic is to be implemented as decision tables, decision tables should also be used as a basis for test case design. But if that's the case, the consistency and completeness of the decision table can and should be checked by the decision-table translation processor; therefore, there would be no need to design those test cases.

Even if you can specify the program's logic as a decision table, it is not always possible or desirable to implement the program as a decision table because the program's logical behavior is only part of its behavior. The program has to interface with other programs, there are restrictions, the decision-table language may not contain other needed facilities. Any of these reasons could be sufficient to reject a decision-table implementation. However, the use of a decision-table *model* to design test cases is warranted when:

1. The specification is given as a decision table or is readily converted to one.
2. The order in which the decisions are evaluated does not affect the interpretation of the rules or the resulting action—that is, any arbitrary permutation of the decision order will not, or should not, affect which action takes place.
3. The order in which the rules are evaluated does not affect the resulting action—that is, any arbitrary permutation of rules will not, or should not, affect which action takes place.
4. Once a rule has been satisfied and an action selected, no other rule need be examined.
5. If multiple actions can result from the satisfaction of a rule, the order in which the actions take place is immaterial.

What these seemingly restrictive conditions mean is that the action is selected strictly on the basis of the combination of decision values and nothing else. It might seem at first that these restrictions would eliminate many potential applications and many potential usages for test case design. However, despite external appearances, the order in which rules are evaluated is often immaterial. For example, if I use a cash machine, the card must be valid, I have to put in the right password, and there must be a sufficient balance in my account. It really doesn't matter in which order these decisions are made. The specific order chosen may be sensible in that it can reduce processing or increase efficiency, but the order is not an inherent part of the program's logic.

The above conditions have further implications: 1) the rules are complete in the sense that every combination of decision values, including the default combinations, are inherent in the decision table, and 2) the rules are consistent if and only if every combination of decision values results in only one action or set of actions. If the rules were inconsistent, that is if at least one combination of decision values was implicit in two or more rules, then the action that would take place could depend on the order in which the rules were examined in contradiction to Requirement 3 above. If the set of rules were incomplete, there could be a combination of input values for which no action, normal or default, were specified and the routine's action would be unpredictable.

2.4. Expansion of Immaterial Cases

Immaterial entries (I) are the source of most contradictions in decision tables. If a decision's value (YES/NO) is immaterial in a rule, the satisfaction of the rule does not depend on the answer. It does not mean that the case is impossible. For example, say the rules are:

R1—"If the persons are male and over 30, then they shall receive a 15% raise."

R2—"But if the persons are female, then they shall receive a 10% raise."

It's clear that age is material for determining a male's raise, but immaterial for determining a female's raise. No one would seriously suggest that females either under or over 30 are impossible. If there are n decisions there must be 2^n cases to consider. You find the cases by expanding the immaterial cases. This is done by converting each I entry into a pair of entries, one with a YES and the other with a NO. Each I entry in a rule doubles the number of cases in the expansion of that rule. Rule 2 in Table 9-1 contains one I entry and will therefore expand into two equivalent subrules. Rule 4 contains two I entries and will therefore expand into four subrules. The expansion of Rules 2 and 4 are shown in Table 9-3.

Rule 2 has been expanded by converting Decision 2's I entry into a separate Rule 2.1 for YES and 2.2 for NO. Similarly, Decision 2 was expanded in Rule 4 to yield intermediate Rules 4.1/4.2 and 4.3/4.4, which were then expanded via Decision 3 to yield the four subrules shown.

The key to test case design based on decision tables is to remove all immaterial entries by expansion and to generate tests that correspond to all the subrules. If some decisions are three-way decisions, an immaterial entry

	RULE 2		RULE 4			
	RULE 2.1	RULE 2.2	RULE 4.1	RULE 4.2	RULE 4.3	RULE 4.4
DECISION 1	YES	YES	NO	NO	NO	NO
DECISION 2	<u>YES</u>	<u>NO</u>	<u>YES</u>	<u>YES</u>	<u>NO</u>	<u>NO</u>
DECISION 3	YES	YES	<u>YES</u>	<u>NO</u>	<u>NO</u>	<u>YES</u>
DECISION 4	YES	YES	YES	YES	YES	YES

Table 9-3. Expansion of Immaterial Cases for Rules 2 and 4.

	RULE 1	RULE 2
DECISION 1	YES	YES
DECISION 2	I	NO
DECISION 3	YES	I
DECISION 4	NO	NO
ACTION 1	YES	NO
ACTION 2	NO	YES

	RULE 1.1	RULE 1.2	RULE 2.1	RULE 2.2
YES	YES	YES	YES	YES
YES	YES	NO	NO	NO
YES	YES	YES	YES	NO
NO	NO	NO	NO	NO
YES	YES	YES	NO	NO
NO	NO	NO	YES	YES

Table 9-4. The Expansion of an Inconsistent Specification.

would expand into three subrules. Similarly, an n-way case statement that was immaterial would expand into n subrules.

If no default rules are given, then all cases not covered by explicit rules are perforce default rules (or are intended to be). If default rules are given, then you must test the specification for consistency. The specification is complete if and only if n (binary) decisions expand into exactly 2^n unique subrules. It is consistent if and only if all rules expand into subrules whose decision combinations do not match those of any other rules. Table 9-4 is an example of an inconsistent specification in which the expansion of two rules yields a contradiction.

Rules 1 and 2 are contradictory because the expansion of Rule 1 via Decision 2 leads to the same set of decision values as the expansion of Rule 2 via Decision 3. Therefore whether Action 1 or Action 2 takes place depends on which rule is evaluated first. Assuming that my boss was rational about the way he determined raises, I would not take kindly to it if my raise was determined by the order in which he took account of inflation and my performance in the previous year.

2.5. Test Case Design

The design of test cases by decision tables begins with examining the specification's consistency and completeness. This is done by expanding all immaterial cases and checking the expanded tables. Efficient methods for doing this are given in Section 3 and in Chapter 10. Once the specifications have been proven correct, the objective of the test cases is to show that the implementation provides the correct action for all combinations of decision values.

1. If there are n binary decisions, there are 2^n cases to consider—no more and no less. Each case is a test case. Find input values that will force each case and confirm the action. Expand the decision table as required for the default cases; this should be considered as just another action.
2. It is not usually possible to change the order in which the *decisions* are evaluated because that order is built into the program.* If however, the implementation does allow that order to be modified by input values, augment the test cases by using different decision-evaluation orders. Try all pairs of interchanges for a representative set of values. For example, if the normal order is decision A followed by B, then try a test in which B is followed by A. For N decisions, there will be $N(N-1)/2$ interchanges for each combination of values of the decisions.
3. It is not usually possible to change the order in which the rules are evaluated because that order is built into the program.* If however, the implementation does allow the rule-evaluation order to be modified, test different orders for the rules by pairwise interchanges. One set of decision values per rule should be sufficient.
4. Identify the place or places in the routine where rules are invoked or where the processors that evaluate the rules are called. Similarly, identify the places where the actions are initiated. Instrument those paths so that you can show that the correct action was invoked for each rule.

---

*Decisions and rule-evaluation order could be variable in a system in which operators use explicit identifiers for every input field in a command. For example, the input specification might be of the form:

$$A = 1, B = 3, C = 17, D = ABCDE. . . .\text{and so on}$$

A tolerant implementation would allow these fields in any order. Similarly, an input packet could consist of several dozen or possibly a variable number of input cards, each of which was self-identifying and could therefore be tolerated in any order. Finally, complicated forms can have conditional subforms, which can result in the same data being input in different orders, depending on what path was taken through the form and on the values of previous data. All such examples can result in variable orders of decision evaluation and/ or variable orders of rule evaluation.

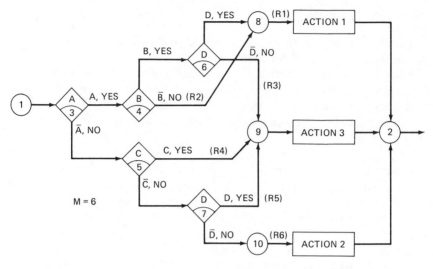

Figure 9-1. A Sample Program

2.6. Decision Tables and Structure

Decision tables can also be useful in examining a program's structure (GOOD75). Figure 9-1 shows a program segment that consists of a tree of decisions. These decisions, in various combinations can lead to actions 1, 2, or 3. Does this flowchart correspond to a complete and consistent set of conditions?

The corresponding decision table is shown in Table 9-5. You can almost read it from the flowchart. If the decision appears on a path, put a YES or NO as appropriate. If the decision does not appear on the path, put in an I. Rule 1 does not contain Decision C, therefore its entries are: YES, YES, I, YES. Expanding the immaterial cases for Table 9-5 leads to Table 9-6.

Sixteen cases are represented in Table 9-5 and no case appears twice. Consequently, the flowchart appears to be complete and consistent. As a first check, before you look for all sixteen combinations, count the number of Y's and N's in each row. They should be equal. I found my bug that way.

Consider the following specification whose putative flowchart is shown in Figure 9-2:

1. If decision A is satisfied, do process A1 no matter what other processes are done or what other decisions are satisfied.
2. If decision B is satisfied, do process A2 no matter what other processes are done or what other decisions are satisfied.

	RULE 1	RULE 2	RULE 3	RULE 4	RULE 5	RULE 6
DECISION A	YES	YES	YES	NO	NO	NO
DECISION B	YES	NO	YES	I	I	I
DECISION C	I	I	I	YES	NO	NO
DECISION D	YES	I	NO	I	YES	NO
ACTION 1	YES	YES	NO	NO	NO	NO
ACTION 2	NO	NO	YES	YES	YES	NO
ACTION 3	NO	NO	NO	NO	NO	YES

Table 9-5. The Decision Table Corresponding to Figure 9-1.

	R1	RULE 2	R3	RULE 4	R5	R6
DECISION A	Y Y	Y Y Y Y	Y Y	N N N N	N N	N N
DECISION B	Y Y	N N N N	Y Y	Y Y N N	N Y	Y N
DECISION C	Y N	N N Y Y	Y N	Y Y Y Y	N N	N N
DECISION D	Y Y	Y N N Y	N N	N Y Y N	Y Y	N N

Table 9-6. The Expansion of Table 9-5.

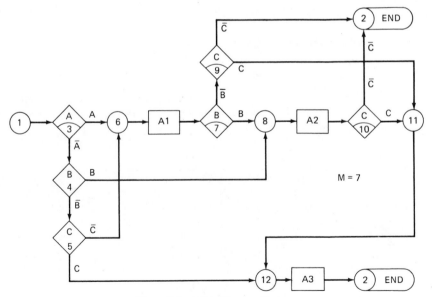

Figure 9-2. A Troublesome Program

3. If decision C is satisfied, do process A3 no matter what other processes are done or what other decisions are satisfied.
4. If none of the decisions is satisfied, then do processes A1, A2, and A3.
5. When more than one process is done, process A1 must be done first, then A2, and then A3. The only permissible cases are: (A1), (A2), (A3), (A1,A2), (A1,A3), (A2,A3) and (A1,A2,A3).

Table 9-7 shows the conversion of this flowchart into a decision table after expansion. There are eight cases and all paths lead to the evaluation of all three predicates, even though some predicates on some paths may be evaluated more than once. We can use the same path and predicate notation we used in Chapter 3 and name the rules by their corresponding combination of predicate values to save a little work and make things clearer.

As clever as this design may seem, and perhaps because it is clever, it has a bug. The programmer attempted to force all three processes to be executed for the $\bar{A}\bar{B}\bar{C}$ cases but forgot that the B and C decisions would be done again, thereby bypassing processes A2 and A3. This would have been easily found by the analytical techniques of the next section, but for the moment, if all three processes had been instrumented and monitored, and if all eight cases were used in test, the failure would have been revealed. Notice that sheer coverage based on structure would reveal nothing because the design was at fault—it did something, but what it did didn't happen to match the specification.

3. PATH EXPRESSIONS AGAIN

3.1. General

Let's say we're working from an implementation flowchart and that what it represents is what has been coded rather than what the programmer or the specification may have intended. Our purpose is to generate path expressions

RULES

	$\bar{A}\bar{B}\bar{C}$	$\bar{A}\bar{B}C$	$\bar{A}BC$	$\bar{A}B\bar{C}$	$AB\bar{C}$	ABC	$A\bar{B}C$	$A\bar{B}\bar{C}$
DECISION A	NO	NO	NO	NO	YES	YES	YES	YES
DECISION B	NO	NO	YES	YES	YES	YES	NO	NO
DECISION C	NO	YES	YES	NO	NO	YES	YES	NO
ACTION 1	YES	NO	NO	NO	YES	YES	YES	YES
ACTION 2	YES	NO	YES	YES	YES	YES	NO	NO
ACTION 3	YES	YES	YES	NO	NO	YES	YES	NO

Table 9-7. Decision Table for Figure 9-2.

by path tracing as in Chapter 6, but this time, our purpose is to convert the path expressions into boolean algebra, using the predicate's values (e.g., A and $\bar{A}$) as weights. This will be adequate in applications in which programs use binary decisions. Nonbinary decisions and case statements can be handled by different kinds of logics, all of which would require more explanation than is within the scope of this book. Those with a morbid interest can look into Post algebras for an example.

3.2. Notation

1. Label each decision with an uppercase letter that represents the truth value of the predicate. The YES or TRUE branch is labeled with a letter and the NO or FALSE branch with the same letter overscored.
2. The truth value of a path is the product of the individual labels. Concatenation or products mean "AND."

For example, the straight-through path of Figure 9-2, which goes via nodes 3, 6, 7, 8, 10, 11, 12, and 2, has a truth value of ABC. The path via nodes 3, 6, 7, 9 and 2 has a value of $A\bar{B}\bar{C}$.

3. If two or more paths merge at a node, the fact is expressed by use of a plus sign (+) which means "OR."

Using this convention, the truth-functional values for several of the nodes can be expressed in terms of segments from previous nodes. Use the node name to identify the point.

$$N6 \ = A + \bar{A}\bar{B}\bar{C}$$
$$N8 \ = (N6)B + \bar{A}B = AB + \bar{A}\bar{B}\bar{C}B + \bar{A}B$$
$$N11 = (N8)C + (N6)\bar{B}C$$
$$N12 = N11 + \bar{A}\bar{B}C$$
$$N2 \ = N12 + (N8)\bar{C} + (N6)\bar{B}\bar{C}$$

3.3. Boolean Algebra

3.3.1. General

The algebraic expressions of the previous sections are examples of boolean algebra expressions. Unlike regular expressions in which useful identities were rare, boolean algebra is complete and also simpler than ordinary algebra. Boolean algebra deals with truth-functional values of statements rather than numbers. The expression for node 6 can be translated into the following.

"Either it is true that decision A is satisfied (YES) *or* it is true that decision A is not satisfied (NO) *and* decision B is not satisfied and decision C is not satisfied, *or* both."

The "or" in boolean algebra is always an **inclusive-or**, which means "A or B or both." The **exclusive-or**, which means "A or B, but not both" is represented by $A\bar{B} + \bar{A}B$. Each letter in a boolean algebra expression represents the truth or falsity of a statement or sentence, such as:

"It is snowing outside."
"Decision A is satisfied."
"A mouse is green when it is spinning."

There are only two numbers in boolean algebra: zero (0) and one (1). One means "always true" and zero means "always false." "Truth" and "falsity" should not be taken in the literal or ordinary sense but in a more specific sense—such as meaning that a particular bit is set. Actually, it doesn't matter if it is or is not snowing outside. If the decision executed in the program is evaluated as corresponding to "it is snowing," then we say that the statement is true or that the value of the variable that represents it is 1.

3.3.2. The Rules of Boolean Algebra

Boolean algebra has three operators:

$\times$ meaning *and*. Also called multiplication. A statement such as AB means "A and B are both true." The multiplication sign is usually left out as in ordinary algebra.

$+$ meaning or. "A + B" means "either A is true or B is true or both."

$\bar{A}$ meaning *not*. Also called "negation" or "complementation." This is read as either "not A" or "A bar." The entire expression under the bar is negated. For example, $\bar{A}$ is a statement which is true only when statement A is false. The statement $\overline{(A + \bar{B})}$ is translated as, "It is not true that either A is true or B is not true or both."

Generally, we dispense with the clumsy phraseology of "it is true" or "it is false" and say "equals 1" or "equals 0" respectively. With these preambles, we can set down the laws of boolean algebra:

1. $A + A$ $= A$ If something is true, saying it twice
   $\bar{A} + \bar{A}$ $= \bar{A}$ doesn't make it any truer—ditto for false-hoods.
2. $A + 1$ $= 1$ If something is always true, then "either A or true or both" must also be universally true.
3. $A + 0$ $= A$
4. $A + B$ $= B + A$ Commutative law.
5. $A + \bar{A}$ $= 1$ If either A is true or not-A is true, then the statement is always true.
6. AA $= A$
   $\bar{A}\bar{A}$ $= \bar{A}$
7. $A \times 1$ $= A$
8. $A \times 0$ $= 0$
9. AB $= BA$
10. $A\bar{\bar{A}}$ $= 0$ A statement can't both be true and false simultaneously.
11. $\bar{A}$ $= A$ "You ain't not going" means you are. How about, "I ain't not never going to get this nohow."?
12. $\bar{0}$ $= 1$
13. $\bar{1}$ $= 0$
14. $\overline{(A + B)}$ $= \bar{A}\bar{B}$ Called "De Morgan's theorem or law."
15. $\overline{AB}$ $= \bar{A} + \bar{B}$
16. $A(B + C)$ $= AB + AC$ Distributive law.
17. $(AB)C$ $= A(BC)$ Multiplication is associative.
18. $(A + B) + C$ $= A + (B + C)$ So is addition.
19. $A + \bar{A}B$ $= A + \bar{B}$ Absorptive law.
20. In all of the above, a letter can represent a single sentence or an entire boolean algebra expression.

3.3.3. Examples

The path expressions of Section 3.2 can now be simplified by applying the rules. The steps are shown in detail to illustrate the use of the rules. Usually, it's done with far less work. It pays to practice.

$$N6 = A + \bar{A}\bar{B}\bar{C}$$
$$= A + \bar{B}\bar{C} \qquad\qquad : \quad \text{Use Rule 19, with "B" = } \bar{B}\bar{C}.$$

$$
\begin{aligned}
N8 &= (N6)B + \bar{A}B \\
&= (A + \bar{B}\bar{C})B + \bar{A}B &&: \text{Substitution.} \\
&= AB + \bar{B}\bar{C}B + \bar{A}B &&: \text{Rule 16 (Distributive law).} \\
&= AB + B\bar{B}\bar{C} + \bar{A}B &&: \text{Rule 9 (Commutative} \\
&&& \quad \text{multiplication).} \\
&= AB + 0C + \bar{A}B &&: \text{Rule 10.} \\
&= AB + 0 + \bar{A}B &&: \text{Rule 8.} \\
&= AB + \bar{A}B &&: \text{Rule 3.} \\
&= (A + \bar{A})B &&: \text{Rule 16 (Distributive law).} \\
&= 1 \times B &&: \text{Rule 5.} \\
&= B &&: \text{Rules 7, 9.}
\end{aligned}
$$

Similarly,

$$
\begin{aligned}
N11 &= (N8)C + (N6)\bar{B}C \\
&= BC + (A + \bar{B}\bar{C})\bar{B}C &&: \text{Substitution.} \\
&= BC + A\bar{B}C &&: \text{Rules 16, 9, 10, 8, 3.} \\
&= C(B + \bar{B}A) &&: \text{Rules 9, 16.} \\
&= C(B + A) &&: \text{Rule 19.} \\
&= AC + BC &&: \text{Rules 16, 9, 9, 4.} \\
N12 &= N11 + \bar{A}\bar{B}C \\
&= AC + BC + \bar{A}\bar{B}C \\
&= C(B + \bar{A}\bar{B}) + AC \\
&= C(\bar{A} + B) + AC \\
&= C\bar{A} + AC + BC \\
&= C + BC \\
&= C \\
N2 &= N12 + (N8)\bar{C} + (N6)\bar{B}\bar{C} \\
&= C + B\bar{C} + (A + \bar{B}\bar{C})\bar{B}\bar{C} \\
&= C + B\bar{C} + \bar{B}\bar{C} \\
&= C + \bar{C}(B + \bar{B}) \\
&= C + \bar{C} \\
&= 1
\end{aligned}
$$

The deviation from the specification is now clear. The correct functions should have been:

$$
\begin{aligned}
N6 &= A + \bar{A}\bar{B}\bar{C} = A + \bar{B}\bar{C} &&: \text{correct.} \\
N8 &= B + \bar{A}\bar{B}\bar{C} = B + \bar{A}\bar{C} &&: \text{wrong, was just B.} \\
N12 &= C + \bar{A}\bar{B}\bar{C} = C + \bar{A}\bar{B} &&: \text{wrong, was just C.}
\end{aligned}
$$

An efficient flowchart to produce the correct functions is tricky if you assume that each process will be called only once and that no flags or loops will be used to record the outcomes of tests already done.

3.3.5. Test Case Design

It is, in principle, necessary to design a test case that corresponds to each possible TRUE/FALSE combination of the variables that define the logic. In general, as in the example, the predicates are correlated so that not all paths are possible. If the predicates were all uncorrelated, then each of the 2^n combinations would correspond to a different path, and the sum of them would correspond to a minimum-covering set. The example in this section is a little different from previous examples. There we wanted to achieve coverage over the various paths from entry to exit. We also want to do that in this case, but there are intermediate points of interest as well.

While it is possible to have ambiguities and contradictions in a specification (say given as a list of conditions or a decision table), it is *not* possible for a program to have contradictions or ambiguities if:

1. The routine has a single entry and a single exit.
2. No combination of predicate values leads to nonterminating loops.
3. There are no pieces of dangling code that lead nowhere.

Under these circumstances, the boolean algebra expression for the entry to the exit must equal 1 exactly. If it doesn't, either you've made a mistake in evaluating it or there are pieces of unreachable code or nonterminating code for some predicate-value combination.

The most complete test case set you can use is one where the paths correspond to all 2^n combinations of predicate values. There can be no more cases than this, but coverage can often be achieved with fewer test cases. In the above example, end-to-end coverage can be achieved by using all the cases except ABC and $A\bar{B}\bar{C}$. Other combinations can be found that do not include all 2^n cases but which still provide full coverage. To find a set of covering paths, write out all 2^n combinations. Each combination specifies a path. Continue to add combinations until coverage has been achieved.

We had three other points of interest in this routine, corresponding to the three processes. Those points were N6, N8, and N12. The boolean algebra expression for those points specifies the test cases needed for each. Each expression consists of a number of "AND" terms joined by "ORs." Each such "AND" term is called a **prime implicant**. Any one prime implicant is sufficient to reach the point of interest. The expansion of the expression for that node specifies all possible ways of reaching that node, although all terms may not be needed to provide coverage to that point. For example:

$$N6 = A + \bar{B}\bar{C}$$
$$= A\bar{B}\bar{C} + A\bar{B}C + AB\bar{C} + ABC + \bar{A}\bar{B}\bar{C}$$

Any term starting with A will get us to node 6, and it doesn't matter what happens subsequently. The only other way to get to node 6 is via $\bar{A}\bar{B}\bar{C}$. This is exactly what the simplified version of the expression for N6 said. A gets you there and the other predicates are immaterial. Consequently, the $A\bar{B}\bar{C}$ obtained from the expansion of $\bar{B}\bar{C}$ is also immaterial, and only the $\bar{A}\bar{B}\bar{C}$ term remains. N8 is reached by B, no matter what values the other predicates may have. In particular, $\bar{A}\bar{B}$ and AB provide all the ways to get to node 8. Node 12 can be reached by C. But all four terms in the expansion of C are required to get there in all four possible ways. The set of paths used to reach any point of interest in the flowchart can be characterized by an increasingly more thorough set of test cases:

1. Simplest—Use any prime implicant in the expression to the point of interest as a basis for a path. The only predicate values that must be investigated are those that appear in the prime implicant. All predicates not appearing in the prime implicant chosen can be set arbitrarily. If we chose the $\bar{B}\bar{C}$ prime implicant for node 6, we could still get to node 6, whether we chose A or $\bar{A}$. If we picked the A prime implicant, it doesn't matter what we do about B or C.
2. Covered—Expand the prime implicants to the fullest form and remove any redundant ones. Pick a sufficient number of prime implicants in the expansion to cover all paths to the node of interest.
3. Complete—Test all expanded terms for that node—for example, five terms for node 6, four for node 8, and four for node 12.

The exit is treated as any other point of interest except that it should have a value of 1 for its boolean expression, which when expanded yields all 2^n combinations of predicate values. (A set of covering paths could be achieved with fewer than 2^n test cases.)

3.4. Boolean Equations

The introduction of loops into the program complicates things because it may be necessary to solve a boolean equation to determine what predicate-value combinations will lead to where. Furthermore, the boolean expression for the end point does not necessarily equal 1. Consider the flowchart of Figure 9-3.

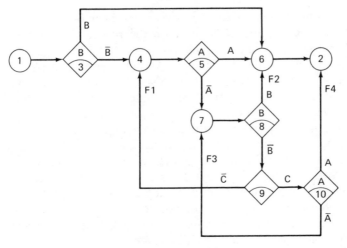

Figure 9-3. A Flowchart with Loops

Assign a name to any node whose value you don't know yet and write the expressions down, one at a time, working backward to something you do know, simplifying as you go. It's usually convenient to give names to links. The names represent the boolean expression corresponding to that link. I've named the links F1, F2, F3, and F4.

$$
\begin{aligned}
N4 &= \bar{B} + F1 \\
F1 &= \bar{B}\bar{C}N7 \\
N4 &= \bar{B} + \bar{B}\bar{C}N7 \\
&= \bar{B} \\
N6 &= B + AN4 \\
&= B + A\bar{B} \\
&= A + B \\
N7 &= \bar{A}N4 + F3 \\
&= \bar{A}\bar{B} + F3 \\
F3 &= N7\bar{B}C\bar{A} \\
N7 &= \bar{A}\bar{B} + \bar{A}\bar{B}CN7 \\
&= \bar{A}\bar{B} \\
N2 &= N6 + F4 \\
&= A + B + F4 \\
F4 &= A\bar{B}CN7 \\
N2 &= A + B + A\bar{B}CN7 \\
&= A + B
\end{aligned}
$$

You might argue that this is a silly flowchart, but it does illustrate some interesting points. The fact that the expression for the end point does not reduce to 1 means that there are predicate-value combinations for which the routine will loop indefinitely. Because the program's exit expression is A + B, the condition under which it does not exit is the negation of this or $\overline{(A + B)}$, which by rule 14 is equal to $\overline{A}\overline{B}$. This term when expanded yields $\overline{A}\overline{B}C + \overline{A}\overline{B}\overline{C}$, which identifies the two ways of looping, via nodes 7,8,9,10 and 4,5,7,8,9, respectively. It is conceivable that this unstructured horror could have been deliberately constructed (other than as a tutorial example, that is), but it's not likely. If the predicate values are independent of the processing, this routine must loop indefinitely for $\overline{A}\overline{B}$. A complete test consisting of all eight predicate-value combinations would have revealed the loops. Alternatively, the fact that the exit expression did not equal 1 implied that there had to be a loop. Feeding the logic back into itself this way, usually in the interest of saving some code or some work, leads to simultaneous boolean equations, which are rarely as easy to solve as the given example; it may also lead to dead paths and infinite loops.

4. SUMMARY

1. Use decision tables as a convenient way to organize statements in a specification—possibly as an intermediate step toward a more compact and more revealing equivalent boolean algebra expression.
2. Label the links following binary decisions with a weight that corresponds to the predicate's logical value and evaluate the boolean expressions to the nodes of interest.
3. Simplify the resulting expressions or solve equations and then simplify if you cannot directly express the boolean function for the node in terms of the path-predicate values.
4. The boolean expression for the exit node should equal 1. If it does not, or if attempting to solve for it leads to a loop of equations, then there are conditions under which the routine will loop indefinitely. The negation of the exit expression specifies all the combinations of predicate values that will lead to the loop or loops.
5. Any node of interest can be reached by a test case derived from the expansion of any prime implicant in the boolean expression for that node.
6. The set of all paths from the entry to a node can be obtained by expanding all the prime implicants of the boolean expression that corresponds to that node. A covering set of paths may, however, not require all the terms of the expansion.

10

BOOLEAN ALGEBRA THE EASY WAY

1. SYNOPSIS

The analysis of boolean functions of up to six variables can be simplified by using the **Karnaugh-Veitch chart** or diagram. More on analyzing inconsistencies and ambiguities in specifications. How to handle impossible and don't-care cases.

2. THE PROBLEM

It's okay to slug through boolean algebra expressions to determine which cases are interesting and which combination of predicate values should be used to reach which node; it's okay, but not necessary. If you had to deal with expressions in four, five, or six variables, you could get bogged down in the algebra and make as many errors in designing test cases as there are bugs in the routine you're testing. The **Karnaugh-Veitch map** (this is known by every combination of "Karnaugh" and/or "Veitch" with any one of "map," "chart," or "diagram") reduces boolean algebraic manipulations to graphical trivia (KARN53, VEIT52). Beyond six variables these diagrams get cumbersome, and other methods such as the Quine-McCluskey (MCCL56, QUIN55) method (which are beyond the scope of this book) must be used.

3. KV CHARTS

3.1. Simple Forms

Figure 10-1 shows all the boolean functions of a single variable and their equivalent representation as a KV chart. The charts show all possible values (0,1 or TRUE/FALSE) that the variable A can have. The heading above each box in the chart denotes this fact. A "1" means the variable's value is "1" or TRUE. A "0" means that the variable's value is 0 or FALSE. The entry in the box (0 or 1) specifies whether the function that the chart represents is true or false for that value of the variable. We usually do not explicitly put in 0 entries but specify only the conditions under which the function is true.

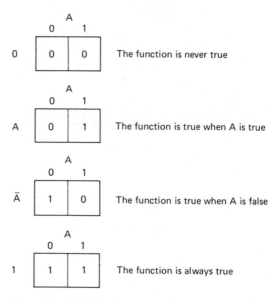

Figure 10-1. KV Charts for Functions of a Single Variable.

Figure 10-2 shows eight of the sixteen possible functions of two variables. Each box corresponds to the combination of values of the variables for the row and column of that box. The single entry for $\overline{A}\,\overline{B}$ in the first chart is interpreted that way because both the A and B variable's value for the box is 0. Similarly, $A\overline{B}$ corresponds to A = 1 and B = 0, $\overline{A}B$ to A = 0 and B = 1, and AB to A = 1 and B = 1. The next four functions all have two nonzero entries, and each entry forms an **adjacent** pair. A pair may be adjacent either horizontally or vertically but not diagonally. Any variable that changes in either the horizontal or vertical direction does not appear in the expression. In the fifth chart, the B variable changes from 0 to 1 going down the column, and because the A variable's value for the column is 1, the chart, is equivalent to a simple A. Similarly, in the sixth chart, it is the A variable that changes in the B = 1 row, and consequently, the chart is equivalent to B. Similarly for $\overline{A}$ and $\overline{B}$.

Figure 10-3 shows the remaining eight functions of two variables. The interpretation of these charts is a combination of the interpretations of the previous charts in Figure 10-2. The first chart has two 1's in it, but because they are not adjacent, each must be taken separately. They are written using a plus sign. Because the first is $\overline{A}\,\overline{B}$ and the second AB, the entire chart is equivalent to $\overline{A}\,\overline{B}$ + AB. Similarly, the second chart is equivalent to $\overline{A}B$ + $A\overline{B}$.

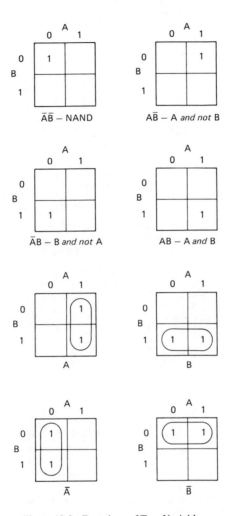

Figure 10-2. Functions of Two Variables.

The next four charts have three 1's in them, and each can be grouped into adjacent groups of two (remember, adjacency is either horizontal or vertical).* Each adjacent group is a prime implicant and is therefore written down connected to the others by a "+." The first example consists of two adjacent groups of two boxes, corresponding to $\overline{A}$ (vertical group) and B (horizontal group), to yield $\overline{A}$ + B. The last case has all boxes filled with 1's and consequently, whatever the value of the variables might be, the function is

*Overlapping and multiple use is allowed because A + AB = A.

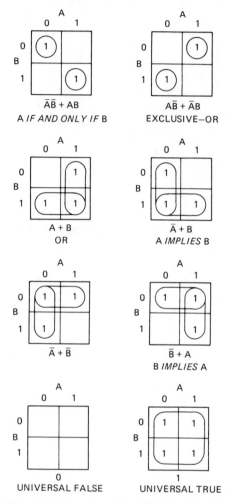

Figure 10-3. Functions of Two Variables Continued.

equal to 1. The four entries in this case form an adjacent grouping of four boxes. It is clear now why there are sixteen functions of two variables. Each box in the KV chart corresponds to a combination of the variables' values. That combination might or might not be in the function (i.e., the box corresponding to that combination might have a 1 or 0 entry).

N variables lead to 2^n combinations of 0 and 1 for the variables, and each such combination (box) can be filled or not filled, leading to 2^{2^n} ways of doing this. Consequently for one variable there are $2^{2^1} = 4$ functions, 16 functions of 2 variables, 256 functions of 3 variables, 16,384 functions of 4 variables, and so on. The third example of Figure 10-3 explains Rule 19 on page 203. In fact, it's trivially obvious:

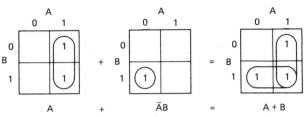

I've used the fact that KV maps also behave like boolean functions. Given two maps over the same variables, arranged the same way, their product is the term by term product, their sum is the term by term sum, and the negation of a map is gotten by reversing all the 0 and 1 entries in the map. The general procedure for simplifying expressions using KV maps is to fill in each term one at a time, and then to look for adjacencies and to rewrite the expression in terms of the largest groupings you can find that cover all the 1's in the chart. Say the expression is:

$$\bar{A}\bar{B} + A\bar{B} + AB$$

then:

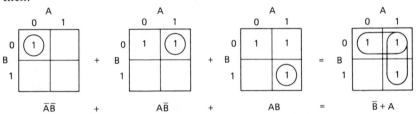

3.2. Three Variables

KV maps for three variables are shown. As before, each box represents an elementary term of three variables with a bar appearing or not appearing according to whether the row-column heading for that box is 0 or 1. Note that I've labeled the column headings in an unusual way "00, 01, 11, 10" rather than with the expected "00, 01, 10, 11." Recall that the variable whose value did not change is the one we ended with. This labeling preserves the adjacency properties of the chart. However, note that adjacencies can go around corners, because 00 is adjacent to 10. The meaning of "adjacency" can now be specified more precisely: two boxes are adjacent if they change in only one bit, and two groupings are adjacent if they change in only one bit. A three-variable map can have groupings of 1, 2, 4, and 8 boxes. A few examples will illustrate the principles:

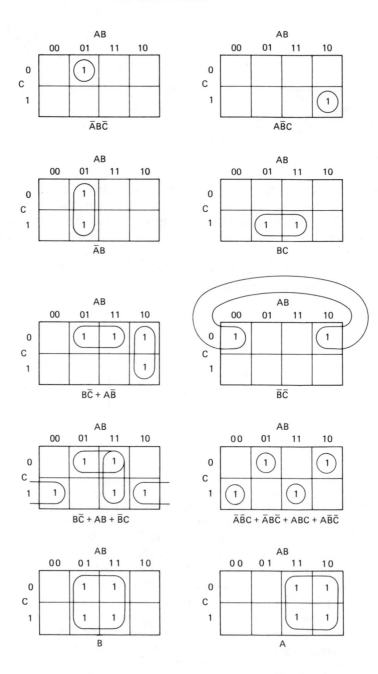

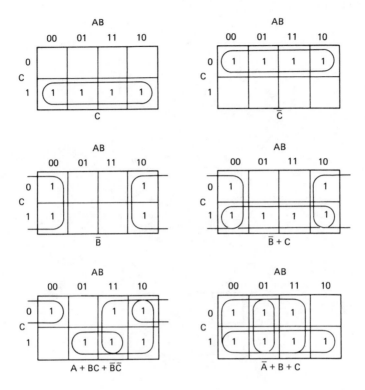

You'll notice that the ways in which you can circle the boxes into maximum-sized groups that cover are not unique. However, all such sets of coverings are equivalent, no matter how different they might appear to be. As an example, consider:

$$BC + \overline{A}\,\overline{B}C + A\overline{B}C$$

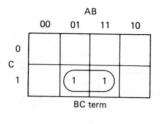

BC term

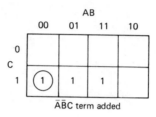

$\overline{A}\overline{B}C$ term added

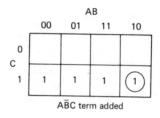

$A\overline{B}C$ term added

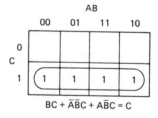

$BC + \overline{A}\overline{B}C + A\overline{B}C = C$

3.3. Four Variables and More

The same principles hold for four and more variables. A four-variable map and several possible adjacencies are shown below. Adjacencies can now consist of 1, 2, 4, 8, and 16 boxes, and the terms resulting will have 4, 3, 2, 1, and 0 literals in them respectively.

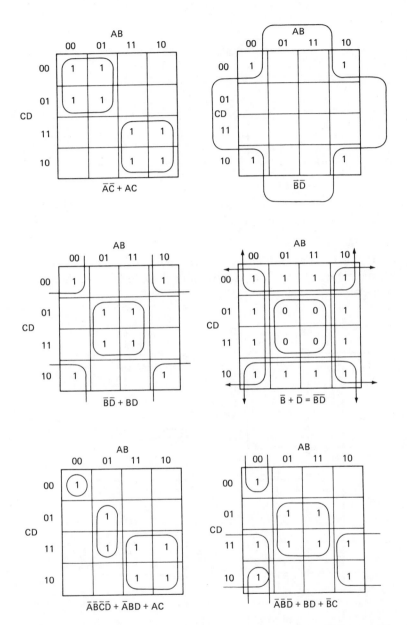

As with three-variable maps, the way you can group adjacent entries to cover all the 1's in the chart is not unique, but all such ways are equivalent, even though the resulting boolean expressions may not look the same.

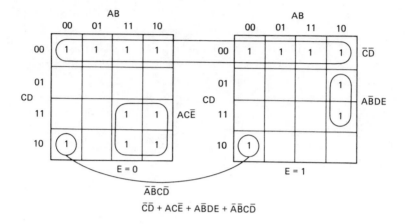

$$\overline{CD} + AC\overline{E} + A\overline{B}DE + \overline{A}\overline{B}C\overline{D}$$

This is a five-variable map with some of the adjacencies shown. You'll notice that things start to get cumbersome. For the hardy, there is a six-variable map.

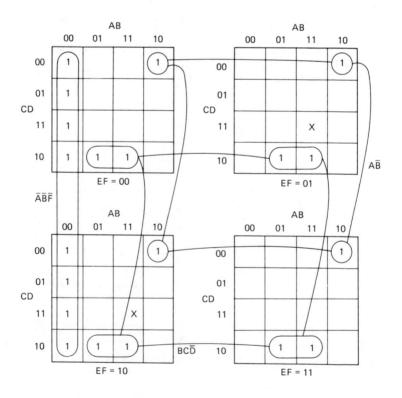

The two points labeled "X" are not adjacent, because the submaps on which they appear are diagonal to one another. If you really have to do a lot of work with six variables, you can build a three-dimensional tic-tac-toe game (4 × 4 × 4) out of transparent plastic. I heard of someone who carried things further and used eight transparent chessboards to handle nine-variable problems.*

4. SPECIFICATIONS

4.1. General

There's no point in getting deep into design and coding until you're sure that the specification is logically consistent and complete. The KV chart substantially reduces the labor required to confirm this. The procedure is straightforward:

1. Rewrite the specification using consistent terminology.
2. Identify the predicates on which the cases are based. Name them with suitable letters, such as A, B, C.
3. Rewrite the specification in English that uses only the logical connectives AND, OR, and NOT, however stilted it might seem.
4. Convert the rewritten specification into an equivalent set of boolean expressions.
5. Identify the default action and cases, if any are specified.
6. Enter the boolean expressions in a KV chart and check for consistency. If the specifications are consistent, there will be no overlaps, except for cases that result in multiple actions.
7. Enter the default cases and check for consistency.
8. If all boxes are covered, the specification is complete.
9. If the specification is incomplete or inconsistent, translate the corresponding boxes of the KV chart back into English and get a clarification, explanation, or revision.
10. If the default cases were not specified explicitly, translate the default cases back into English and get a confirmation.

4.2. Finding and Translating the Logic

This is the most difficult part of the job, because it takes intelligence to disentangle intentions that are hidden by ambiguities inherent in English and

---

*I admit to it. It didn't work very well, although it was impressive as hell.

by poor English usage. We cast the specifications into sentences of the following form:

"IF logical expression THEN action."

The logical expressions are written using the AND, OR, and NOT boolean connectives. Therefore, the problem should be one of finding the key words: IF, THEN, AND, OR, and NOT. Unfortunately we have to deal with the real world of specifications and specification writers, where clarity ranges from elusive, through esoteric, into incomprehensible. Here is a sample of phrases that have been or can be used (and abused) for the basic words we need:

IF—
based on, based upon, because, but, if, if and when, only if, only when, provided that, when, when or if, whenever.

THEN—
applies to, assign, consequently, do, implies that, infers that, initiate, means that, shall, should, then, will, would.

AND—
all, and, as well as, both, but, in conjunction with, coincidental with, consisting of, comprising, either . . . or, furthermore, in addition to, including, jointly, moreover, mutually, plus, together with, total, with.

OR—
and, and if . . . then, and/or, alternatively, any of, anyone of, as well as, but, case, contrast, depending upon, each, either, either. . . .or, except if, conversely, failing that, furthermore, in addition to, nor, not only . . . but, although, other than, otherwise, or, or else, on the other hand, plus.

NOT—
but, but not, by contrast, besides, contrary, conversely, contrast, except if, excluding, excepting, fail, failing, less, neither, never, no, not, other than.

EXCLUSIVE OR—but, by contrast, conversely, nor, on the other hand, other than, or.

IMMATERIAL— independent of, irregardless, irrespective, irrelevant, regardless, but not if, whether or not.

Remember that I'm including examples of poor usage. The above list is *not* a list of recommended synonyms for specification writers. Several entries appear in more than one list—a source of danger. There are other dangerous phrases, such as "respectively," "similarly," "conversely," "and so forth," and "etc." More than one project's been sunk by an "etc." The main point, maybe the only point, of translating the specification into unambiguous English that uses IF, THEN, AND, OR, and NOT, is that this form is less likely to be misinterpreted.

Start rewriting the specification by getting rid of ambiguous terms, words, and phrases and expressing it all as a long list of IF. . .THEN statements. Then identify the actions and give them names such as A1, A2, A3, etc. Break the actions down into small units at first. All actions at this point should be mutually exclusive in the sense that no one action is part of another. If some actions always occur in conjunction with other actions and vice versa, then lump them into a single action and give it a new name. Now substitute the action names in the sentences. Identify the "OR" components of all sentences and rewrite them so that each "OR" is on a separate line (i.e. each prime implicant). You now have a specification of the form:

IF A AND B AND C, THEN A1,
IF C AND D AND F, THEN A1,
IF A AND B AND D, THEN A2,

. . .

Now identify all the NOTs, which can be knotty, because some sentences may have the form $\overline{(A + B + C)}$ or $\bar{A}\bar{B}\bar{C}$. Put phrases in parentheses if that helps to clarify things. The only English now remaining are the A's, B's and C's, which should resemble predicates of the form, "A is true" or "NOT A . . ." Identify all the predicates in both negated and unnegated form and group them. Select a single representative for each, preferably the clearest one, or rewrite the predicates if that helps. Give each predicate a letter. You now have a set of boolean expressions that can be retranslated back into English preparatory to confirmation. An alternative is a table. List the predicates on one side and the actions on the other—a decision table is a handy format—and use that instead of English sentences. It's helpful to expand the immaterial cases and show the 2^n combinations of predicate values explicitly. Immaterial cases are always confusing.

This process should be done as early as possible because the translation of the specification into boolean algebra may require discussion among the specifiers, especially if contradictions and ambiguities emerge. If the specification has been given as a decision table or in another equally unambiguous tabular form, then most of the above work has been avoided and so has much of the potential confusion and many of the bugs that inevitably result therefrom.

4.3. Ambiguities and Contradictions

Here is a specification:

$$
\begin{aligned}
A1 &= B\bar{C}\bar{D} + A\bar{B}\bar{C}D \\
A2 &= A\bar{C}\bar{D} + A\bar{C}D + A\bar{B}\bar{C} + AB\bar{C} \\
A3 &= BD + BC\bar{D} \\
ELSE &= B\bar{C} + \bar{A}\bar{B}\bar{C}\bar{D}
\end{aligned}
$$

Here is the KV chart for this specification (I've used the numerals 1, 2, 3, and 4 to represent the actions and the default case):

There is a clear ambiguity, probably related to the default case. The $\bar{A}\bar{B}\bar{C}D$ case is missing. The specification layout seems to suggest that this term also belongs to the default action. I would ask the question twice:

1. Is the $\bar{A}\bar{B}\bar{C}D$ also to be considered a default action?
2. May the default action be rephrased as $\bar{B}C + \bar{A}\bar{B}$?

You might get contradictory answers, in which case, you may have to rephrase your question, or better yet, lay out all the combinations in a table and ask for a resolution of the ambiguities. There are several boxes that call for more than one action. If the specification did not explicitly call out both actions in a sentence, such as, "IF $AB\bar{C}\bar{D}$ then *both* action 1 and action 2 shall be taken," I would treat each box that contained more than one action as a potential conflict. Similarly, if the specification did say, ". . . both A1 and A2 . . ." but did not mention A3, as in the $AB\bar{C}D$ entry, I would also question that entry.

If no explicit default action is specified, then fill out the KV chart with explicit entries for the explicitly specified actions, negate the entire chart, and present the equivalent expression as a statement of the default. In the above example, had no default action been given, all the blank spaces would have been replaced with 1's and the $\overline{B}C + \overline{A}\overline{B}$ expression would have resulted.

Be suspicious of almost complete groups of adjacencies. For example, if a term contains seven adjacent boxes and lacks only one to make a full eight adjacency, question the missing box. I would question 3 out of 4, 6 or 7 out of 8, 13 through 15 out of 16, and so on, especially if the missing boxes are not themselves adjacent.

It's also useful to present the new version of the specification as a table that shows all cases explicitly and also as a compact version in which you've taken advantage of the possibility of simplifying the expression by using a KV map. You present the table and say that, "This table can also be expressed as . . . ." There may be disagreement. The specifier might insist that the table does not correspond to the specification and that the table also does not correspond to your compact statement, which you know was derived from the table by using boolean algebra. Don't be smug if that happens. Just as often as the seeming contradiction will be due to not understanding the equivalence, it will be due to a predicate that has not been explicitly stated.

4.4. Don't-Care and Impossible Terms

There are only three things in this universe that I'm certain are impossible:

1. Solving a provably unsolvable problem, such as creating a universal program verifier.
2. Knowing both the exact position and the exact momentum of a fundamental particle.
3. Knowing what happened before the "big bang" that started the universe.

Everything else is improbable, but not impossible. So-called "impossible" cases can be used to advantage to simplify logic and consequently, to simplify the programs that implement that logic. There are two kinds of so-called impossible conditions: the condition that cannot be created or is seemingly contradictory or improbable, and the condition that results from our insistence on forcing a complex, continuous world into a binary, logical mold. Most program illogical conditions are of the latter kind. There are twelve cases for something, say, and we represent those cases by four bits. Our conversion from the real world to the binary world has "created" four impossible cases. The external world can also contain "impossible" and "mutually exclusive" cases, such as female fighter pilots, consistent specifications, honest mechanics and politicians, insincere used-car salesmen and funeral directors, and blind editors. The seemingly impossible cases of semantic origin can appear to occur within a program because of malfunctions or alpha particles. The supposed impossibilities of the real world can come into being because the world changes. Consequently, you can take advantage of an "impossible" case only when you are sure that there is data validation or protection in a preceding module or when appropriate illogical condition checks are made elsewhere in the program. Taking advantage of "impossible" and "illogical" cases is an inherently dangerous practice and should be avoided, but if you insist on doing that sort of thing, you might as well do it right:

1. Identify all "impossible" and "illogical" cases and confirm them.
2. Document the fact that you intend to take advantage of them.
3. Fill out the KV chart with the possible cases and then fill in the impossible cases. Use the combined symbol "$\emptyset$," which is to be interpreted as a 0 or 1, depending on which value provides the greatest simplification of the resulting logic. These terms are called **"don't-care"** terms, because the case is impossible, and we don't care which value (0 or 1) is used.

Here is an example:

	AB				
		00	01	11	10
CD	00	$\emptyset$	1		
	01	1	$\emptyset$	$\emptyset$	
	11	$\emptyset$	1	1	1
	10	1	1	1	1

By not taking advantage of the impossible conditions, we get the resulting boolean expression:

$$C\bar{D} + CB + CA + \bar{A}B\bar{D} + \bar{A}\bar{B}\bar{C}D$$

By taking advantage of the impossible conditions, we get:

$$C + \bar{A}$$

The corresponding flowcharts are shown in Figure 10-4. The B and D decisions have disappeared for the second case. This a two-edged sword.

By reducing the logic's complexity we have reduced instructions, data references for B and D, and the routine's complexity, thereby reducing the probability of bugs. However, the routine now depends on nature's good graces, how thoroughly preceding routines have done data validation, and how thoroughly data validation will be done after this design has been modified in maintenance. It is not obvious whether long-term quality has been improved or degraded.

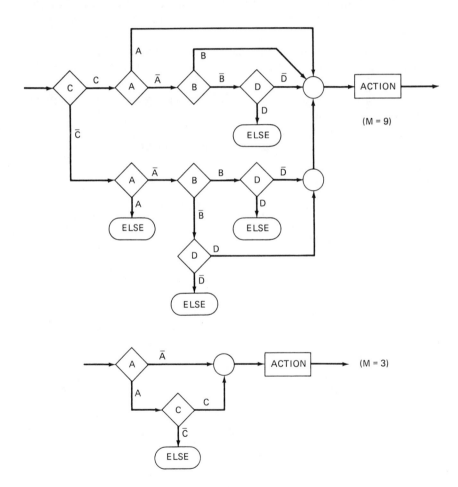

Figure 10-4. Reducing Complexity by Simplifying the Logic.

5. SUMMARY

1. You don't do boolean algebra by algebra. You use KV charts for up to six variables. Keep quadrille-ruled paper pads handy.
2. When a routine seems to be dominated by logic, particularly if many of the decisions are correlated, examine the completeness and consistency of the specification using boolean algebra via KV charts.
3. Be careful in translating English into boolean algebra. Retranslate and discuss the retranslation of the algebra with the specifier.
4. Question all missing entries, question overlapped entries if there was no explicit statement of multiple actions, question all almost-complete groups.
5. Avoid taking advantage of don't-care cases or impossible cases, but if you must, make sure you get the maximum payoff by making the resulting logic as simple as you can.
6. Document, document, document, all instances in which you take advantage of don't-care cases.
7. Document the don't-care assumptions.
8. Be sure the don't-care assumptions are clearly documented.

11

STATES, STATE GRAPHS, AND TRANSITION TESTING

1. SYNOPSIS

The **state graph** and its associated **state table** are useful models for describing the behavior of some programs. Methods analogous to path testing are described and discussed.

2. STATE GRAPHS

2.1. States

The word "**state**" is used in much the same way it is used in ordinary English, as in "state of the Union," or "state of health." The Oxford English Dictionary defines "state" as: "A combination of circumstances or attributes belonging for the time being to a person or thing."

A program that detects the character sequence "ZCZC" can be in the following states:

1. Neither ZCZC nor any part of it has been detected
2. Z has been detected
3. ZC has been detected
4. ZCZ has been detected
5. ZCZC has been detected

A moving automobile whose engine is running can have the following states with respect to its transmission:

1. Reverse gear
2. Neutral gear

3. First gear
4. Second gear
5. Third gear
6. Fourth gear

A person's checkbook can have the following states with respect to the bank balance:

1. Equal
2. Less than
3. Greater than

States are represented by circles, or nodes. The states are numbered or may be identified by words or whatever else is convenient. Figure 11-1 shows a typical state graph. A state usually depicts a combination of attributes or conditions of interest at the moment. The automobile example is really more complicated because: 1) the engine might or might not be running, 2) the car itself might be moving forward or backward or be stopped, and 3) the clutch might or might not be depressed. These factors would multiply the above six states by 2 × 3 × 2 = 12, for a total of 72 rather than 6 states. Each additional factor that has alternatives multiplies the number of states in a model by the number of alternatives. The number of states of a computer is 2 raised to the power of the number of bits in the computer; that is, all the bits in main memory, registers, discs, tapes, and so on. Because most interesting factors are binary, and because each new factor doubles the number of states, state graphs are most useful for relatively simple functional models involving at most a few dozen states and only a few factors.

2.2. Inputs and Transitions

That which is being modeled is subjected to inputs, and as a result of those inputs, the state changes, or is said to have made a **transition**. The transitions are denoted by links that join the states. The input or inputs that caused the transition are marked on the link. The ZCZC detection example can have the following kinds of inputs:

1. Z
2. C
3. Any character other than Z or C, which we'll denote by A

The state graph of Figure 11-1 is interpreted as follows:

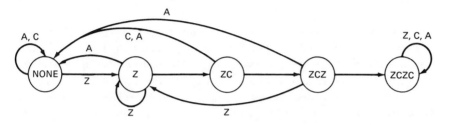

Figure 11-1. One-Time ZCZC Sequence-Detector State Graph.

1. If the system is in the "NONE" state, any input other than a Z will keep it in that state.
2. If a Z is received, the system transitions to the "Z" state.
3. If the system is in the "Z" state, and a Z is received, it will remain in the "Z" state. If a C is received it will go to the "ZC" state, and if any other character is received, it will go back to the "NONE" state because the sequence has been broken.
4. A Z received in the "ZC" state progresses to the "ZCZ" state, but any other character breaks the sequence and causes a return to the "NONE" state.
5. A C received in the "ZCZ" state completes the sequence and the system enters the "ZCZC" state. A Z breaks the sequence and causes a transition back to the "Z" state; any other character causes a return to the "NONE" state.
6. No matter what is received in the "ZCZC" state, the system stays there.

As you can see, the state graph is a compact representation of all this verbiage.

2.3. Outputs

An output or action can be associated with every combination of input and transition. An output is denoted by a letter or label and is separated from the input by a slash as follows: "input/output." If every input associated with a transition causes the same output, then denote it as: "input 1, input 2, input 3/output." If there are many different combinations of inputs and outputs, it's best to draw a separate parallel link for each output. Consider now an example that's closer to home—a simplified specification for a tape transport write-error recovery procedure, such as might be found in a tape control routine:

If there are no write errors detected, (input = OK), no special action is taken (output = NONE). If a write error is detected (input = BAD), backspace the tape one block and rewrite the block (output = REWRITE). If the rewrite is successful (input = OK), ignore the fact that there has been a rewrite. If the rewrite is not successful, try another backspace and rewrite. Return to the original state if and only if there have been two successive successful writes. If there have been two successive rewrites and a third error occurs, backspace ten centimeters and erase forward from that point (output = ERASE). If the erasure works (input = OK), return to the initial state. If it does not work, backspace and erase another ten centimeters of tape and treat the next write attempt as for the first erasure. If the second erasure does not clear the problem, put the tape transport out of service.

The state graph is shown in Figure 11-2. As in the previous example, the inputs and actions have been simplified. There are only two kinds of inputs (OK, ERROR) and four kinds of outputs (REWRITE, ERASE, NONE, OUT-OF-SERVICE). Do not confuse outputs with transitions or states. This can be confusing, because sometimes the name of the action or output is the same as the name of a state.*

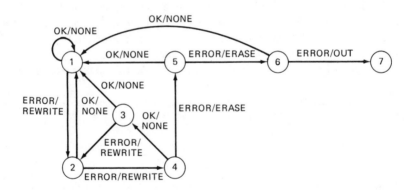

Figure 11-2. Tape-Control Recovery-Routine State Graph.

---

*An alternate, but equivalent, representation of behavior, called a "**Moore model**" (MOOR56), associates outputs with the state rather than with the transition. The model used in this book is called a "**Mealy model**" (MEAL55), in which outputs are associated with transitions. This is a generally more useful model because of the typical way in which software of this kind is implemented.

INPUT

STATE	OKAY	ERROR
1	1/NONE	2/REWRITE
2	1/NONE	4/REWRITE
3	1/NONE	2/REWRITE
4	3/NONE	5/ERASE
5	1/NONE	6/ERASE
6	1/NONE	7/OUT
7	...	...

2.4. State-Table Representation

State graphs tend to become cluttered and hard to follow. It's more convenient to represent the state graph as a table, that specifies the states, the inputs, the transitions, and the outputs. The following conventions are used:

1. Each row of the table corresponds to a state.
2. Each column corresponds to an input condition.
3. The box at the intersection of a row and column specifies the next state (the transition) and the output, if any.

The state table for the tape control example is shown in the above table.

I didn't specify what happens in state 7 because it's not germane to the discussion. You would have to complete the state graph for that state and for all the other states (not shown) that would be needed to get the tape back into operation. Compare the tabular representation with the graphical representation so that you can follow the action in either notation.

2.5. Software Implementation

There is almost never a direct correspondence between code and the behavior of a process described as a state graph. In the tape-control example, for instance, it is clear that the actual inputs would occur over a period of time. The routine is probably activated by an executive, and the inputs might be status-return interrupts from the tape-control hardware. Alternatively, the inputs might appear as status bits in a word in memory reserved for that transport. The tape-control routine itself probably is reentrant so that it can be simultaneously used for all transports.

The state diagram represents the total behavior consisting of the transport, the software, the executive, the status returns, interrupts, et cetera. There is no simple correspondence between lines of code and states. The state table, however, forms the basis for a widely used implementation shown in Figure 11-3. There are four tables involved:

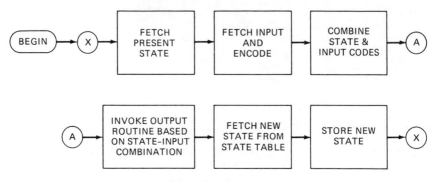

Figure 11-3. State-Table Implementation Overview

1. A table that encodes the input values into a compact list.
2. A table that specifies the next state for a given combination of state and input code.
3. A table or case statement that specifies the output, if any, associated with that state-input combination.
4. A table that stores the present state of every device or process that uses the same state table (e.g., one entry per tape transport).

This set of tables is collectively called a **state table** or a **state-transition table**. The routine operates as follows:

1. The present state is fetched from memory.
2. The present input value is fetched. If it is already numerical, it can be used directly; otherwise, it may have to be encoded into a numerical value, say by use of a case statement.
3. The present state and the input code are combined to yield an address (row and column) of the state table and its logical image (the output table).
4. The output table, either directly or via a case statement, contains the address of the routine to be executed (the output) for that state-input combination. The routine is invoked (possibly a trivial routine if no output is required).

5. The same index is used to fetch the new state value, which is then stored. Thereafter, the routine starts over with the new state.

Actually, there would be a whole lot of code between the end of this flow and the start of a new pass. Typically, there would be a return to the executive, and the state-control routine would only be invoked upon an interrupt. Many variations are possible. Sometimes, no input encoding is required. In other situations, the routine invoked is itself a state-table-driven routine that uses a different table. In assembly language programs, the input code and state are combined directly to provide an index, which, when used with a base address and offset, indirectly executes the required routine.

An explicit state-table implementation is advantageous when either the control function is likely to change in the future or when the system has many similar, but slightly different control functions. Their use in telecommunications, particularly telephony, is almost universal. This technique, when implemented in assembly language, provides very fast response time—one pass through the above flowchart can be done in ten to fifteen instruction execution times. It is not an effective technique for very small (four states or less) or very large (256 states or more) state graphs. In the small case, the overhead required to implement the state-table software would exceed any time or space savings that one might hope to gain. In very large state tables, the product of input values and states is large—in the thousands—and the memory required to store the tables becomes significant.

We are not, however, concerned with either implementation details or the economics of this approach but with how a state-table or state-graph representation of the behavior of a program or system can help us to design effective tests. If the programmers have implemented an explicit state-table approach, much of our work has been done for us. There is an interesting correlation, though: when a state-graph model appears to be appropriate, a state-table implementation is usually also appropriate. Sometimes, showing the programmers the kinds of tests developed from state-table descriptions can lead them to consider it as an implementation technique.

3. GOOD STATE GRAPHS AND BAD

3.1. General

This is a book on testing, and consequently, we must deal not with good state graphs, but with bad ones. What constitutes a good and a bad state graph is to some extent biased by the kinds of state graphs that are likely to be used in a software test design context. Here are some principles for judging:

1. The total number of states is equal to the product of the possibilities of factors that make up the state.
2. For every state and input there is exactly one transition specified to exactly one, possibly the same, state.
3. For every transition there is one output action specified. That output could be trivial, but at least one output does something sensible.*
4. For every state there is a sequence of inputs that will drive the system back to the same state.**

Figure 11.4 shows examples of improper state graphs.

Looking at these state graphs, you should realize that this kind of state diagram must have at least two different input codes. Don't confuse an input to the state diagram with an input from the world. The two "input" codes to a state graph could be "any real input from the world," and "no real input from the world"—which is why I've called them "input codes" rather than "inputs." With only one input code, there are only a few kinds of state graphs you can build: a bunch of disconnected individual states, disconnected strings of states that end in loops and variations thereof, or a strongly connected state graph in which all states are arranged in one grand loop. The latter can be implemented by a simple counter that resets at some fixed maximum value and therefore this elaborate modeling apparatus is hardly necessary.

I seem to have violated my own rules regarding outputs—I have. None of the examples showed output codes. There are two aspects to state graphs: the states with their transitions and the inputs that cause them, and the outputs associated with specific transitions. Just as in the flowchart model we concentrated on the control structure and tended to ignore the processing that did not directly affect the control flow, in state testing, we may ignore outputs, because it is the states and transitions that are of primary interest. Two state graphs with identical states, inputs, and transitions could have vastly different outputs, yet from a control point of view and from a state testing point of view, they would be almost identical. Consequently, we reduce the clutter caused by explicit output specifications if outputs are not interesting at the moment.

---

*State graphs without outputs can't do anything in the pragmatic world and can consequently be ignored. For output, include anything that could cause a subsequent action—perhaps setting only one bit.

**In other words, we've restricted the state graphs to be strongly connected (see Chapter 5). This may seem overly narrow, because many state graphs are not strongly connected. However, in a software context, the only nonstrongly connected state graphs are those used to set off bombs and other infernal machines or those that deal with failure, recovery, and illogical, irrecoverable conditions. A state graph that is not strongly connected usually has a bug.

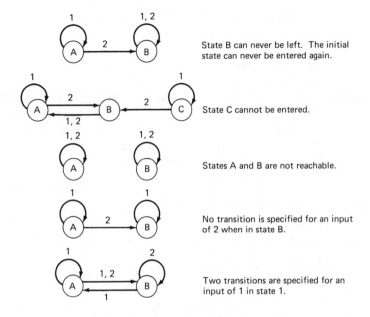

State B can never be left. The initial state can never be entered again.

State C cannot be entered.

States A and B are not reachable.

No transition is specified for an input of 2 when in state B.

Two transitions are specified for an input of 1 in state 1.

Figure 11-4. Improper State Graphs

3.2. State Bugs

3.2.1. Number of States

The number of states in a state graph is the number of states we choose to recognize or model. However, in practice, the state is directly or indirectly recorded as a combination of values of variables that appear in the data base. As an example, the state could be composed of the value of a counter whose possible values ranged from 0 to 9, combined with the setting of two bit flags, leading to a total of $2 \times 2 \times 10 = 40$ states. When the state graph represents an explicit state-table implementation, this value is encoded, and consequently, bugs in the number of states are less likely. However, the encoding can be wrong. Failing to account for all the states is one of the more common bugs related to software that can be modeled by state graphs. Because an explicit state-table mechanization is not typical, the opportunities for missing states abound. Find the number of states as follows:

1. Identify all the component factors of the state.
2. Identify all the allowable values for each component.

3. The number of states is the product of the number of allowable values of all the components: Period—Exactly—Precisely.

Before you do anything else, before you consider a single test case, go over the number of states you think there are with the number of states the programmer (or you, if you're wearing a programmer's hat) thinks there are. Differences of opinion are common. There's no point in designing tests that are intended to check the system's behavior in various states if there's no agreement on how many states there are. And if there's no agreement on how many states there are, there must be disagreement on what the system does in which states and on the transitions and the outputs. If it seems that I'm giving undue emphasis to the seemingly trivial act of counting states, it's because that act often exhumes fundamental design deficiencies. You don't need to wait until the design is completed. A functional specification is usually sufficient—as state testing is primarily a functional test tool. I read the functional specification and identify the factors and then the number of possible values for each factor. Then I question the designer. I want to get an identification or recognition for each state—with one state corresponding to each combination of condition values. It's gratifying work. It's gratifying to hear, "Oh yeah, I forgot about that one." Make up a table, with a column for every factor, such that all combinations of factors are represented. Before you get concurrence on outputs or transitions or the inputs that cause the transitions, get concurrence (or confirm for yourself) from the designer that every combination listed makes sense.

3.2.2. Impossible States

Some combinations of factors may appear to be impossible. Say that the factors are:

GEAR	R, N, 1,2,3,4	= 6 factors
DIRECTION	Forward, reverse, stopped	= 3 factors
ENGINE	Running, stopped	= 2 factors
TRANSMISSION	Okay, broken	= 2 factors
ENGINE	Okay, broken	= 2 factors
TOTAL		= 144 states

However, a broken engine cannot run, and consequently, the combination of factors for engine condition and engine operation yields only 3 rather than 4 states, so the total number of states is at most 108. A car with a broken transmission won't move for long, thereby further decreasing the number of feasible states. The discrepancy between the programmer's state count and the tester's state count is often due to a difference of opinion concerning "impossible states."

We should say "supposedly impossible" rather than "impossible." There are always alpha particles to contend with, as well as bugs in other routines. The implicit or explicit record of the values of the factors in the computer is not always the same as the values of those factors in the world—as was learned at Three Mile Island. One of the contributing factors to that fiasco was a discrepancy between the actual position of an actuator and the reported position of that actuator. The designers had falsely assumed that it was "impossible" for the actuator's actual position to be at variance with it's reported position. Two states, "Actuator-UP/Actuator Indicates-DOWN" and "Actuator-DOWN/Actuator-Indicates-UP" were incorrectly assumed to be impossible.

Because the states we deal with inside computers are not the states of the real world but rather a numerical representation of real-world states, the "impossible" states can occur. Wrack your brains for a devious scenario that gets the program into the impossible states, even if the world can't produce such states. If you can't come by such states honestly, invoke alpha particles or lighting storms. A robust piece of software will not ignore impossible states but will recognize them and invoke an illogical-condition handler when they appear to have occurred. That handler will do whatever is necessary to reestablish the system's correspondence to the world.*

3.2.3. Equivalent States

Two states are **equivalent** if *every* sequence of inputs starting from one state produces *exactly* the same sequence of outputs when started from the other

---

*The most bizarre case I know of of loss of correspondence between the computer's notion of the state and the world's notion of the state occurred at a major international air-freight depot more than a decade ago. The computer's purpose was to control a vast, automated warehouse that was used to transship and rearrange air-cargo loads. Pallets were taken off aircraft and loaded into the automatic warehouse. Automated fork-lift trucks trundled up and down the aisles and lofted the pallets into push-through bins that were stacked six stories high. Other fork-lift trucks pulled the pallets out and automatically put them onto conveyors bound for the aircraft on which the pallets belonged. Unfortunately, the designers had made several slight errors: 1) the power-transient protection was inadequate for the environment, 2) the hardware was not duplicated, 3) there appeared to be no automatic-recovery software, 4) the data-validation checks that should have continually verified the correspondence between the computer's notion of what the bins contained (stored as disc sectors) and the real contents of the bins were either missing or faulty, but surely inadequate, and 5) test sophistication matched design sophistication. It worked fine for a few days; then, came the lighting storm. Correspondence between the computer's version of the bins and the real bins was lost—but the system kept on doing it's thing—a thing out of Walt Disney's Fantasia (The Sorcerer's Apprentice). The warehouse was glutted and gutted in hours as automatic fork-lift trucks tried to stuff more pallets into full bins and remove nonexistent pallets from empty bins. They shut down. The old warehouse, of course, had been decommissioned by then. They then hired hundreds of university students to clamber about the six-story warehouse to identify just what was where. The several tons of frozen liver that not been placed into a refrigerated section were found in a few days. It took much longer to find the corpses in their coffins.

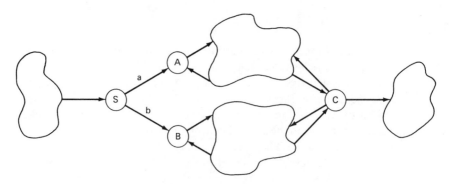

Figure 11-5. Equivalent States.

state.This notion can also be extended to sets of states. Figure 11-5 shows the situation:

Say that the system is in state S and that an input of *a* causes a transition to state A while an input of *b* causes a transition to state B. The blobs indicate portions of the state graph whose details are unimportant. If, starting from state A, *every* possible sequence of inputs produces *exactly* the same sequence of outputs that would occur when starting from state B, then there is no way that an outside observer can determine which of the two sets of states the system is in without looking at the record of the state. The state graph can be reduced to that of Figure 11-6 without harm:

The fact that there is a notion of state equivalency means that there is an opportunity for bugs to arise from a difference of opinion concerning which states are equivalent. If you insist that there exists another factor, not recognized by the programmer, such that the resulting output sequence for a given input sequence is different depending on the value of that factor, then you are asserting that two nonequivalent sets of states have been inadvertently merged. Conversely, if you cannot find a sequence of inputs which results in at least one different output when starting from either of two supposedly inequivalent states, then the states are equivalent and should be merged if only to simplify the software and thereby reduce the probability of bugs. Be careful, though, because equivalent states could come about as a result of good planning for future enhancements. The two states are presently indistinguishable but could in the future become distinguished as a result of an enhancement that brings with it the distinguishing factor.

Equivalent states can be recognized by the following procedures:

1. The rows corresponding to the two states are identical with respect to input/output/next state. However, the name of the next state could differ.

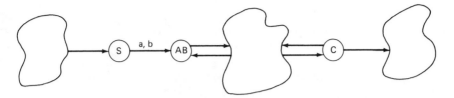

Figure 11-6. Equivalent States of Figure 11-5 Merged.

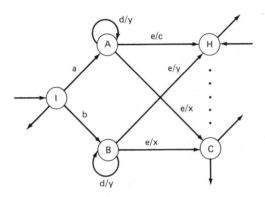

Figure 11-7. Equivalent States.

The two states are differentiated only by the input that distinguishes between them. This situation is shown in Figure 11-7. Except for the *a,b* inputs, which distinguish between states A and B, the system's behavior in the two states is identical for every input sequence. Therefore, they can be merged.

2. There are two sets of rows which, except for the state names, have identical state graphs with respect to transitions and outputs. The two sets can be merged (See Figure 11-8).

   The rows are not identical, but except for the state names (A1 = B1, A2 = B2, A3 = B3), the system's action, when judged by the relation between the output sequence produced by a given input sequence, is identical for either the A or the B set of states. Consequently, this state graph can be replaced by the simpler version shown in Figure 11-8c.

Don't expect to have corresponding states or sets of states so neatly labeled in terms of equivalences. There are more formal methods (beyond the scope of this book—see MILL66) for identifying and spotting such equivalences. It

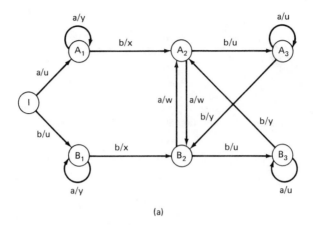

(a)

INPUT

STATE	a	b
I	A_1/Y	B_1/U
A_1	A_1/Y	A_2/X
B_1	B_1/Y	B_2/X
A_2	B_2/W	A_3/U
B_2	A_2/W	B_3/U
A_3	A_3/U	B_2/Y
B_3	B_3/U	A_2/Y

(b)

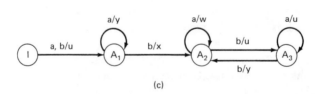

(c)

Figure 11-8. Merged Equivalent States.

is also possible to automate the process. However, because we are using state graphs as a test design tool rather than a design tool, and because the state graphs we deal with are usually small, a quick sketch of the state graphs of the two versions (the tester's and the designer's) will usually suffice to expose the similarities and the possibility of merging equivalent states.

Bugs, however, are often the result of the unjustifiable merger of seemingly equivalent states. Two states or two sets of states appear to be equivalent

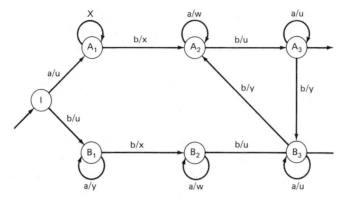

Figure 11-9. Unmergeable States.

because the programmer has failed to carry through to a proof of equivalence for *every* input sequence. The first few sequences looked good. Figure 11-9 is an example:

The input sequence <u>a</u>bbbb produces the output sequence <u>u</u>xuyy, while the input sequence <u>b</u>bbbb produces the output sequence <u>u</u>xuyu. The two sets of states are not equivalent although an incomplete analysis might lead you to believe that they are.

3.3. Transition Bugs

3.3.1. Unspecified and Contradictory Transitions

Every input/state combination must have a specified transition. If the transition is impossible, then there must be a mechanism that prevents that input from occurring in that state—look for it. If there is no such mechanism, what will the program do if, through a malfunction or an alpha particle, the impossible input occurs in that state? The transition for a given state/input combination may not be specified because of an oversight. *Exactly one transition must be specified for every combination of input and state.* However you model it or test it, the system will do *something* for every combination of input and state. It's better that it does what you want it to do, which you assure by specifying a transition, rather than what some bugs want it to do.

An actual program cannot have contradictions or ambiguities. Ambiguities are impossible because the program will do *something* (right or wrong) for every input. Even if the state does not change, by definition this is a transition to the same state. Similarly, real software cannot have contradictory transitions because computers can only do one thing at a time. A seeming contradiction could come about in a model if you don't account for all the factors that constitute the state and all the inputs. A single bit that escaped your notice, if that bit participates in the definition of the state, can double the number of states. However, if you are not monitoring that component of the state, it would appear that the program had performed contradictory transitions or had different outputs for what appeared to be the same input from the same state. If you say while debugging "sometimes it works and sometimes it doesn't," you have admitted that there is a component to the state that you are not aware of—a component that is probably caused by a bug. Exploring the real-state diagram and recording the transitions and outputs for each combination of input and state may lead you to discover the bug.

3.3.2. An Example

One of the most common source of ambiguities and contradictions is the specification. Specifications, unlike real programs, can be full of ambiguities and contradictions. The following example illustrates how to convert a specification into a state graph and how contradictions can come about. The tape-control routine will be used. Start with the first statement in the specification, and add to the state graph one statement at a time. Here is the first statement of the specification:

Rule 1   The program will maintain an error counter which will be incremented every time there is an error.

I don't yet know how many states there will be, but I might as well start by naming them with the values of the error counter. The initial state diagram might look like this:

OK/NONE

There are only two input values, "okay" and "error." A state-table will be easier to work with, and it's much easier to spot ambiguities and contradictions. Here is the first state table:

INPUT

STATE	OKAY	ERROR
0	0/none	1/
1		2/
2		3/
3		4/
4		5/
5		6/
6		7/
7		8/

There are no contradictions yet, but lots of ambiguities. It's easy to see how ambiguities come about—just stop the specification before it's finished. Let's add the rules one at a time and fill in the state graph as we go. Here are the rest of the rules; study them for a moment and see if you can find the problems, if any:

Rule 2   If there is an error, rewrite the block.

Rule 3   If there have been three successive errors, erase ten centimeters of tape and then rewrite the block.

Rule 4   If there have been three successive erasures and another error occurs, put the unit out of service.

Rule 5   If the erasure was successful, return to the normal state and clear the error counter.

Rule 6   If the rewrite was not successful, increment the error counter, advance the state, and attempt another rewrite.

Rule 7   If the rewrite was successful, decrement the error counter and return to the previous state.

Adding Rule 2, we get:

INPUT

STATE	OKAY	ERROR
0	0/NONE	1/REWRITE
1		2/REWRITE
2		3/REWRITE
3		4/REWRITE
4		5/REWRITE
5		6/REWRITE
6		7/REWRITE
7		8/REWRITE

Rule 3   If there have been three successive errors, erase ten centimeters of tape and then rewrite the block.

		INPUT
STATE	OKAY	ERROR
0	0/NONE	1/REWRITE
1		2/REWRITE
2		3/REWRITE, ERASE, REWRITE
3		4/REWRITE, ERASE, REWRITE
4		5/REWRITE, ERASE, REWRITE
5		6/REWRITE, ERASE, REWRITE
6		7/REWRITE, ERASE, REWRITE
7		8/REWRITE, ERASE, REWRITE

Rule 3, if followed blindly, causes an unnecessary rewrite. It's a minor bug, so let it go for now. However, it pays to check such things. There might be an arcane security reason for rewriting, erasing, and then rewriting again.

Rule 4   If there have been three successive erasures and another error occurs, put the unit out of service.

		INPUT
STATE	OKAY	ERROR
0	0/NONE	1/RW
1		2/RW
2		3/ER, RW
3		4/ER, RW
4		5/ER, RW
5		6/OUT
6		
7		

Rule 4 terminates our interest in this state diagram; consequently, we can dispose of states beyond 6. The details of state 6 will not be covered by this specification; presumably there is a way to get back to state 0. Also, we can credit the specifier with enough intelligence to not have expected a useless rewrite and erase prior to going out of service.

Rule 5   If the erasure was successful, return to the normal state and clear the counter.

INPUT

STATE	OKAY	ERROR
0	0/NONE	1/RW
1		2/RW
2		3/ER, RW
3	0/NONE	4/ER, RW
4	0/NONE	5/ER, RW
5	0/NONE	6/OUT
6		

Rule 6   If the rewrite was not successful, increment the error counter, advance the state, and attempt another rewrite.

Because the value of the error counter is the state, and because Rules 1 and 2 specified the same action, there seems to be no point to Rule 6 unless yet another rewrite was wanted. Furthermore, the order of the actions is wrong. If the state is advanced before the rewrite, we could end up in the wrong state. The proper order should have been: output = attempt-rewrite and then increment the error counter.

Rule 7   If the rewrite was successful, decrement the error counter and return to the previous state.

INPUT

STATE	OKAY	ERROR
0	0/NONE	1/RW
1	0/NONE	2/RW
2	1/NONE	3/ER, RW
3	0/NONE 2/NONE	4/ER, RW
4	0/NONE 3/NONE	5/ER, RW
5	0/NONE 4/NONE	6/OUT
6		

Rule 7 got rid of the ambiguities but created contradictions. The specifier's intention probably was:

Rule 7A   If there have been no erasures and the rewrite is successful, return to the previous state.

We're guessing, of course, and we could guess wrong, especially if the issue is obscure and the technical details unfamiliar. The only thing you can assume is that it's unlikely that a satisfactory implementation will result from a contradictory specification. If the state graph came from a design specification, be especially stupid. Be literal in your interpretation and smile when the designer accuses you of nit-picking over semantics. It's funny, (tragic, really) how such "purely semantic" issues turn out to cause tough bugs.

3.3.3. Unreachable States

An **unreachable state** is like unreachable code. It is a state that no input sequence will get you to. An unreachable state is not impossible, just as unreachable code is not impossible. Furthermore, it may be possible that there are transitions from the unreachable state to other states. In fact, there usually are, because the state became unreachable because of one or more incorrect transitions.

Unreachable states can come about from previous "impossible" states. You listed all the factors and laid out a table listing all states. Some of these corresponded to previously "impossible" states. The designer, perhaps after some rough persuasion, agrees that something should be done about the unreachable states. "Easy," he thinks, "provide no transitions into them." However, there should still be a transition out of all such states. At the least, a transition to an error-recovery procedure or an exception handler.

An isolated, unreachable state here and there, which clearly relates to impossible combinations of real-world state-determining conditions are acceptable. However, if you find groups of connected states that are isolated from others, there is reason for concern. There are two possibilities: 1) there is a bug; some transitions are missing, 2) the transitions are there, but you don't know about it; there are other inputs and associated transitions to reckon with. Typically, such hidden transitions are caused by software operating at a higher priority level or by interrupt processing.

3.3.4. Dead States

A **dead state**, or set of dead states, is a state which once entered cannot be left. This is not necessarily a bug, but it is suspicious. If the software was designed to be the fuse for a bomb, we would expect at least one such state. A set of states may appear to be dead because the program has two modes of operation. In the first mode it goes through an initialization process that consists of several states. Once initialized, it goes to a working set of states, which, within the context of the routine, cannot be exited. The initialization states are unreachable to the working states, and the working states are dead to the initialization states. The only way to get back might be after a system crash and restart. Legitimate dead states are rare. They occur mainly with system-level issues and device handlers. In normal software, if it's not possible to get from any state to any other, there's reason for concern.

3.4. Output Errors

The set of states, the transitions, and the inputs that cause those transitions could be correct, there could be no dead or unreachable states, but the output for the transition could be incorrect. Output actions must be verified independently of states and transitions. That is, you should distinguish between a program whose state graph is correct but has the wrong output for a transition and one whose state graph is incorrect. The most likely reason for an incorrect output is an incorrect call to the routine that executes the output. This is usually a localized and minor error. Errors in the state graph are more serious because they tend to be related to fundamental control-structure problems. If the routine is implemented as a state table, both types of errors are of comparable severity.

3.5. Impact of Bugs

Let's say that a routine is specified as a state graph and that the state graph has been verified as correct in all details. Code or tables or a combination of both must still be implemented. A bug can manifest itself as one or more of the following symptoms:

1. Wrong number of states.
2. Wrong transition for a given state-input combination.
3. Wrong output for a given transition.
4. Pairs of states or sets of states are inadvertently made equivalent (factor lost).
5. States or sets of states are split to create nonequivalent duplicates.
6. States or sets of states become dead.
7. States or sets of states become unreachable.

4. STATE TESTING

4.1. General Principles

The approach for state testing is analogous to that used for path-testing flowcharts. Just as it's impractical to go through every possible path in a flowchart, it's impractical to go through every path in a state graph. A path in a state graph, of course, is a succession of transitions caused by a sequence of inputs. The notion of coverage is identical to that used for flowcharts—pass through each link (i.e., each transition must be exercised). Assume that some state is particularly interesting—call it the initial state. Because most realistic state graphs are strongly connected, it should be possible to go through all states and back to the initial state, when starting from there. The starting point of state testing is:

1. Define a set of covering input sequences that get back to the initial state when starting from the initial state.
2. For each step in each input sequence, define the expected next state, the expected transition, and the expected output (if any).

A set of tests then, consists of three sets of sequences:

1. Input sequences
2. Corresponding transitions or next-state names
3. Output sequences

Because the state graph is probably strongly connected, McCabe's metric tells us the minimum number of input sequences it will take to provide coverage. Do it by state-transition counts, where states are nodes and transition links, or equivalently, treat each node with outgoing transitions as a decision node or a case-statement node.

4.2. Limitations

Just as node-link coverage in a flowchart model of program behavior did not guarantee complete testing, state-transition coverage in a state-graph model does not guarantee complete testing. However, things are slightly better because it's not necessary to consider any sequence that is longer than the total number of states. NOTE: Everything discussed in this section applies equally well to flowchart graphs with suitable translation.

Chow (CHOW78) defines a hierarchy of paths and methods for combining paths to produce covers of a state graph. The simplest is called a "0 switch," and it corresponds to testing each transition individually. The next level consists of testing transition sequences that consist of two transitions, called "1 switches." The maximum-length switch is an $n-1$ switch, where n is the number of states. Chow's primary result shows that in general, a 0 switch cover (which I've called a "full" cover for a flowchart) is capable of catching output errors but may not catch some transition errors. In general, one must use longer and longer covering sequences to catch transition errors, missing states, extra states, et cetera. The theory of what constitutes a sufficient number of tests (i.e., input sequences) to catch specified kinds of state-graph errors is still in its infancy and is beyond the scope of this book. Furthermore, practical experience with such theory as there is is limited, and the efficacy of such methods as bug catchers has yet to be demonstrated sufficiently well to earn these methods a solid place in the tester's tool repertoire. However, work continues and progress in the form of semiautomatic test tools and effective methods are sure to come. Meanwhile, we have the following experience:

1. Simply identifying the factors that contribute to the state, calculating the total number of states, and comparing this number to the designer's notion catches some bugs.
2. Insisting on a justification for all supposedly dead, unreachable, and impossible states and transitions catches a few more bugs.
3. Insisting on an explicit specification of the transition and output for every combination of input and state catches many more bugs.
4. A set of input sequences that provide coverage of all nodes and links is a mandatory minimum requirement.
5. In executing state tests, it is essential that means be provided (e.g., instrumentation software) to record the sequence of states (e.g., transitions) resulting from the input sequence and not just the outputs that result from the input sequence.

4.3. What to Model

Because every combination of hardware and software can in principle be modeled by a sufficiently complicated state graph, this representation of software behavior is applicable to every program—the utility of such tests, however, is more limited. The state graph is a behavioral model—it is functional rather than structural and is therefore far removed from the code. As a method of testing, it is a bottom-line method that ignores structural detail to focus on behavior. However, it is advantageous to look into the data base to see how the factors that create the states are represented in order to get a state count. More than most test methods, state-graph tests yield their biggest payoffs during the design of the tests rather than during the running thereof. Because they can be constructed from a design specification long before flowcharting and coding, they help catch deep bugs early in the game when correction is inexpensive. Here are some generic situations in which it may prove useful to design state-graph tests:

1. Any processing where the output is based on the occurrence of one or more sequences of events, such as detection of specified input sequences,

sequential format validation, and other situations in which the order of inputs is important.

2. Most protocols between systems, between humans and machines, between modules within a system.

3. Device handlers such as tape handlers, disc handlers, and the like, that involve complicated retry and recovery procedures if the action depends on the state.

4. Transaction flows where the transactions are such that they can stay in the system indefinitely. For example, online users, tasks in a multi programming system.

5. High-level control functions within an operating system. Transitions between user states, supervisor's states, and so on. Security handling of records, permission for read/write/modify privileges, priority interrupts and transitions between interrupt states and levels, recovery issues and the safety state of records and/or processes with respect to recording recovery data.

6. The behavior of the system with respect to resource management and what it will do when various levels of resource utilization are reached. Any control function that involves responses to thresholds where the system's action depends not just on the threshold value, but also on the direction in which the threshold is crossed. This is a normal approach to control functions. A threshold passage in one direction stimulates a recovery function, but that recovery function is not suspended until a second, lower threshold is passed going the other way.

7. Whenever a function is directly and explicitly implemented as one or more state-transition tables.

5. SUMMARY

1. State testing is primarily a functional testing tool whose payoff is best in the early phases of design.

2. A real program cannot have contradictory or ambiguous transitions or outputs, but a specification can and does. Use a state-table to verify the specification's validity.

3. Count the states.

4. Insist on a specification of transition and output for every combination of input and states.

5. Apply a minimum set of covering tests.

6. Instrument the transitions to capture the sequence of states and not just the sequence of outputs.

7. Count the states.

12

GRAPH MATRICES
AND APPLICATIONS

1. SYNOPSIS

Graph matrices are introduced as another representation for graphs; some useful path-tracing tools resulting therefrom are examined.

2. THE PROBLEM

Graphs, as an abstraction of software structure, were introduced early in this book and used throughout. Yet another graph that modeled software behavior was introduced in Chapter 11. There are many other kinds of graphs, not discussed in this book, that are useful in software testing. Whenever a graph is used as a model, sooner or later we trace paths through it—to find a set of covering paths, a set of values that will sensitize paths, what logic function controls the flow from one node to another, the processing time of the routine, if the routine pushes or pops, or if a state is reachable or not. Even the seemingly algebraic representation, such as BNF and regular expressions, can be converted to equivalent graphs. Much of test design consists of tracing paths through a graph.

Path tracing is not easy, and it's subject to error. You can miss a link here and there or cover some links twice—even if you do use a marking pen to note which paths have been taken. You're tracing a long complicated path through a routine when the telephone rings—you've lost your place before you've had a chance to mark it. I get confused tracking paths, so naturally I assume that other people also get confused.

One solution to this problem is to represent the graph as a matrix and to apply operations to that matrix that are equivalent to path tracing. These methods are not necessarily easier than path tracing, but because they are more methodical and mechanical and do not depend on your ability to "see" a subtle path, they are more reliable. Furthermore, tools which automate path tracing are based on the use of these methods or their equivalences. Two methods are provided:

1. Matrix multiplication, which is used to get the path expression from every node to every other node
2. A collapsing process (analogous to the determinant of a matrix), which gets the path expression from any node to any other specified node

3. THE MATRIX OF A GRAPH

3.1. Basic Principles

A **graph's matrix** is a square array with one row and one column for every node in the graph. Each row-column combination corresponds to a potential relation between the node corresponding to the row and the node corresponding to the column. The relation, for example, could be the link name, if there is a link between the nodes. Some examples of graphs and their associated matrices are shown in Figure 12-1. Observe the following:

1. The size of the matrix (i.e., the number of rows and columns) is equal to the number of nodes.
2. There is a place to put every possible direct connection or link between any node and any other node.
3. The entry at a given row and column intersection is the link weight for the link (if any) that connects the two nodes in that direction.
4. A connection from node i to node j does not imply a connection from node j to node i. Note that in Figure 12-1h, the (5,6) entry is *m*, but the (6,5) entry is *c*.
5. If there are several links between two nodes, then the entry is a sum, with the "+" sign indicating parallel links as usual.

In general, an entry is not just a simple link name but a path expression corresponding to the paths between the pair of nodes. Furthermore, as with the graphs, an entry can be a link weight or an expression in link weights (see Chapter 6 for a refresher). Finally, all arithmetic operations must be understood to imply the arithmetic operations that are appropriate to the weights that the links represent.

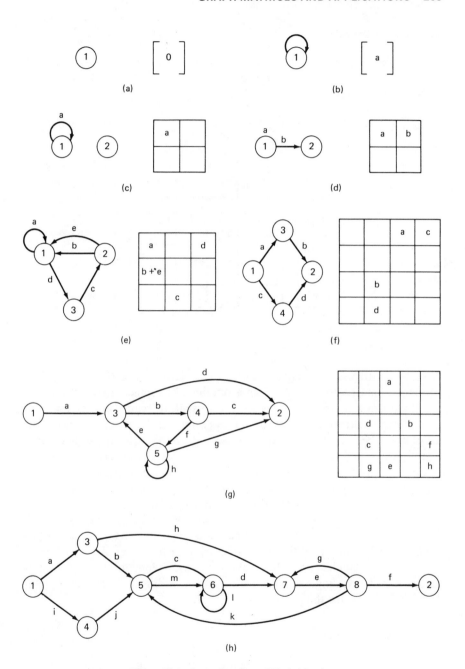

Figure 12-1. Some Graphs and Their Matrices.

3.2. A Simple Weight

The simplest weight we can use is to note that a connection exists or does not exist. Let "1" mean that a connection exists and "0" that it does not. The arithmetic rules are:

$$1 + 1 = 1, 1 + 0 = 1, 0 + 0 = 0, 1 \times 1 = 1, 1 \times 0 = 0, 0 \times 0 = 0.$$

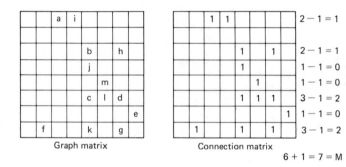

Graph matrix   Connection matrix

$$6 + 1 = 7 = M$$

A matrix with weights defined like this is called a **connection matrix**. The connection matrix for Figure 12-1h is obtained by replacing each entry with 1 if there is a link and 0 if there isn't. As usual, to reduce clutter we don't write down 0 entries. Each row of matrix (whatever the weights) denotes the set of links that exit the node that corresponds to that row, and each column denotes the set of links that enter the node that corresponds to that column. A decision node is a node with more than one nonzero entry in its row. A junction node is a node with more than one nonzero entry in its column. A self-loop is an entry along the diagonal. Because rows 1, 3, 6, and 8 of the above matrix all have more than one entry, those nodes are decision nodes. Using the principle that a case statement is equivalent to n − 1 decisions, by subtracting 1 from the total number of entries in each row and ignoring rows with no entries (such as node 2), we obtain the equivalent number of decisions for each row. Adding these values and then adding 1 to the sum yields McCabe's metric for the graph.

3.3. Further Notation

Talking about the "entry at row 6, column 7" is wordy. To compact things, the entry corresponding to node i and column j, which is to say the link or link weights between nodes i and j, is denoted by a_{ij}. A self-loop about node i is denoted by a_{ii}, while the link weight for the link between nodes j and i is denoted by a_{ji}. The path segments expressed in terms of link names and, in this notation, for several paths in the graph of Figure 12-1h are:

$$
\begin{aligned}
abmd &= a_{13}a_{35}a_{56}a_{67}; \\
degef &= a_{67}a_{78}a_{87}a_{78}a_{82} \\
ahekmlld &= a_{13}a_{37}a_{78}a_{85}a_{56}a_{66}a_{66}a_{67}
\end{aligned}
$$

because:

$$a_{13} = a, a_{35} = b, a_{56} = m, a_{66} = l, a_{67} = d, \text{etc.}$$

The expression "$a_{ij}a_{jj}a_{jm}$" denotes a path from node i to j, with a self-loop at j and then a link from node j to node m. The expression "$a_{ij}a_{jk}a_{km}a_{mi}$" denotes a path from node i back to node i via nodes j, k, and m. An expression such as "$a_{ik}a_{km}a_{mj} + a_{in}a_{np}a_{pj}$" denotes a pair of paths between nodes i and j, one going via nodes k and m and the other via nodes n and p. By convention, when we don't want to be explicit about which pair of nodes we are talking about, node "i" is the first node and node "j" is the second node of the pair.

This notation may seem cumbersome, but it's not intended for working with the matrix of a graph but for expressing operations on the matrix. It's a very compact notation. For example:

$$\sum_{i=1}^{n} a_{ik}a_{kk}a_{ki}$$

This denotes the set of all possible paths between nodes i and j via one intermediate node. But because "i" and "j" denote any node, this expression is the set of all possible paths between any two nodes via one intermediate node.

4. THE POWERS OF A MATRIX

4.1. Principles

Each entry in the graph's matrix, that is, each link, expresses a relation that exists between the pair of nodes that corresponds to that entry. It is a direct relation. But we are usually interested in indirect relations that may exist by virtue of intervening nodes between the two nodes of interest. Multiplying the matrix by itself (using suitable arithmetic for the weights) yields a new matrix which expresses the relation between each pair of nodes via one intermediate node. That is, it is a matrix that represents all path segments that are two links long. Similarly, the third power of the matrix represents all path segments that are three links long. And the k'th power of the matrix represents all path segments that are k links long. Because a matrix has at most n nodes, and no path can be more than n − 1 links long without incorporating some path segment that has already been accounted for, it is generally not necessary to go beyond the n − 1 power of the matrix. As usual, concatenation of links or the weights of links is represented by multiplication, and parallel links or path expressions by addition.

Let A be a matrix whose general entries are a_{ij}. Then the set of all paths between any node i and any other node (possibly i itself) j, via all possible intermediate nodes, is given by:

$$a_{ij} + \sum_{k=1}^{n} a_{ik}a_{kj} + \sum_{k=1}^{n}\sum_{m=1}^{n} a_{ik}a_{km}a_{mj} + \sum_{k}^{n}\sum_{m}^{n}\sum_{l}^{n} a_{ik}a_{km}a_{ml}a_{lj} +$$

$$\cdots \sum_{k=1}^{n}\sum_{m=1}^{n}\sum_{l=1}^{n} \cdots \sum_{p=1}^{n} a_{ik}a_{km}a_{ml} \cdots a_{qp}a_{pj}$$

As formidable as this expression might appear it states nothing more than:

1. Consider the relation between every node and its neighbor.
2. Extend that relation by considering each neighbor as an intermediate node.
3. Extend further by considering each neighbor's neighbor as an intermediate node.
4. Continue until the longest possible, nonrepeating path has been established.
5. Do this for every pair of nodes in the graph.

4.2. Matrix Powers and Products

Given a matrix whose entries are a_{ij}, the square of that matrix is obtained by replacing every entry with:

$$a_{ij} = \sum_{k=1}^{n} a_{ik}a_{kj}$$

More generally, given two matrices A and B, with entries a_{ik} and b_{kj} respectively, their product is a new matrix C, whose entries are c_{ij}, where:

$$c_{ij} = \sum_{k=1}^{n} a_{ik}b_{kj}$$

$$\begin{bmatrix} a_{11}\,a_{12}\,a_{13}\,a_{14} \\ a_{21}\,a_{22}\,a_{23}\,a_{24} \\ a_{31}\,a_{32}\,a_{33}\,a_{34} \\ a_{41}\,a_{42}\,a_{43}\,a_{44} \end{bmatrix} \times \begin{bmatrix} b_{11}\,b_{12}\,b_{13}\,b_{14} \\ b_{21}\,b_{22}\,b_{23}\,b_{24} \\ b_{31}\,b_{32}\,b_{33}\,b_{34} \\ b_{41}\,b_{42}\,b_{43}\,b_{44} \end{bmatrix} = \begin{bmatrix} c_{11}\,c_{12}\,c_{13}\,c_{14} \\ c_{21}\,c_{22}\,c_{23}\,c_{24} \\ c_{31}\,c_{32}\,c_{33}\,c_{34} \\ c_{41}\,c_{42}\,c_{43}\,c_{44} \end{bmatrix}$$

$$c_{11} = a_{11}b_{11} + a_{12}b_{21} + a_{13}b_{31} + a_{14}b_{41}$$
$$c_{12} = a_{11}b_{12} + a_{12}b_{22} + a_{13}b_{32} + a_{14}b_{42}$$
$$c_{13} = a_{11}b_{13} + a_{12}b_{23} + a_{13}b_{33} + a_{14}b_{43}$$
$$\cdots$$
$$\cdots$$
$$\cdots$$
$$c_{32} = a_{31}b_{12} + a_{32}b_{22} + a_{33}b_{32} + a_{34}b_{42}$$
$$\cdots$$
$$\cdots$$
$$\cdots$$
$$c_{44} = a_{41}b_{14} + a_{42}b_{24} + a_{43}b_{34} + a_{44}b_{44}$$

The indexes of the product (e.g. (3,2) in c_{32}) identify respectively, the row of the first matrix and the column of the second matrix that will be combined to yield the entry for that product in the product matrix. The c_{32} entry is obtained by combining, element by element, the entries in the third row of the A matrix with the corresponding elements in the second column of the B matrix. I use two hands. My left hand points and traces across the row while the right points down the column of B. It's like patting your head with one hand and rubbing your stomach with the other at the same time: it takes practice to get the hang of it. Applying this to the matrix of Figure 12-1g yields:

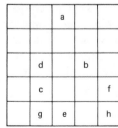

A

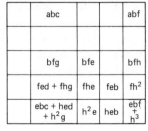

A²   A³

It can be shown that $A^2A = AA^2$—that is, matrix multiplication is associative. Consequently, you can get A^4 in any of the following ways: A^2A^2, $(A^2)^2$, A^3A, AA^3. However, because multiplication is not necessarily commutative, you must remember to put the contribution of the left-hand matrix in front of the contribution of the right-hand matrix and not to inadvertently reverse the order. The loop terms are important. These are the terms that appear along the principal diagonal (the one that slants down to the right). The initial matrix had a self-loop about node 5, link *h*. No new loop is revealed with paths of length 2, but the cube of the matrix shows additional loops about node 3 (*bfe*), and node 4(*feb*) and another link about node 5 (*ebf*). It's clear that these are really the same loop that incorporates the three nodes.

If instead of link names you use some other weight, as in Chapter 6, and use the appropriate arithmetic rules, the matrix displays the property corresponding to that weight. Successive powers of the matrix display the property when considering paths of length exactly 2, exactly 3, et cetera. The entire development of Chapter 6 and the applications discussed there carries over virtually unchanged into an equivalent matrix method.

4.3. The Set of All Paths

Recall that our objective is to use matrix operations to obtain the set of all paths from every node to every other node or, equivalently, a property (described by a link weight) over the set of all paths from every node to every other node, using of course, the appropriate arithmetic rules for such weights. The set of all paths from every node to every other node is easily expressed in terms of matrix operations. It's given by the following infinite series of matrix powers:

$$\sum_{i=1}^{\infty} A^i = A + A^2 + A^3 \cdots A^{\infty}$$

This is an eloquent, but practically useless, expression. Consider for the moment graphs that have no loops. Let I be a matrix whose size is n by n, where n is the number of nodes in the graph of interest. Let I's entries consist of multiplicative identity elements along the principal diagonal. For link names, this can be the number "1." For other kinds of weights, it is that entity, such that $a \times \lambda = a$, where a is the link weight and λ is the multiplicative identity for that kind of weight. The above product can be rephrased as:

$$A(I + A + A^2 + A^3 + A^4 \cdots A^{\infty})$$

But in general, because $A + A = A$, $(A + I)^2 = A^2 + A + A + I = A^2 + A + I$. Furthermore, for any finite n,

$$(A + I)^n = I + A + A^2 + A^3 \ldots . A^n.$$

Therefore, the original infinite sum can be replaced with the simpler:

$$\sum_{L=1}^{\infty} A^i = A(A + I)^{\infty}$$

This is an improvement, because in the original expression we had both infinite products and infinite sums, and now we have only one infinite product to contend with. The above is valid whether or not there are loops. If we restrict our interest for the moment to paths of length n − 1, where n is the number of nodes, the set of all paths is given by:

$$\sum_{L=1}^{n-1} A^i = A(A + I)^{n-2}$$

This is an interesting set of paths because with n nodes, no path can exceed n − 1 nodes without incorporating some path segment which is already incorporated in some other path or path segment. Finding the set of all such paths is somewhat easier because it is not necessary to explicitly do all the intermediate products. The following algorithm is effective:

1. Express n − 2 as a binary number.
2. Take successive squares of $(A + I)$, leading to $(A + I)^2$, $(A + I)^4$, $(A + I)^8$, and so on.
3. Retain only those binary powers of $(A + I)$ that correspond to a 1 value in the binary representation of n − 2.
4. The set of all paths of length n − 1 or less is obtained as the product of the matrices you got in Step 3 with the original matrix.

As an example, let the graph have 16 nodes. We want the set of all paths of length less than or equal to 15. The binary representation of n − 2 (14) is $2^3 + 2^2 + 2$. Consequently, the set of paths is given by:

$$\sum_{L=1}^{15} A^i = A(A + I)^8 (A + I)^4 (A + I)^2$$

This required one multiplication to get the square, squaring that to get the fourth power, and squaring again to get the eighth power, then three more multiplications to get the sum, for a total of six matrix multiplications without additions, compared to fourteen multiplications and additions if gotten directly.

4.4. Loops

Every loop forces us into a potentially infinite sum of matrix powers. The way to handle loops is similar to what we did for regular expressions. Every loop shows up as a term in the diagonal of some power of the matrix—the power at which the loop finally closes. The impact of the loop can be obtained by preceding every element in the row of the node at which the loop occurs by the path expression of the loop term starred and then deleting the loop term. For example, using the matrix for the graph of Figure 12-1e, we obtain the following succession of powers for $A + I$:

1	a			
	1			
	d	1	b	
	c		1	f
	h*g	h*e		1

$(A + I)*$

1	ad	a	ab	
	1			
	d+ bc	1	b	bf
	c + fh*g	fh*e	1	f
	h*g+ h*ed	h*e	h*eb	1

$(A + I)^2 *$

1	ad + abc	a	ab	abf
	1			
	d + bc + bfh*g	1 + bfh*e	bf	bf
	c + fh*g + fh*ed	fh*e	1 + fh*eb	f
	h*e(d + bc) + h*g + h*ed	h*e	h*eb	1 + h*ebf

$(A + I)^3 *$

The first matrix $(A + I)$ had a self-loop about node 5 link h. Moving link h out to the other entries in the row, leaving the "1" entry at the (5,5) position, yielded the $h*g$ and the $h*e$ entries at (5,2) and (5,3) respectively. No new loops were closed for the second power. The third power matrix has a loop about node 3, whose expression is $bfh*e$. Consequently, all other entries in that row must be premultiplied by $(bfh*e)*$, to yield $(bfh*e)*(d + bc + bfh*g)$ for (3,2), $(bfh*e)*b$ for (3,4), and $(bfh*e)*bf$ for (3,5). Similarly, the $fh*eb$ term in the (4,4) entry will be removed by multiplying every other nonzero term in the fourth row by $(fh*eb)*$, and the elements in the fifth row will be multiplied by $(h*ebf)*$ to get rid of the loop.

The application of this method of characterizing all possible paths is straightforward. The above operations are to be interpreted in terms of the arithmetic appropriate to the weights used. Note however, if you are working with predicates and you are after the logical function (predicate function, truth-value function) between every node and every other node, this may lead to loops in the logical functions. The specific "arithmetic" for handling predicate loops has not been discussed in this book. The information can be found in any good text on switching and automata theory, such as MILL66. The methodology is a combination of the methods of Chapters 9 and 11. The kind of code that leads to predicate loops is not very nice, not well-structured, hard to understand, and harder to test—and anyone who codes that way deserves the analytical difficulties arising therefrom. Predicate loops come about from declared or undeclared program switches. This means that the routine's code remembers, which is another way of saying that the code is probably not reentrant. If you didn't realize that you put such a loop in you probably didn't intend to. If you did intend it, you should have expected the loop.

5. NODE-REDUCTION METHOD

5.1. General

The matrix powers usually tell us more than we want to know about most graphs. In the context of testing, we are usually interested in establishing a relation between two nodes, typically the input node and the output node. In a debugging context, it is unlikely that we would want to know the path expression between every node and every other node; there also, it is the path expression or some other related expression between a specific pair of nodes that is sought. For example, "How did I get *here* from *there*? The method of this section is a matrix equivalence to the node-by-node reduction procedure of Chapter 6. The advantage of this matrix-reduction method is that it is more methodical than the graphical method presented in Chapter 6 and does not entail continually redrawing the graph. The procedure is almost identical to the graphical method. It consists of the following steps:

1. Select a node for removal; replace the node by equivalent links that bypass that node and add those links to the links they parallel.
2. Combine the parallel terms and simplify as you can.
3. Observe loop terms and adjust the outgoing links from every node that had a self-loop to account for the effect of the loop.
4. The result is a matrix whose size has been reduced by 1. Continue until only the two nodes of interest exist.

5.2. Some Matrix Properties

If you numbered the nodes of a graph from 1 to n, you would not expect that the behavior of the graph or the program that it represents would change if you happened to number the nodes differently. Node numbering is arbitrary and cannot affect anything. The equivalent to renumbering the nodes of a graph is to interchange the rows and columns of the corresponding matrix. Say that you wanted to change the names of nodes "i" and "j" to "j" to "i," respectively. You would do this on the graph by erasing the names and rewriting them. To interchange node names in the matrix you must interchange both the corresponding rows and the corresponding columns. Interchanging the names of nodes 3 and 4 in the graph of Figure 12-1g results in the following.

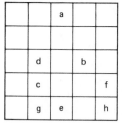

a) Original

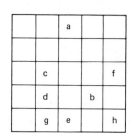

b) Rows 3 and 4 interchanged

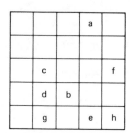

c) Interchange complete

If you redraw the graph based on c, you will see that it is identical to the original except that node 3's name has been changed to 4, and node 4's name to 3.

5.3. The Algorithm

The first step is the most complicated one: eliminating a node and replacing it with a set of equivalent links. Using the example of Figure 12-1g, we must first, as with the matrix multiplication, remove the self-loop at node 5. This produces the following matrix:

The reduction is done one node at a time by combining the elements in the last column with the elements in the last row and putting the result into the entry at the corresponding intersection. In the above case, the f in column 5 is first combined with $h*g$ in column 2, and the result ($fh*g$) is added to the c term just above it. Similarly, the f is combined with $h*e$ in column 3 and put into the 4,3 entry just above it. The justification for this operation is that the column entry specifies the links entering the node, while the row specifies the links leaving the node. Combining every column entry with the corresponding row entries for that node produces exactly the same result as the node-elimination step in the graphical-reduction procedure. To make things clearer, what we did was: $a_{45}a_{52} = a_{42}$ or $f \times h*g = a_{52}$, but because there was already a c term there, we have effectively created a parallel link in the (5,2) position leading to the complete term of $c + fh*g$. The matrix resulting from this step is:

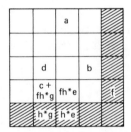

If any loop terms had occurred at this point, they would have been taken care of by eliminating the loop term and premultiplying every term in that row by the loop term starred. There are no loop terms at this point. The next node to be removed is node 4. The b term in the (3,4) position will combine with the (4,2) and (4,3) terms to yield a (3,2) and a (3,3) term respectively. Carrying this out and discarding the unnecessary rows and columns yields:

		a
d + bc + bfh*g	bfh*e	

Removing the loop term yields:

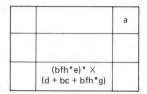

There is only one node to remove now, node 3. This will result in a term in the (1,2) entry, whose value is:

$$a(bfh^*e)^*(d + bc + bfh^*g)$$

This is the path expression from node 1 to node 2. Stare at this one for awhile before you object to the $(bfh^*e)^*$ term that multiplies the d; any fool can see the direct path via d from node 1 to the exit, but you could miss the fact that the routine could circulate around nodes 3, 4, and 5 before it finally took the d link to node 2.

5.4. Applications

5.4.1. General

The path expression is usually the most difficult and complicated to get. The arithmetic rules for most applications are simpler. In this section we'll redo applications from Chapter 6, using the appropriate arithmetic rules, but this time using matrices rather than graphs. Refer back to the corresponding examples in Chapter 6 to follow the successive stages of the analysis.

5.4.2. Maximum Number of Paths

The matrix corresponding to the graph on page 123 follows. The successive steps are shown. Recall that the inner loop about nodes 8 and 9 was to be taken from zero to three times, while the outer loop about nodes 5 and 10 was to be taken exactly four times. This will affect the way the diagonal loop terms are handled.

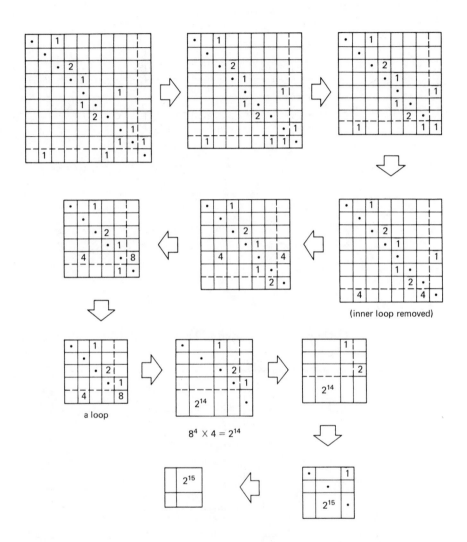

5.4.3. The Probability of Getting There

A matrix representation for the probability problem on page 130 is:

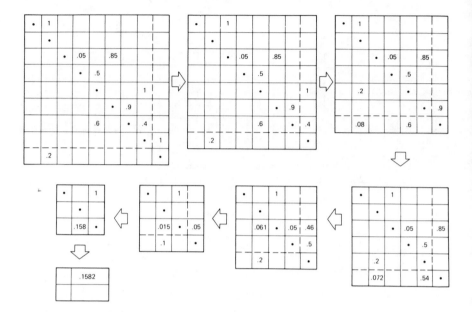

5.4.4. Get/Return Problem

The GET/RETURN problem on page 139 has the following matrix reduction:

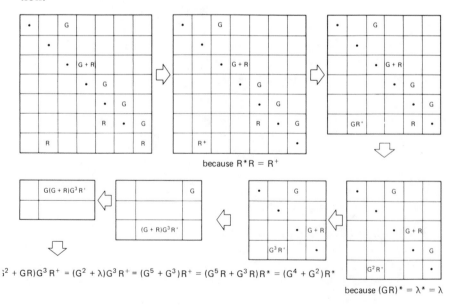

5.5. Some Hints

Redrawing the matrix over and over again is as bad as redrawing the graph to which it corresponds. You actually do the whole job in place. Things get more complicated, and expressions get larger as you progress, so you make the low-numbered boxes larger than the boxes corresponding to higher-numbered nodes, because those are the ones that are going to be removed first. Mark the diagonal lightly so that you can easily see the loops. With these points in mind, the worksheet for the flowchart timing-analysis graph on page 135 looks like this:

171.2143 (1)	61.5 (1)				
60 109.71 (.7) (1.0)	116 (.3)	10 (1)			
50 (.7)	106 (.3)	20 (.6)	13 43 (.4) (1)		8 (1)
7 (.7)	63 (.3)				
			12 (.6)	5 (.4)	

This may appear difficult to follow, but it becomes obvious when you try it out for yourself. A lot of tedium can be saved by judicious node numbering. Leave complicated, knotty areas until last so that you won't have to carry a whole lot of ugly terms all through the analysis. And because the last node to be removed is node 2 in the matrix, I've made it a practice to label the first node in the graph "node 1" and the last node in the graph "node 2," as I've done throughout this book.

REFERENCES

REFERENCES

AKIY71   Akiyama, K. An example of software system debugging. Proceedings of the 1971 IFIP Congress, Amsterdam: North-Holland, 1971.

          Bug statistics on routines ranging in size from 700 to 5500 instructions with correlation to the number of decisions and subroutine calls. Proportion of bugs found in unit testing, integration testing, and system testing.

ALBE76   Alberts, David S. The economics of software quality assurance. Proceedings of the 1976 National Computer Conference, Montvale, NJ: AFIPS Press, 1976.

ALLE72   Allen, F.E. and Cocke, J. Graph theoretic constructs for program control flow analysis. IBM Research Report RC3923, T.J. Watson Research Center, Yorktown Heights, New York, 1972.

ANDE79   Anderson, Robert B. *Proving Programs Correct.* New York: John Wiley and Sons, 1979.

BACK59   Backus, J. The syntax and the semantics of the proposed international algebraic language of the ACM-GAMM Conference. Information Processing, Paris, 1959.

BAKE79A   Baker, A.L. and Zweben, S.H. A comparison of measures of control flow complexity. Proceedings COMSAC'79, New York: IEEE, 1979.

BAKE80   Baker, A.L. A comparison of measures of control flow complexity. *IEEE Transactions on Software Engineering* SE-6: 506-511 (1980).

BARN72   Barnes, B.H. A Programmer's view of automata. *Computing Surveys,* 4: 222-239 (1972).

          General introduction to the concept of state graphs and related automata theory topics from a software-application perspective.

BAUE79   Bauer, J.A. and Finger, A.B. Test plan generation using formal grammars. IEEE, Proceedings of the Fourth International Conference on Software Engineering, Munich, September 1979.

          Use of state-graph model for processes and the automated generation of test cases based on such models. Examples of application to telephone call control.

BEIZ78   Beizer, Boris. *Micro-Analysis of Computer System Performance.* New York: Van Nostrand Reinhold, 1978.
Analytical models of software processing time, memory utilization, queueing theory, system models, mass memory latency models, model validation, and system tuning.

BEIZ79   Beizer, Boris. *Organizacja Systemow Komputerowyc.* Warsaw: Panstwowe Wydawnictwo Naukowe, 1979.
Polish edition of B. Beizer, The *Architecture and Engineering of Digital Computer Complexes.* Volume I, New York: Plenum Press, 1971.

BEIZ83   Beizer, Boris. *Software System Testing and Quality Assurance.* New York: Van Nostrand Reinhold, 1983.
Companion to this book. Focuses on management and system-level techniques. Organization of testing, functional testing, formal-acceptance testing, stress testing, software reliability, bug-prediction methods, software metrics, test teams, adversary teams, design reviews, walkthroughs, etc.

BELF76   Belford, P.C. and Taylor, D.S. Specification verification—a key to improving software reliability. PIB Symposium on Computer Software Engineering, Polytechnic Institute of New York, April 1976.
Examines the verification of specifications, use of specification languages, and related subjects.

BELF79   Belford, P.C. and Berg, R.A. Central flow control software development: A case study of the effectiveness of software engineering techniques. IEEE CH 1479, May 1979, 85-93.
Use of decision-to-decision paths as a measure of complexity. Statistics on bugs caught during design review, unit testing, and system testing based on 24,000 lines of executable code. Statistics show that limiting the module size is not effective and that module sizes of 100 to 200 lines would be better than 50 lines of executable code. Decision-to-decision paths are a better predictor of the number of test cases and development effort required than are lines of code.

BOEH73   Boehm, B.W., Software and its impact: A quantitative assessment. *Datamation* 19: 48-59 (May 1973).

BOEH75A   Boehm, B.W., McClean, R.K., and Urfrig, D.B. Some experience with automated aids to the design of large-scale reliable software. *IEEE Transactions on Software Engineering* SE-1: 125-133 (March 1975). (Also in IEEE, Proceedings of the International Conference on Reliable Software, Los Angeles, Calif., April 1974).
Statistics on software errors.

BOEH75B   Boehm, B.W. Software design and structuring. In *Practical Strategies for Developing Large Software Systems,* Edited by Ellis Horowitz, Reading, MA: Addison-Wesley, 1975.

BOEH75C Boehm, B.W. The high cost of software. In *Practical Strategies for Developing Large Software Systems.* Edited by Ellis Horowitz. Reading, MA: Addison-Wesley, 1975.

BOEH79 Boehm, B.W. Software engineering—as it is. IEEE, Proceedings of the Fourth International Conference on Software Engineering, Munich, September 1979.
   Survey of the state of the art in testing and software engineering. Lots of good aphorisms.

BOHM66 Bohm, C., and Jacopini, G. Flow diagrams, Turing machines, and languages with only two formation rules. *Communications of the ACM* 9: 366-371 (1966).
   Proof that single-entry, single-exit programs can be constructed without GOTOs using only the IF-THEN-ELSE and DO-WHILE constructs.

BOIE72 Boies, S.J., and Gould, J.D. A behavioral analysis of programming—on the frequency of syntactical errors. IBM Research Report RC-3907, T.J. Watson Research Center, Yorktown Heights, New York, June 1972.

BROW73 Brown, J.R., and Lipow, M. The quantitative measurement of software safety and reliability. TRW Report SDP-1176, 1973.

BRZO62 Brozozowski, J.A. A survey of regular expressions and their application. *IRE Transactions on Electronic Computers* EC-11: 324-335, (1962).
   Survey of regular expression theory and its application to logic design and finite automata.

BRZO63 Brzozowski, J.A., and McCluskey, E.J., Jr. Signal flow graph techniques for sequential circuit state diagrams. *IEEE Transactions on Electronic Computers* EC-12: 67-76 (1963).
   Basic paper that applies Mason's flow graph techniques to regular expressions and state diagrams of finite state automata.

CHEN78A Chen, E.T. Program complexity and programmer productivity. *IEEE Transactions on Software Engineering* SE-4: 187-194 (1978). (Also in Proceedings COMSAC '77, New York: IEEE, 1977.)

CHOW78 Chow, T.S. Testing software design modeled by finite state machines. *IEEE Transactions on Software Engineering* SE-4: 78-186 (1978). (Also in Proceedings COMSAC '77, New York: IEEE, 1977).
   Testing of software that can be effectively modeled by state graphs with examples from telephony. Definition of n-switch cover as a generalization of covering. Categorizes types of state-graph errors and shows relation between type of cover and the kind of errors that can and cannot be caught.

CHUN78 Chung, Paul, and Gaiman, Barry. Use of state diagrams to engineer communications software. IEEE, Proceedings of the Third International Conference on Software Engineering, Atlanta, Georgia, May 1978.

CICU75   Cicu, A., Maiocchi, M., Polillo, R., and Sardoni, A. Organizing tests during software evolution. IEEE, Proceedings of the 1975 International Conference on Reliable Software, Los Angeles, April 1975.

CURT79A   Curtis, B., Sheppard, S.B., and Milliman, P. Third time charm: stronger predictions of programmer performance by software complexity metrics. IEEE, Proceedings of the Fourth International Conference on Software Engineering, Munich, March 1979.
          Continuation of related experiments (see SHEP79C). Correlation between McCabe, Halstead, and program-length metrics. Halstead's metric appears to be a better predictor than either length or McCabe's metric. Study dealt with small FORTRAN routines.

CURT80B   Curtiss, B. Measurement and experimentation in software engineering. *Proceedings of the IEEE* 68: 1144-1157 (1980)
          Survey of various complexity metrics including McCabe's and Halstead's. State of the art and current research on software metrics.

DEMI78   DeMillo, R.A., Lipton, R.J., and Sayward, F.G. Hints on test data selection: help for the practicing programmer. *Computer* 4: 34-43 (April 1978).

DEON74   Deo, Narsingh. *Graph Theory With Applications to Engineering and Computer Science.* Englewood Cliffs, New Jersey: Prentice-Hall, 1974.

DNIE78   Dniesirowski, A, Guillaume, J.M., and Mortier, R. Software engineering in avionics applications. IEEE, Proceedings of the Third International Conference on Software Engineering, Atlanta, Georgia, May 1978
          Good bug categories. Statistics on bugs caught during specification, design, and coding and the kind of testing used to catch them. Also effort required to catch bugs.

ELSH76B   Elshoff, J.L. An analysis of some commercial PL/I programs. *IEEE Transactions on Software Engineering* SE-2: 113-120 (1976).

ELSH78B   Elshoff, J.L., and Marcotty, M. On the use of the cyclomatic number to measure program complexity. *ACM SIGPLAN Notices* 13: 33-40 (1978).

ENDR75   Endres, A. An analysis of errors and their causes in system programs. IEEE, Proceedings of the 1975 International Conference on Reliable Software, Los Angeles, April 1975. (Also in *IEEE Transactions on Software Engineering* SE-1: 140-149 (1975).
          Detailed error categories and statistics on bugs for each.

FEUE79A   Feuer, A.R., and Fowlkes, E.G. Some results from an empirical study of computer software. IEEE, Proceedings of the Fourth International Conference on Software Engineering, Munich, April 1979.
          Study of 197 PL/I routines averaging 54 statements. Focus is on maintainability. Shows that program size is a good guide to maintainability as measured by error density, time to repair, and subjective judgement. Shows that decision density (related to McCabe's metric) is probably better suited to large programs.

FEUE79B   Feuer, A.R., and Fowlkes, E.B. Relating computer program maintainability to software measures. *Proceedings of the 1979 National Computer Conference*, Montvale NJ: AFIPS Press, 1979.
Study of 123 PL/I modules in business data processing applications. Relates complexity measure to maintainability. Applies Halstead's metric to maintainability question.

FISC79   Fischer, K.F., and Walker, M.J. Improved software reliability through requirements verification. *IEEE Transactions on Reliability* R-28: 233-240 (1979).

FOSD76A   Fosdick, L.D., and Osterweil, L.J. Data flow analysis in software reliability. *ACM Computing Surveys* 8: 305-330 (1979).
Use of graphs, survey of symbolic execution methods, path expressions derived from flow graphs, detection of data-flow anomalies.

FOST80   Foster, K.A. Error sensitive test case analysis (ESTCA). *IEEE Transactions on Software Engineering* SE-6: 258-264 (1980).
Three rules for structural testing based on input-data domains: useful rules for arithmetic processing.

GABO76   Gabow, H.N., Maheshwari, S.N., and Osterweil, L.J. On two problems in the generation of program test paths. *IEEE Transactions on Software Engineering* SE-2: 227-231 (1976).
Construction of constrained paths.

GANN76   Gannon, J.D. Data types and programming reliability—some preliminary evidence. *PIB Symposium on Computer Software Engineering*, Polytechnic Institute of New York, April 1976.
Discussion of data types and data-type operands. Summary of errors related to data types.

GANN79   Gannon, C. Error detection using path testing and static analysis. *Computer* 12: 26-31 (August 1979).

GILB77   Gilb, T. *Software Metrics.* Cambridge, Mass: Winthrop, 1977.

GOEL78B   Goel, A.L., and Okumoto, K. Analysis of recurrent software errors in a real-time control system. ACM, Proceedings of the 1978 Annual Conference.

GOOD75   Goodenough, J.B., and Gerhart, S.L. Toward a theory of test data selection. *IEEE Transactions on Software Engineering* SE-1: 156-173 (1975).
Limitations of structure-based testing and formal methods of proof. Formal definitions for reliable tests, valid tests, complete tests, and successful tests. Use of decision tables as aid to test case design.

GOOD79   Goodenough, J.B. A survey of program testing issues. In *Research Directions in Software Technology.* Edited by Peter Wegner. Cambridge Mass: MIT Press, 1979.

GREE76   Green, T.F., Schneidewind, N.F., Howard, G.T., and Parisequ, R. Program structures, complexity, and error characteristics. PIB Symposium on Computer Software Engineering, Polytechnic Institute of New York, April 1976.

HALS75   Halstead, M.H. Software physics: basic principles. IBM Technical Report RJ-1582, T.J. Watson Research Center, Yorktown Heights, New York, 1975.

HALS77   Halstead, M.H. *Elements of Software Science.* New York: Elsevier North-Holland, 1977.

HANF70   Hanford, K.V. Automatic generation of test cases. *IBM System Journal* 9: 242-257 (1979).
          Use of BNF and syntax-directed software to generate syntactically valid test cases of PL/I code for testing a PL/I compiler.

HANS78   Hanson, W.J. Measurement of program complexity by the pair cyclomatic number, operator count. *ACM SIGPLAN Notices* 13: 29-32 (1978).

HAUG64   Haugk, G., Tsiang, S.H., and Zimmerman, L. System testing of the number 1 electronic switching system. *Bell System Technical Journal* 43: 2575-2592 (1964).

HECH72   Hecht, M.S., and Ullman, J.D. Flow graph reducibility. *SIAM Journal on Computing* 1: 188-202 (1972).

HECH77B   Hecht, M.S. *Flow Analysis of Computer Programs.* New York: Elsevier North-Holland, 1977.
          A clearly written, deep, exposition of the application of graph theory to the analysis of programs. Primarily aimed at questions related to compiler design and code optimization. Large bibliography. For the mathematically mature.

HEND75   Henderson, P. Finite state modeling in program development. IEEE, Proceedings of the 1975 International Conference on Reliable Software, Los Angeles, April 1975.

HETZ73   Hetzel, W.C. (Editor) *Program Test Methods.* Englewood Cliffs, New Jersey: Prentice-Hall, 1972.
          Basic book on testing. Comprehensive pre-1972 bibliography on testing and related subjects.

HOFF77   Hoffmann, H.M. An experiment in software error occurrence and detection. MS Thesis, Naval Postgraduate School, Monterey, California, June 1977.

HORE79   Horejs, J. Finite semantics for program testing. IEEE, Proceedings of the Fourth International Conference on Software Engineering, Munich, September 1979.

HOWD76   Howden, W.E. Reliability of the path analysis testing strategy. *IEEE Transactions on Software Engineering* SE-2: 208-215 (1976).

Proof that the automatic generation of a finite test set which is sufficient to test a routine is not a computable problem. Formal definition of computation error, path error, and other kinds of errors.

HOWD78A Howden, W.E. A survey of static analysis methods. In Miller, E., and Howden, W.E. *Software Testing and Validation Techniques.* IEEE Tutorial, New York: IEEE, 1978. (IEEE Catalog No. EHO-138-8)

HOWD78B Howden, W.E. A survey of dynamic analysis methods. In Miller, E., and Howden, W.E. *Software Testing and Validation Techniques.* IEEE Tutorial, New York: IEEE, 1978. (IEEE Catalog No. EHO-138-8)

HOWD78C Howden, W.E. Empirical studies of software validation. In Miller, E., and Howden, W.E. *Software Testing and Validation Techniques.* IEEE Tutorial, New York: IEEE, 1978. (IEEE Catalog No. EHO-138-8)

HOWD78D Howden, W.E. Theoretical and empirical studies of program testing. *IEEE Transactions on Software Engineering* SE-4: 293-298 (1978). (Also in IEEE, Third Conference on Software Engineering, Atlanta, Georgia, 1978)
Symbolic trace, algebraic value trace, reliability of various methods.

HOWD78E Howden, W.E. An evaluation of the effectiveness of symbolic testing. *Software Practice and Experience* 8: 381-397 (1978). (Also, University of California at San Diego, Computer Science Technical Report, No. 16, (1977).
Shows that path testing is 64% effective.

HOWD80 Howden, W.E. Functional program testing. *IEEE Transactions on Software Engineering* SE-6: 162-169 (1980). (Also in Proceedings COMSAC'78, IEEE, November 1978).
Role and use of functional testing as applied mostly to the testing of mathematical software—proposes combined functional/structural testing.

HUAN75 Huang, J.C. An approach to program testing. *ACM Computing Surveys* 7: 113-128 (1975).
Structure-based testing, graph models, path coverage, path count, path predicates; discusses use of inserted counters in links to measure test thoroughness.

HUAN79 Huang, J.C. Detection of data flow anomaly through program instrumentation. *IEEE Transactions on Software Engineering* SE-5: 226-236 (1979).

ITOH73 Itoh, Daiju, and Izutani, Takao. Fadebug-1, a new tool for program debugging. IEEE, Record of the 1973 Symposium on Computer Software Reliability, April-May 1973.
Summary of findings on the utility of path-tracing test tool. Statistics on bug types.

KARN53 Karnaugh, M. The map method for synthesis of combinational logic circuits. *Transactions of the AIEE Part I* 72: 593-598 (1953).

KERN76   Kernighan, B.W., and Plauger, P.J. *Software Tools.* Reading, Mass: Addison-Wesley, 1976.

KRAU73   Krause, K.W., Smith, R.W., and Goodwin, M.A. Optimal software test planning through automated network analysis. IEEE, Proceedings of the 1973 Symposium on Computer Software Reliability.
Early example of path testing, graph models, coverage, and automated generation of paths.

LEIB74   Leibholz, S.W., and Wilson, L.D. *User's Guide to Computer Crime.* Radnor, PA: Chilton, 1974.
One of your better "How To Do It" books.

LITE76   Litecky, C.R., and Davis, G.B. A study of errors, error proneness, and error diagnosis in COBOL. *Communications of the ACM* 19: 33-37 (1976).

MANN78   Manna, Zohar, and Waldinger, Richard. The logic of computer programming. *IEEE Transactions on Software Engineering* SE-4: 199-229 (1978).
Survey of methodology and limitation of formal proofs of program correctness. State of the art. Examples drawn from numerical problems.

MANZ80   Manzo, John. Private communication.

MAYE72   Mayeda, Wataru. *Graph Theory.* New York: John Wiley & Sons, 1972
Still one of the best introductions to graph theory and related subjects. Application to many different areas.

MARI60   Marimont, R.B. Application of graphs and boolean matrices to computer programming. *SIAM Review* 2: 259-268 (October 1960).

MCCA76   McCabe, T.J. A complexity measure. *IEEE Transactions on Software Engineering* SE-2: 308-320 (1976).
Definition of cyclomatic complexity, subgraphs that lead to structured code, relation of covering paths to complexity. Basic paper.

MCCL56   McCluskey, E.J., Jr. Minimization of boolean functions. *Bell System Technical Journal* 35: 1417-1444 (1956).
A "must" method for more than six boolean variables and for any boolean function minimization software design.

MCNA60   McNaughton, R., and Yamada, H. Regular expressions and state graphs for automata. *IRE Transactions on Electronic Computers* EC-9: 39-47 (1960).
Survey of the theory of regular expressions as applied to finite state automata. Proof of several fundamental theorems.

MEAL55   Mealy, G.H. A method for synthesizing sequential circuits. *Bell System Technical Journal* 34: 1045-1079 (1955).

MILL66   Miller, R.E., *Switching Theory.* Volumes I and II. New York: John Wiley and Sons, 1966.
Basic reference on switching and automata theory.

MILL74   Miller, E.F., et. al, Structurally based automatic program testing. IEEE, EASCON Proceedings, 1974.

MILL75   Miller, E.F., and Melton, R.A. Automated generation of test case data sets. IEEE, Proceedings of the 1975 International Conference on Reliable Software, Los Angeles, April 1975.

MILL77C   Miller, E.F. Program testing: art meets theory. *Computer* 10: 42-51. Survey of the state of the art of testing, vis-a-vis theory and practice.

MILL78A   Miller, E.F., and Howden, W.E. (Editors). *Tutorial: Software Testing and Validation Techniques.* IEEE Computer Society, 1978. (IEEE Catalog No. EHO-138-8).

MILL78B   Miller, E. F. Program testing—an overview for managers. Proceedings COMSAC'78, Chicago, November 1978. (IEEE Catalog No. 78C-H1338-3C).

MOOR56   Moore, E.F. Gedanken experiments on sequential machine. In *Automata Studies. Annals of Mathematical Studies, No. 34.* Princeton, New Jersey: Princeton University Press, 1956.

MORA78   Moranda, P.B. Limits to program testing with random number inputs. Proceedings COMSAC'78, New York: IEEE, 1978.

MYER77   Myers, G.J. An extension to the cyclomatic measure of program complexity. *ACM SIGPLAN Notices* 12: 62-64 (1977).

MYER79   Myers, G.J. *The Art of Software Testing.* New York: John Wiley and Sons, 1979.

NAFT72   Naftaly, S.M., and Cohen, M.C. Test data generators and debugging systems . . . workable quality control. *Data Processing Digest* 18: (February and March 1972). Survey of automatic test data generation tools.

NTAF78   Ntafos, S.C. A graph theoretic approach to program testing. PhD Dissertation, Northwestern University, Evanston, Illinois, 1978. Path-covering problems and other subjects applicable to automatic test-data generation.

PAIG73   Paige, M.R., and Balkovich, E.E. On testing programs. IEEE, Proceedings of the 1973 Symposium on Computer Software Reliability, New York, April 1973. Structural testing based on graph model; covering.

PAIG75A   Paige, M.R., Program graphs, an algebra, and their implication for programming. *IEEE Transactions on Software Engineering* SE-1: 286-291 (1975).

PAIG77   Paige, M.R., and Holthouse, M.A. On sizing software testing. IEEE, International Symposium on Fault Tolerant Computing, June 1977.

PAIG78   Paige, M.R. An analytical approach to software testing. IEEE, Proceedings COMSAC'78, New York: IEEE, November 1978.

PETE76   Peters, L.J., and Tripp, L.L. Software design representation schemes. PIB Symposium on Computer Software Reliability, Polytechnic Institute of New York, April 1976.
Survey of methods and models for representing the behavior of programs, including: HIPO charts, activity charts, structure charts, control graphs, decision tables, flowcharts, transaction diagrams, and others. Comments on use and experience with various methods. Critiques and suggestions for new representations. One of the most complete surveys of its kind.

PETE80   Peters, L.J. Software representation and composition techniques. *IEEE Proceedings* 68: 1085-1093 (1980).
Survey of software description models including Leighton diagrams, design trees, structure charts, SADT diagrams, flowcharts, Hamilton-Zeldin diagrams, decision tables, Nassi-Shneiderman model, data-flow diagrams. Design methodologies that use these models.

QUIN55   Quine, W.V. A way to simplify truth functions. *The American Math Monthly* 52: 627-631 (1955).
Like the McCluskey method (MCCL56), but cumbersome notation.

RAMA66   Ramamoorthy, C.V. Analysis of graphs by connectivity considerations. *Journal of the ACM* 13: 211-222 (1966).
Early paper on graph models of programs.

RAMA75A   Ramamoorthy, C.V., and Ho, S.F. Testing large software with automated evaluation systems. *IEEE Transactions on Software Engineering* SE-1: 46-58 (1975).

RAMA75B   Ramamoorthy, C.V., and Kim, K.H. Optimal placement of software monitors aiding systematic testing. *IEEE Transactions on Software Engineering* SE-1: 403-410 (1975).
Discussion of monitor software inserted in code to measure path traversals and to detect errors. Discussion of algorithm for optimum placement of a minimum number of probes.

RAMA76   Ramamoorthy, C.V., Ho, S.F., and Chen, W.T. On the automated generation of program test data. *IEEE Transactions on Software Engineering* SE-2: 293-300 (1976).
Structured-based testing; generation of paths followed by symbolic execution, test constraints on input variables, problems of arrays, difficulty of solving constraint equations, random generation of test cases that satisfy contraints. FORTRAN CASEGEN and automated test case generator.

REIF79   Reifer, D.J. Software failure modes and effects analysis. *IEEE Transactions on Reliability* R-28: 247-249 (1979).

RUBE75   Rubey, R.J., Dana, J.A., and Biche, P.W. Quantitative aspects of software validation. *IEEE Transactions on Software Engineering* SE-1: 150-155 (1975)

SCHI78   Schick, G.J., and Wolverton, R.W. An analysis of competing software reliability models. *IEEE Transations on Software Engineering* SE-4: 104-120 (1978).
A survey of the history, development, and experience with various models of software reliability.

SCHE65   Scheff, B. Decision-table structure as input format for programming automatic test equipment systems. *IEEE Transactions on Electronic Computers* EC-14: 248-250 (1965).
Use of decision tables in automatic generation of test cases.

SCHN75   Schneidewind, N.F. Analysis of error processes in computer software. IEEE, Proceedings 1975 Conference on Reliable Software, Los Angeles, April 1975.

SCHN79A Schneidewind, N.F., and Hoffman, H.M. An experiment in software error data collection and analysis. *IEEE Transactions on Software Engineering* SE-5: 276-286 (1979).
Study of 500 modules averaging 480 statements each with a total sample of 250K statements (including comments). Job was a modification of an operating system. Breakdown by error types and the project phase during which the error was discovered. Relation between McCabe's metric and the fundamental circuit matrix or basis. Shows that McCabe's metric correlates well with the number of bugs and the time needed to correct them, but not with the time required to find them. Shows qualitative change in bug density and labor in the region of M = 5. This last result, however, is based on a small sample.

SCHN79B Schneidewind, N.F. Software metrics for aiding program development debugging. Proceedings of the 1979 National Computer Conference, Montvale NJ: AFIPS Press, 1979.
Comparison of several measures of complexity and their relation to discovered bugs. Reachability matrix and uses thereof.

SCHN79C Schneidewind, N.F. Application of program graphs and complexity analysis to software development and testing. *IEEE Transactions on Reliability* R-28: 192-198 (1979).
Tutorial overview of graph-related concepts. Fundamental circuit matrix and relation to McCabe's metric. Experiments on ALGOL code; 173 bugs found in 2000 statements. Semi automatic test tools described.

SCHN79D Schneidewind, N.F. Case study of software complexity and error detection simulation. IEEE, Proceedings of the Third International Software Application Conference, Chicago, November 1979.

SCHW71   Schwarts, J.T. An overview of bugs. In *Debugging Techniques in Large Systems*. Edited by R. Rustin. Englewood Cliffs, NJ: Prentice-Hall, 1971
Nature of bugs and their sources. Debugging and test tools. Difference between debugging and testing.

SHED80   Shedley, Ethan I., *The Medusa Conspiracy*. New York: Viking, 1980.
Espionage thriller dealing with bugs that lead to potential nuclear holocaust and Middle East war. Shedley claims to be a professional software type.

SHEP79C   Sheppard, S.B., Curtis, W., Milliman, P., Borst, M.A., and Love, T. First-year results from a research program on human factors in software engineering. Proceedings of the 1979 National Computer Conference, Montvale NJ: AFIPS Press, 1979.
Experiment using thirty-six programmers working in FORTRAN on small (fifty-statement) programs. The experiment tested the ease of modification and how well the subjects could recall the control structure. The study shows good correlation between McCabe's and Halstead's metrics, but neither metric particularly effective for small routines.

SHOO75   Shooman, M.L., and Bolsky, M.I. Types, distributions and test and correction times for programming errors. IEEE, Proceedings 1975 Conference on Reliable Software, Los Angeles, April 1975.

THAY77   Thayer, T.A. Software reliability study. Rome Air Development Center, Report No. RADC-TR77-216. (Also: Thayer, T.A., Lipow, A.M., and Nelson, E.C. Software reliability study. TRW Defense and Space Systems Group, Final Technical Report, February 1976. (AD-A030798).
The watershed study on software reliability. More than 300 pages of software-related statistics.

VEIT52   Veitch, E.E. A chart method for simplifying truth functions. ACM, Proceedings of the 1952 Annual Conference.

VOGE80   Voges, U., Gmeiner, L., and von Mayrhauser, A.A. SADAT—An automated test tool. *IEEE Transactions on Software Engineering* SE-6: 286-290 (1980).

WAGO73   Wagoner, W.L. The final report on a software reliability measurement study. The Aerospace Corporation, El Segundo, California, August 1973.

WALS79   Walsh, T.J. A software reliability study using a complexity measure. Proceedings of the 1979 National Computer Conference, Montvale New Jersey: AFIPS Press, 1979.
McCabe's measure applied to 276 routines in the Aegis system. Discusses break at M = 10.

WHIT80   White, L.J., and Cohen, E.I. A domain strategy for computer program testing. *IEEE Transactions on Software Engineering* SE-6: 247-257 (1980).
Use of linear predicates and associated inequalities to establish test cases, boundary choices, etc. Generalization to n-dimensional problems.

WILK77   Wilkens, E.J. Finite state techniques in software engineering. Proceedings COMSAC'77, New York: IEEE, 1977.
Application of finite-state machine models to software design.

WOLV75   Wolverton, R.W. The cost of developing large scale software. In *Practical Strategies for Developing Large Software Systems.* Edited by E. Horowitz. Reading Mass: Addison-Wesley 1975.

WOOD78   Woods, J.L. Path selection for symbolic execution systems. PhD Dissertation, University of Massachusetts, 1978.

WOOD80   Woodward, M.R., Hedley, D., and Hennell, M.A. Experience with path analysis and testing of programs. *IEEE Transactions on Software Engineering* SE-2: 278-286 (1976).
          Using link count as a metric; path testing; and two measures of cover.

YERH80   Yeh, R.T., and Zave, P. Specifying software requirements. *IEEE Proceedings* 68: 1077-1085 (1980).
          Examines specifications as a source of program bugs and suggests methodology for specification design.

ZELK78   Zelkowitz, M.V. Perspective on software engineering. *ACM Computing Surveys* 10: 197-214 (1978).
          Survey of the state of the art and the issues in software engineering.

ZOLN77   Zolnowski, J.C., and Simmons, R.B. Measuring program complexity. Proceedings COMPCON Fall 1977, New York: IEEE, 1977.

INDEX

INDEX

acceptance test, 9, 168
action entry, **191**
action stub, **191**
addressing, 42, 43
ad-lib test, 167
alpha particles, **30**, 148, 150, 224, 237, 241
ambiguity
, format, 164
, natural language, 219
, program, 205-241
, specification, 222-223, 242
arc, **90**
architecture, system, 19, 21, 174
arithmetic
, get/return, 136, 139, 266
, increment/decrement, 139
, maximum path count, 122-125
, minimum path count, 125-128
, processing time, 134
, push/pop, 136
, set/reset, 136, 140, 142
, weight, 252
assembly, conditional, **71**-72
assembly language, 32, 40, 42, 142, 185
automatic test generation, 67, 96

Backus-Naur form, 148, **151**-154, 274
base set of circuits, 92-**93**-96, 106
behavioral model, 249
bias, 6, 17, 46, 49, 67
binary decision, **37**, 55, 97, **191**
binary limit test, 161
bit field, 183
bit, reserved, 188
black box testing. *See: functional testing*
boolean algebra, 191-226
equation, 206
rules, 201, 203
in test design, 205

, translation of specifications to, 221
branch probability, 129, 133
branch, unconditional, 39, 125
bug, 11-12
, absolute address, 42
, accountability for, 7
, arithmetic, 23
, assembler, 28
, call, 19
, characteristics of, 3
, coding, 32-33, 66, 85
, compiler, 28
, control, 21, 24, 32
, consequences of, 15-16, 30, 148
, cost of, 3
, dangling code, 32
, data, 25, 27, 34
-base, 23-33, 54
declaration, 25-26
initialization, 27
residue, 27-28
type, **31**
validation, 29
, firmware, 11
, floating point, 23
, functional, 17
, future, 61, 184, 188
, hardware, 11
, hook, 188-190
, initialization, 20, 21, 24, 25, 50-52, 53, 55,
144, 188
, instrumentation, 68, 69, 71
, interactive, 21
, interface, 7, 18-19, 54, 103
, interlock, 84
, intermittent, 242
, language, 85-86
, latent, 150
, location dependent, 72

, logic, 25, 46, 242
, loop, 24
, manipulative, 23
, output, 247
, parameter conflict, 26, 28
, peek-a-boo, 72
, preprocessor, 28
, prevention, 3, 22, 61, 173
, private vs. public, 3
, process, 23
, protocol, 19
, race condition, 72
, resource, 22-23
, relative address, 43
, sequence, 21, 24, 142
, source of, 18
, source syntax, 32-33
, specification, 17
, state-transition, 233-235, 241, 247
statistics, 2, 33-35, 61, 104, 105, 269, 270,
    272, 275, 279, 280
, symptoms of, 4, 16
, syntax, 32, 164-165
, system, 17, 18, 22
, taxonomy of, 15-35
, test, 7, 11-12, 13, 14, 17
, timing, 19, 20, 72
, translation, 40
, typographical, 33, 46, 65
, unreachable code, 45
, utility program, 28

capability machine, **86**
case statement, 37, **38**, 97, 183, 186
checkout procedure, 70
circuit, **93**
   base set, **93**
code comparison, 65-66
coding bug, 32
coding conventions, 65
communication system, 156
compilation, conditional, **71**-72
compiler, 32
compile-time process, **28**-29
complementary operation, **136**
complementation, **202**
complete
   cover, **46**
   decision table, **195**
   specification, 219

testing, 12, 13, 44, 100, 206
complexity 96-**97**-106, 225, 270
, data-base, 26
, interface, 19
, subroutine, 100-103
concatenated loops, 50, 51, **53**
conditional assembly, compilation, **71**-72
condition entry, **191**
condition stub, **191**
connection matrix, **254**
context dependent format, 155, **161**
contradiction, 177, 181-182
, format, 164
, program, 205, 241
, specification, 196, 222-223, 242
, state-transition, 241
control, 11, 250
   bug, 21, 24
   table, 26
correctness, functional, 18
correctness proof, 13-14
correlated
   field, 155, 164
   predicate, **57**, 60, 122, 129, 134, 141, 205
   variable, **57**, 172
cover, **46**, 54-55, 58, 68, 95, 96, 100, 106, 122,
    128, 200, 205
, bug free assumption, 68
, complete, **46**, 47, 121, 128
, decision table, 192
, minimum set, 121-122, 128, 205
, prime implicant, 206
   set probability, 67, **133**
, state, 248
, transaction flow, 83, 84
, weird path, 85
criminals, 149
cross reference
   check, 64
, documentation, 173
, specification, 177
cross-term, **114**
cyclomatic complexity. *See: McCabe's Metric*

dangling code, 32, 205
data
   attribute, **30**, 32
   -base 9, 56, 79
      bugs 25-32, 34, 54
      coordinator 185

declarations 25-26, 27, 28, 31, 170, 171, 174
  design 31, 171
  generator, 169
  management, 31-32
  size, 170
  solitaire, 177-178
  structure, 174
  test, 166, 170
, boundary value, 161, 183, 186
content, **30**
dependency, 134
dictionary, 27, **31**, 32, 171, 173, 188, 189
, dynamic, 27-28, 170
, excluded values, 52, 58, 161, 186
private, 31, 190
representation change, 186
, static, 27, 28-29
structure, **30**, 172, 188
type, **31**, 32
  bug, **31**
  change, 185, 186
  input test, 161
validation, 27, 29, 148, 150, 151, 154, 182
, vulnerability to bad, 29
deadlock, **22**
dead state, **246**
debug labor, 96, 102, 104, 105
decision. *See also: predicate, branch.* **37**
, binary, **37**, 191
order, 197
table, **191**-200
  , complete, **195**
  , consistent, **195**
  cover, 192
  default specification, 192
  immaterial case, **191**, 195-196
  language, 192-194
  processor, 194
  rule, **191**, 195
  and structure, 198
  test design, 166, 194, 197
declaration, 24, 25, 26, 27, 28, 31, 170, 171, 174
definition tree, **158**
delimiter error, 155, 159-161
DeMorgan's theorem, 203
designer, 5-6, 152, 156, 159, 172, 179-181, 188, 236
dependent predicate, **56**, 62, 122, 129

dependent variable, **56**, 172
desk check, 64-67, 73, 100
  effectiveness, 66
  objectives, 64
device handler, 26, 43, 250
documentation, 31, 173, 174, 224, 226
don't care case, 25, **223**-224
dynamic analysis, **45**

ego, 46
enhancements, 17, 188, 238
environment, **11**, 150
equate file, 174
equivalent states, **237**-241
error recovery, 246
exception handler, 23, 246
excluded paths, 83, 84, 141-142
exclusive-or, **202**
exit expression of program, **208**

field
  access, 187
  access macro, **32**, 183
  , bit, 183
  , case control, 183
  , correlated, 155, 162, 164
  merger, 187
  , numerical, 183
  overlap, 187
  splatter, 187
  syntax, 155
  value test, 161
finite state machine. *See also: state.* 26, 231, 247
firmware, 11
flag, 136, 140-141
flowchart, **37**-41
  check, 65-66
  program, 40
  specification, 60
  translation, 39-40
format, 151
  ambiguity, 164
  , context dependent, 161-162
  contradiction, 164
  , correlated, 164
  definition tree, **158**
  grammar, 151
  , internal, 156

processor, 169
syntax, source of, 165
state dependency, 164
tolerance, 160
validation test, 156, 160, 168
function(al), 49-50, 249
bug, 17
correctness, 18
test(ing), **4**, 5, **12**, 13, 64, 82, 85, 250

garbage, 148, 151
, creative, 150, 165
, data residue, 28
get/return problem, 136, 139, 266
GIGO, 148
glass-box testing. *See: structural testing.* **5**
Gödel numbering, 71
GOTO. *See: branch*
graph, 89-**90**-96
matrix, 251, **252**, 261
loop, 260
node reduction, 262
, power of, 255
, product of, 256
, properties of, 261
guilt, 1, 29-30

hardware, 11, 19-20, 150
hooks, 17, 188, 238
horrible loops, 51, 54
Huang's theorem, 50, 53, 143-146
Hulk, The Incredible, 6, 150
human engineering, 156
hunches, 50
hypermodularity, 102

idiot. *See: user*
illogical condition, 41, 223, 224
immaterial case (decision table), **191**, 195-196
impossible case, 25, 189, 195, 223-224
impossible state, 236-237
inclusive-or, 202
increment/decrement arithmetic, 139
independent
predicate, **56**, 60, 122, 129
testing, 6, 17, 18, 84, 156, 173
variable, **56**
index, field access, 187
initialization, 142-146, 246
bug, 24, 32, 55, 144, 188

initial state, **248**
input
error
, delimiter, 155, 159, 160
, field correlation, 155
, multiple, 157
, state dependent, 155
, syntax, **155**, 157
format, 151
tolerance, 160
validation, 156
sequence for state cover, 248
, state graph, **228**
test, 150, 161, 163, 172
variable. *See: variable*
instrumentation, 67-**68**-72, 139, 197, 200, 242
bug, 68, 69, 71, 72
limitations, 72
, state transition, 242, 249
strategy, 69-70
, transaction flow, 86-87
interface, 7, 8, 18-19, 31, 150
bug, 103
complexity, 19
design, 20
, internal, 19, 42, 156, 169
standards, 9, 19
testing, 20
integration, 19
intermittent bug, 242
interpreter, 86
interrupt routine, 43, 250
interview, 178-181
intuition, 50, 176

job control language, 22, 85
jumping into and out of code, 61, 127
junction, 37, **38**

Karnaugh-Veitch chart, **209**-219

labor, debug, 92, 96, 102, 104
labor, test, 1, 4, 33, 42, 49, 96, 102, 104, 105
language, 185
, assembly, 142, 185
, decision table, 192-193
, hidden, 22, 26-27, 85-86, 169
, higher order, 18, 142
processor, 64, 156, 169, 174

, source, 24, 29, 31, 32, 142
, strongly typed, **24**, **32**, 183, 186
lines-of-code metric, 102, 104
link, **41**, 90
   counter, 69
   name, **20**, 91, 107
   weight, **91**-92, 121
logic bug, 25, 46
logical expression, 220
loop, 206
   , concatenated, 50, 51, **53**-54
   , excluded values, 52
   , graph matrix, 260
   , horrible, 51, 54
   , instrumentation of, 69, 139
   , jumping into and out of, 127
   , nested, **50**, 51, 52-53
   , non-terminating, 205
   , path expression for, 112
   , probability, 129-130
   term, node reduction, **117**
   testing, 48, 50-54, 73
   , time spent in, 53, 54

maintenance, 29, 61, 184, 193, 225, 273
   , data dictionary, 171
malicious user (idiot), 19, 149
matrix. *See: graph matrix*
McCabe's metric, 89, 96-**97**-106, 248, 254,
     272, 279, 280
Mealy model, **230**
memory cost, 22, 26, 27, 170
metalanguage, **152**
metric, **96**
minimum covering set, 205
model, 5, 10, 12, 278
   , behavioral, 233, 249
   , decision table, 194
modularity, 7, 101-103
Moore model, **230**
multi entry/exit routine, 41-44, 121
multiple input errors, 157

naive tester, 6
natural language ambiguity, 219
negation, **202**
nested loop, **50**, 51, 52
node, **41**, 89, 90
   probability, 129-133, 265
   reduction algorithm, 113-117, 261, 262-264

removal order, 119
null path, **110**, 113, 122, 127
null set, path, **113**

operating system, 11, 20-21, 26, 85
operator (human), 8, 149-150, 157, 161
operator commands, 156
output, state graph, **229**

path, **41**
   cover, 54, 68, 95, 100, 106, 122, 128
   , excluded, 83-84, 141-142
   expression, 107-**108**, 120, 123, 152, 200, 252
     applications, 120-147
     , equivalent, 114
     identities, 119
     laws, 112
     , loop, 112
     , non-path, **113**
   , high probability, 46
   length, 122
   name, **70**, 73, **92**, 107-109
   , normal, 46, 48, 67, 85, 122, 165
   , null, 110, **113**, 122, 127
   , number of, 13, 44, 47, 61, 121-128, 264
   , parallel, 110, 116
   probability, 46, 67-68, 129-133, 265
   product, 107-**108**-109
   segment, **41**
   selection, 41-50, 73, 83
   sensitizing, **55**, **56**-63, 66, 73, 182, 278
   , backward, 62-63
   , forward, 63
   , set of all, 258
   sum, **110**, 111
   testing, 13, **22**, 23, **37**-73, 75-87, 166
     effectiveness, 54-55, 275
     limitations, 54, 200
     summary, 72
   tracing, 48, 63, 70, 146, 201, 251
   , weird, 23, 84
peek-a-boo bug, 72
Petri-net, 81
predicate, 55, **56**, 104
   , compound, 103-104
   , correlated, **57**, 60, 122, 141, 205
   count, 106
   notation, 59, 200
   , process dependent, **56**, 62, 122
   , process independent, **56**, 60, 122

, uncorrelated, **57**, 122
value, 208
prime implicant, **205**-206
private space, 31, 190
proof. *See: correctness*
process, **37**
bug, 23
dependent predicate, **56**, 62, 122
dependent variable, **56**
independent predicate, **56**, 60, 122
independent variable, **56**
processing, 11
time, 22, 53, 54, 133-136, 141, 267, 270
program
ambiguity, 205, 241
as data, 25, 26
behavior model, 230, 233
contradiction, 205, 241
design language (PDL), 39, 60, 65-66
exit expression, **208**
structure, 4
structured, 125-127
programming productivity, 2, 3, 33
protocol, 19, 26, 250
pseudo-code. *See: program design language*
push/pop arithmetic, 136

random data test, 67-68
recognizer, string, **154**, 159
redundant code, 61
regular expression, **107**, 142-**143**-146, 152
requirements, functional. *See also: specification.* 5, 89, 176, 177, 182, 183
reserved value, 188
resource
bug, 22-23
deadlock, **22**
garbage, 28
, fractioned, 22
holding time, 22
loss, 23
management, 27, 187, 250
size, 23

security, 250
segment, **41**
semantic shift, **183**-185
sequence bug, 21, 24, 142
series term, node reduction, **114**
set/reset arithmetic, 136, 140

software
architecture, 21
cost, 3, 26, 170
reliability, 14
source language, 24, 29, 31, 32, 142
specification, 5, 14, 18, 24, 64, 82, 172, 175, 184, 185, 194, 208
ambiguity, 9, 12, 14, 222-223, 242-246
, BNF, 155
bug, 17
, consistent, 14, 196, 197, 219
contradiction, 196, 197, 219, 222-223, 242-246
cross reference, 177
, default, 192
flowchart, 60
language, 18
, PDL, 60
, syntax, 156
, transaction flow, 78
: translation to boolean algebra, 221
, unit level, 24
writers, 220
standards, 19
state, **227**
bug, 235
cover, 248
, dead, **246**
dependent errors, 155, 163-164
, equivalent, **237**-241
graph, **227**
bug, 233, 234
input, **228**
implementation, 231
model, 233
output, **229**
, strongly connected, 234, 248
, impossible, 236-237
, initial, **248**
machine, 26, 231, 247
merger, 240
, non-equivalent, 240
, number of, 228, 235-236
test, 166, 227, 247
limitations 248-249
transition, **228**
bug, 241, 247
contradiction, 241
instrumentation, 242
sequence, 248

table, **227**, 231, 232
, unspecified, 241
, unreachable, 246
state/world correspondance, 237
static analysis, **45**, 142
string
  generator, **155**
  recognizer, **154**, 159
strong connection, **93**
, state graph, 234, 248
strongly typed language, **24**, **32**, 183, 186
structure(d), 13, 49, 157, 166
, decision table and, 198
  program, 118, 125-**126**-127
structural complexity, 96-**97**-106
structural testing, **5**, **13**-14, 64
stupidity, inspired, 73, 185, 246
style, 5, 31, 33, 65
subroutine, 91
  complexity, 100-103
  design, 101
  size, 101-102
subsystem, 190
symptoms, 4
syntax
  bug, 32, 164-165
  check, 64
  input errors, **155**, 157
  specification, 156
  test, 86, 148, 154, 157, 165, 166, 169
system
  architecture, 174
  documentation, 82
  test, 6, 17, 68, 82-83, 85, 167

task, **75**
taxonomy of bugs, 15-35
tables. *See: data base*
test(ing), 12, 49, 61
, ad-lib, 167
, automatic generation, 67, 96
, black-box. *See: test, functional.* 4
, boundary, 161, 183, 186
, bugs in, 7, 11-12, 13, 14, 17, 18
, comlete(ness), 12, 13, 44, 100, 121
  cost, 3, 26, 84, 166
  criteria, 18
  data-base, 7
, data-base, 166, 170
  data, random, 67-68

, data validation, 150-169, 182
debugging, 18
, decision table, 166, 194, 197
design, 3, 4, 33, 38, 55, 182, 190
design labor, 4, 33, 37, 55, 66, 159, 166, 169, 174, 182, 190
documentation, 3, 12, 73, 173
efficiency, 7
, format validation, 156, 160, 168
, functional, **4**, **5**, **12**, 13, 24, 64, 82, 172, 182, 250
, glass box, 5, 13
goals, 3, 14, 61
ideas, 172, 177
, independent, 6, 17, 18, 84, 156, 173
, initialization, 144
, interface, 20
labor, 1, 4, 33, 42, 49, 96, 102, 104, 105
, limitations of, 12-14, 54, 165, 248, 273
, loop, 50-54
modularity, 7
, multi-entry/exit routine, 42-44
overview, 10-11
, path. *See also: path testing.* 13, **22**, **37**, 166
rules for loops, 50
results, 10, 11
running, 73, 166
set-up, 49
, state, 166, 227, 247, 248, 271
, structural 5, **13**, 24, 64
, syntax, 86, 148, 154, 165, 169
, system, 6, 17, 19, 83
testing, 18
, threat of, 165
, transaction flow, 82-85
tools, 96, 142
unit level, 6, 24, 46, 55, 172
tester, 5-6, 152, 154, 156, 159, 179-181
token, **79**
transaction, **74**-78
  control, 169
    block, **26**, 79
    language, 26
    table, 86
  flow, **22**, 75-87, 250
    cover, 83, 84
    , forbidden path, 83
    implementation, 78-82
    instrumentation, 71, 86

loop, 83
  path selection, 83, 84
, merging, **81**
, split, **81**
testing, 82-85
traversal marker, **70**-71
truth value, 56, 141, 202
type. *See: data type*
typographical bug, 33, 46, 65

uncorrelated predicate, **57**, 122, 129
uncorrelated variable, **57**
unspecified state transition, 241
unstructured program, **127**
untested code, 46-47

user, 4, 7, 19, 75, 78, 149, 157, 161
utility program, 174

variable
  , correlated, **57**, 162-163
  , process dependent, **56**
  , process independent, **56**
  , uncorrelated, **57**
vulnerability to bad data, 29, 148, 151

weight
  arithmetic, 252
  , link, **91**-92, 121
weird path, 23, 84, 85
wild card. *See: bug, coding*